EY
BENTLE

RACING IN THE DARK

Also by Peter Grimsdale

High Performance:
When Britain Ruled the Roads

RACING IN THE DARK

When the Bentley Boys Conquered Le Mans

PETER GRIMSDALE

Sourced from the W.O. Bentley Memorial Foundation

SIMON &
SCHUSTER

London · New York · Sydney · Toronto · New Delhi

First published in Great Britain by Simon & Schuster UK Ltd, 2021

1 3 5 7 9 10 8 6 4 2

Simon & Schuster UK Ltd
1st Floor
222 Gray's Inn Road
London WC1X 8HB

www.simonandschuster.co.uk
www.simonandschuster.com.au
www.simonandschuster.co.in

Simon & Schuster Australia, Sydney
Simon & Schuster India, New Delhi

A CIP catalogue record for this book
is available from the British Library

Hardback ISBN: 978-1-4711- 9826-7
eBook ISBN: 978-1-4711- 9827-4

Typeset in Sabon by M Rules
Printed and bound by CPI Group (UK) Ltd, Croydon, CR0 4YY

For Vivian

Contents

‘All men dream: but not equally. Those who dream by night in the dusty recesses of their minds wake up in the day to find it was vanity, but the dreamers of the day are dangerous men, for they may act their dreams with open eyes, to make it possible.’

T.E. LAWRENCE, *Seven Pillars of Wisdom*

‘Though the machines themselves are interesting beyond belief, it is knowledge of men that counts.’

S.C.H. DAVIS, *Motor Racing*

Le Mans Circuit (1923–28)

Lap length 10.726 miles

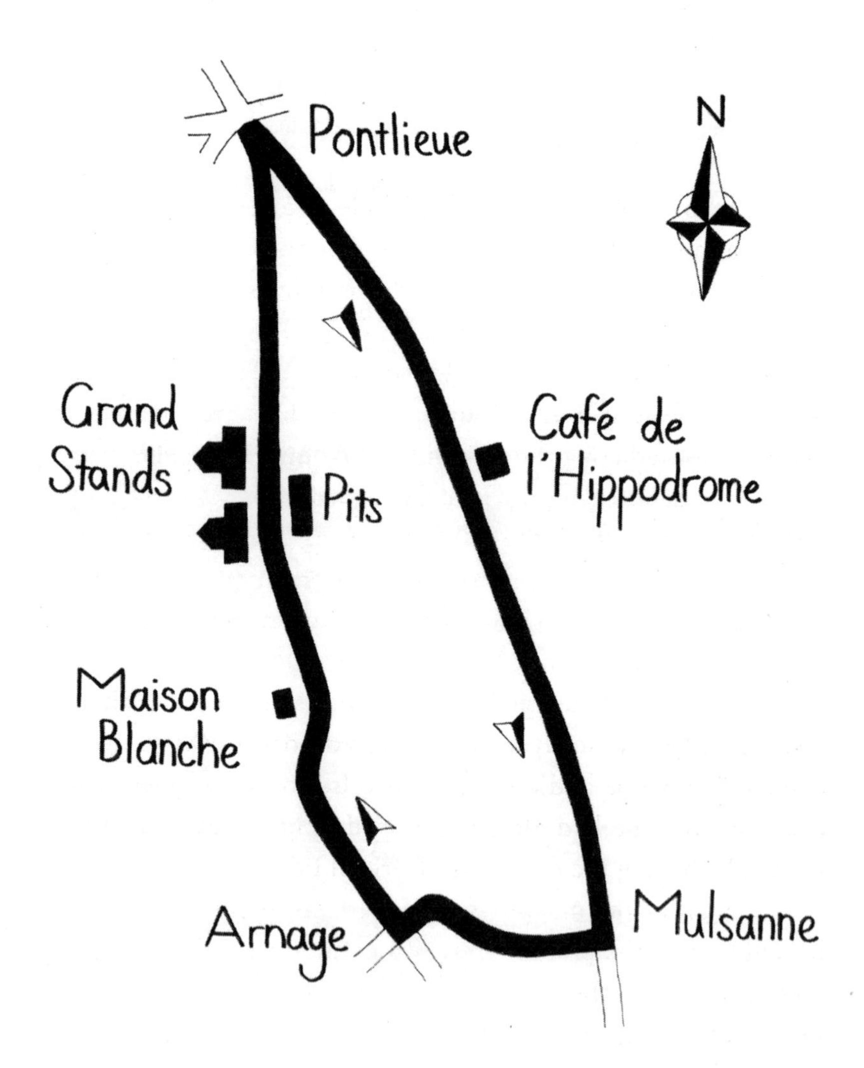

PROLOGUE

Duel on a Golf Course

On the 28th of July 1998 at the 19th hole on a golf course outside the Bavarian city of Ingolstadt, two of Germany's most powerful autocrats met to settle a dispute – which of them would take control of Britain's automotive crown jewel, Rolls-Royce.

Ferdinand Piëch was the grandson of Ferdinand Porsche, designer of the Volkswagen. Bullet-headed, with ice-blue eyes, famous in Germany for fathering thirteen children by three wives, Piëch was also a formidable engineer. He had designed the Le Mans-winning Porsche 917 as well as the rally-conquering Audi Quattro. And, having rescued Volkswagen from near bankruptcy, he was now on a buying spree, bent on building the biggest car maker in the world. Only the previous month he had acquired Lamborghini and Bugatti.

His rival for the hallowed British brand was Bernd Pischetsrieder, the softly spoken, goateed boss of BMW. A confirmed Anglophile and cousin of Alec Issigonis, designer of the original Mini, he had already scooped up a handful of British brands by buying the remnants of British Leyland.

As a sign of the magnitude of what was at stake, Piëch had brought along the premier of VW's home state, Lower Saxony, and alongside Pischetsrieder was the prime minister of BMW's Bavaria, the future Chancellor, Gerhard Schroeder.

All this for a tiny, struggling company with a clapped-out factory that the year before had made only 1,900 cars – at a loss.

By the time they emerged from the clubhouse, they had a deal that neither party expected, for there had been an eleventh-hour intervention. Although Rolls-Royce Aerospace had severed almost all their links with the car business, they still controlled the trademark. And having built the Merlin engine that supercharged the Battle of Britain, they were not about to let their name be associated with the producer of Hitler's 'People's Car'.

The consequence was a carve-up: BMW would get the Rolls-Royce name only, a brand with a reach out of all proportion to its output and a reputation for excellence unmatched by the current product. Piëch and VW, for a cool billion Deutschmarks, got Rolls-Royce's antiquated factory in the Cheshire city of Crewe. His consolation prize – another piece of British automotive heraldry: Bentley.

~

Many thought the acquisitive Piëch had finally lost his head. Ever since Rolls acquired it in 1931, Bentley had been little more than a product of what the motor industry sneeringly calls 'badge-engineering' – the famous 'flying B' grafted on to a slightly rounded-off version of the Grecian Rolls-Royce grille. But Piëch was doing something he rarely ever did; he was smiling. He had forced his board into letting him make an offer no one could refuse. 'One billion marks is cheap,' he insisted.

What did he think he was buying?

Being a details man, Piëch could answer that question with typically withering precision. He could point to an exact moment – not just a year or a day, but an exact time – 9.28 p.m. on 18 June 1927. And a location, between the villages of Arnage and

Pontlieue in the Sarthe region of France, a whitewashed single-storey building known as Maison Blanche. For it was at that place at that time that a motor car designed by Walter Owen Bentley found fame. And that is where this story begins.

1

Dangerous Men

The race had been underway for six hours: another eighteen to go. Dusk settled over the Le Mans circuit. Behind the pit counter, Walter Owen – W.O. – Bentley glanced again at the stopwatch hanging from a leather strap around his neck, then stared back to where the empty stretch of track disappeared into the darkness. Apart from the dull thump inside his head, there was nothing but silence.

They were late – all of them. All of his cars.

One of the three timekeepers looked up at his boss, perched on a stool just behind them. W.O.'s lips were pressed tightly together, his face white in the ghostly glow of the French army arc lights that illuminated the darkening pits. He was a man of few words at the best of times, and this was not the best of times. His mind raced, but he said nothing.

His first thoughts were for his drivers, Callingham, Duller and Davis. There had already been one fatality and four injuries that weekend. As the seconds climbed towards a full minute, the enormity of what was happening started to sink in. For one car to be overdue was not unusual, but for all three ...

The Bentleys had led from the start. The latest model, the 4½ Litre, had smashed the lap record at a commanding 73.2 mph, while the two 3 Litre cars kept close. W.O.'s machines were fast but durable, his drivers prudent and drilled not to cane the vehicles, in the hope that they would last the full twenty-four hours – an awesome feat in 1927. But now, along with his fears for the drivers, back came his misgivings about being there at all.

The previous two years' events had been pure humiliation; none of the Bentleys finished either race. In 1926 S.C.H. Davis ploughed car number 7 into a sandbank just minutes from the flag. After that, W.O. vowed to give up racing and put the team cars up for sale. But Davis's co-driver Dudley Benjafield was determined to have another go. He bought 'Old No. 7' and put his name down for the 1927 event, as a privateer. In the end W.O. succumbed, unable to resist one more crack at *Les Vingt-Quatre Heures du Mans*, like a gambler pushing all his chips onto one number. And once again he was staring into a void.

In its eight years of existence, Bentley Motors had yet to make a penny. Only a last-minute bailout had saved it from collapse. Common sense should have told W.O. to focus on building and selling more cars to turn that elusive profit. But other forces were at work.

W.O., Davis and Benjafield, born in the reign of Queen Victoria, enjoyed a lifestyle undreamed of by their ancestors as Britain crested the wave of imperial prosperity and industrial progress. But that carefree life had been vaporised in the cataclysm of world war.

In August 1914, each had seized the chance to serve their country; to do otherwise would have been unthinkable. Their duty to King and Country had been drilled into them at their public schools. But nothing in their history textbooks had prepared them for what was coming – W.O. neck deep in a freezing canal as the Red Baron Manfred von Richthofen's Fokker Triplane strafed a Dunkirk airfield; Davis marooned in his armoured car in the mud of Ypres as the Kaiser's chlorine gas rolled over them; Benjafield, aboard his mobile laboratory in the ferocious Palestine sun, grappling with another enemy, the terrifying virus yet to become known as Spanish flu.

None of what they wrote afterwards dwells on the impact of what they saw and did. Benjafield's account in the June 1919 *British Medical Journal* is a model of clinical reportage. And Davis's enthusiasm misfires only fleetingly as he records the fates of all the other men in his family in 1915 and makes the all-too-brief admission that he 'cracked up entirely and went to live in hospital'. W.O., by far the most tight-lipped of the trio, captured some of the madness, witnessing five pilots from one flight on the Western Front 'spiralling down in flames' and the 'grief, courage and fear thrown together in hectic drunken parties among the survivors in the evening'. But his own very personal loss of his young wife to the pandemic, just days after the Armistice, is dispatched in a single line.

Only by reading between the lines these men wrote can the pain and emotion behind their monstrous losses be detected. It was a legacy that left them less biddable, more stubborn, more committed to living by their own rules, with no thought of danger. As survivors, they carried the burden of responsibility to do something of value, to find some restorative nobility. For years after they didn't discuss it because they didn't need to – they all felt it. Fellow veterans Robert Graves and T.E. Lawrence, friends since school, made a pact never to speak of it.

Instead, Davis, Benjafield and W.O. found an outlet in racing cars through the night. Tim Birkin, former RFC pilot and fellow Bentley driver, broke ranks and tried to shed some light on this choice for future generations in a memoir he dedicated 'to all schoolboys':

> Motor racing provided the energy, adventures and risks most like those of the battlefield. It had, moreover, the promise of

> a great future, and there was the same chance of unexpected disaster, the same need of perfect nerves, with a presence of mind that must never desert you, the same exhilaration of living in the shadow of death that often came so suddenly and gloriously, that it seemed to have no shadow. There was, besides, the peculiar delight of being responsible for your own calamities, since, once off the mark, you were at liberty to take risks or avoid them as you pleased, a state of independence few individuals enjoyed in the war.

But as night shrouded the Le Mans circuit, there was little of that sense of glory in the Bentley pit.

Out of the darkness came a single headlight beam and the unmistakable thump of a four-cylinder engine struggling at low revs.

The crew leapt to their feet. It was a Bentley! But which one?

The grandstand lights swept across a familiar bonnet. One wheel, badly bent, wobbled as it turned, a mudguard pointed skyward and the driver's-side headlamp was completely crushed. On the mesh of the radiator grille the white '3' was still clear.

W.O. surveyed the wreckage as Davis, haggard and still in shock, climbed out from behind the wheel to face his boss. He coughed out the words, a crash at Maison Blanche like nothing he had ever seen, five, six cars, piled on each other, the other two Bentleys utterly destroyed. Under the arc lights Old No. 7 looked like it had been savaged by some metal-eating monster.

All eyes were on W.O. Was this how it would end – in the dark, in a trackside pit in France?

2

Seven Tons of Coal

Walter Owen Bentley was sixteen years old before he got his first ride in a motor vehicle. He was in no hurry; like many growing up in the last days of the nineteenth century, he had already dismissed the automobile as 'a slow, inefficient, draughty and anti-social means of transport'. What fascinated him from as far back as he could remember were steam locomotives. 'They filled my dreams and ambitions.'

From the family home in Avenue Road, just north of London's Regent's Park, it was a fifteen-minute walk to the point where Loudoun Road spanned the northerly portals of Robert Stephenson's Primrose Hill tunnel. With careful timing, his long-suffering governess in tow, the infant enthusiast could hail the *Flying Scotsman* as it blasted out of the darkness and streamed past them towards Willesden and points north.

Born in 1888, he was the youngest of nine – three girls and six boys. He hated the name Walter and always preferred 'W.O.', but as a child, on account of his round face and dark eyes, was known as 'The Bun'.

His affluent circumstances came courtesy of family money. Father Alfred was a painfully shy man who liked reading his bible and according to W.O. was not much good at business. He retired early from his family's wool and silk firm. What powered the Bentley family was his mother Emily's inheritance from her father, Thomas Waterhouse, who had made a fortune in Australia from copper mines and banking. From childhood, W.O. exhibited the defining characteristics of both his parents: his father's diffidence and his mother's passionate determination. As the youngest, W.O. was doted on.

His boyhood coincided with the arrival in England of the first clockwork model railways from Märklin in Germany. One of these sets, along with a model steam stationary engine, were treasured gifts which consumed his waking hours. And his favourite activity was taking them apart to find out how they worked.

This charmed life hit the buffers when, at ten, W.O. was packed off to Lambrook Preparatory School near Ascot. Public schools at that time prioritised discipline and obedience and learning by rote, with the emphasis firmly on the classics, not science. Used to getting his way, W.O. did not take to this regimen and was frequently caned. 'I didn't like doing things I didn't like and that was that.'

A stubbornness was emerging which would become a key characteristic. But even in the lessons he did like, physics and chemistry, he also got into trouble. Methodical and meticulous, he refused to accept the word of his teachers or take things as read, and had to be convinced by every argument or statement of fact.

'I had to know I was getting somewhere and I had to know why I was going and this made for slow progress and frequent canings.'

He enjoyed cricket and was at The Oval on 13 August 1902 to witness history being made when Gilbert Jessop scored the fastest-ever Test century for England – 'slashing and stroking 104 in 75 minutes'.

Inspired, W.O. made it into the Lambrook First XI and at an away match in Reading he went out first and scored 79 not out. It was a rare high point which 'gave me more satisfaction than anything that happened at Le Mans thirty years later'.

From Lambrook he followed his five brothers to Clifton College in Bristol, but for W.O. this was just a waiting room. After three undistinguished years there he made his escape and, having at last turned sixteen, realised his dream: a place at the Great Northern and Eastern Railway engine sheds in Doncaster, where they were building the fastest machines on earth.

There were two kinds of apprenticeships: 'trade', for the sons of GNER railwaymen who were paid five shillings a week; and 'premium' for those who could afford the £75 upfront for the privilege, to be paid back as weekly wages over five years. It was not unheard of for public-school boys to join Britain's great engine sheds. Sir Nigel Gresley, who would design the *Mallard*, the world's fastest steam engine, had attended Marlborough before his apprenticeship at Crewe.

Up north, the eager teenager faced a tough regime: sixty hours over five and a half days, with a six o'clock start every morning, and penalties for being even thirty seconds late. At first, W.O. was ragged for his southern accent and being 'a snob', but he refused to be cowed. His methodical determination soon began to win him respect; in his words, 'the barrier dissolved and that was that'.

The work was exhausting, grimy, noisy and dangerous, and he loved every minute. This was just as well, because it was eighteen months before he got near an actual steam engine and another three entire years before he finally realised his ultimate boyhood dream: to 'fire' a locomotive.

'The sensation of being on the footplate of a Great Northern Atlantic, heading an express north out of London, was more thrilling and wonderful than I had ever thought it could have been. I was fascinated by the feeling of power as we pulled out of Kings Cross, up the steep gradients and tunnels of north London, up the steady grind for another eleven miles to Potter's Bar, and by the sudden irresistible surge of acceleration when the track levelled off and fell away. There is nothing I know to compare with the sensation of rushing through the night without lights and with the soothing mechanical rhythm beating away continuously, even leading to a dangerous tendency to surrender to the power quivering beneath the steel floor. And then the signals flash into view, your absolute guide and master, and from time to time the lights of a town, the searing white flash of a station – and back into darkness.' Four hundred miles, shovelling what came to seven tons of coal. 'Not a bad day's exercise.'

But it was not to last. In the summer of 1910, as W.O. neared the end of his apprenticeship, he woke up one day and realised with a jolt that he'd had a change of heart.

Steam power had transformed the world and powered Britain's industrial revolution. But by the dawn of the twentieth century the locomotive had pretty much been perfected; there was little scope for innovation. The railway industry was no longer expanding and in the engine sheds the plum jobs were scarce, with long waiting lists. He realised the railway would not be his life after all.

Meanwhile the motor vehicle, which had so failed to impress W.O. as a small boy in the 1890s, was no longer a spluttering alternative to the horse. The internal combustion engine, noisy and temperamental, was compact, adaptable and ripe for development. And for a mechanically minded man on the threshold of his twenties, cars and motorcycles – unconstrained by rails and timetables – promised undreamed-of independence.

In 1906, to get to the locomotive sheds from his lodgings across Doncaster for that early start, he had bought himself a belt-driven Quadrant 3hp motorcycle – the first mechanically propelled vehicle any Bentley had ever owned.

Having quickly mastered it, he decided to forego the train and attempt the entire journey home on the Great North Road, 'a rough, narrow and second-rate highway', arriving at the Bentley front door one Saturday evening caked in dust. Although the youngest, 'The Bun' was the trailblazer; two of his brothers soon got their own machines.

'For a brief time motorcycles ruled our lives,' W.O. recalled as they began to explore further and wider. They signed up for the London to Edinburgh trial, undaunted by the mostly unmetalled roads. For the mechanically resourceful Bentley, this opened up a whole new avenue of discovery – and all on his own terms.

He traded up to a 5hp Rex and did what he'd done with his clockwork railway: pulled it all apart. He then dramatically improved its performance with his own modification – a pipe which fed a film of oil from the crankcase into the carburettor. In the Great Northern sheds, you did exactly what you were told according to time-honoured customs and practices by your elders and betters. But the internal combustion petrol engine was still in its infancy. Trial and error were the order of the day: fertile ground for Bentley to innovate. It also brought him into contact with a similarly eager fellow enthusiast.

3

The Outlaws

Sydney Charles Houghton Davis – 'Sammy' to all who knew him – was born in 1897, one year before W.O. He came from a similarly well-heeled north London household, but unlike the more conventional Bentleys, the Davis family were inclined to rebellion.

As a boy, Davis's maternal grandfather, Arthur Boyd Houghton, lost an eye playing with a toy cannon, which did nothing to deter him from becoming an accomplished artist and illustrator. He spent time in Russia and America, where he painted Native Americans. Back home in Hampstead, he enthralled his grandson with his habit of 'blow[ing] loudly on a coach horn from his studio window to attract beer from a neighbouring public house'.

Davis's paternal grandfather, Edwin, was also something of an adventurer. He eloped with his future wife, Sarah Latham, then further scandalised the family by becoming a shopkeeper in Hull. Against their expectations, Edwin Davis became the city's foremost department store, and guaranteed his descendants a life of leisure.

The family made only a cursory effort at seeming respectable. Davis remembered Grandma Sarah passing her Sundays apparently reading her bible – with a Wilkie Collins novel sewn between the covers. His mother had gone one further and raised eyebrows – in public – as an early devotee of the bicycle when 'such things were not done'. His father Edwin Jr was, according to the 1901 census, a 'tea importer', but this appears to have been wishful thinking. Davis described him as 'a dandy' and 'so much in love with my mother that nothing else really mattered to him'.

So in this apparently carefree household, where they 'never thought about money', there was no controversy when Sammy announced that he wanted to emulate his one-eyed grandfather and become an artist.

In contrast with W.O., Davis was smitten by the motorcar almost from birth, at a time when motorists were still widely regarded with hostility – which infuriated him. 'Persecuted by police, called evil names, assaulted if possible, the pioneers of motoring were a race without the law, untouchables, tinkers – people who were not – repeat not – gentlemen.'

The incident that fired his passion was an encounter with a Mercedes. The racing car was a reserve machine for the 1903 Gordon Bennett Cup race in Ireland, standing stationary on the Finchley Road, shrouded in steam. The desperate driver was calling for water to anyone who would listen. Davis seized the moment, procured a pailful from an astonished nearby householder and was rewarded with a ride all the way to Barnet.

At Westminster School he found himself in the same year as Malcolm Campbell, the future breaker of world land and water speed records, and two other enthusiasts, Roy Geddes and 'Fatty' Bowes-Scott, who procured a Rex motorcycle. Budding mechanics all, they eagerly took it apart to find out how it worked. Davis was soon hooked, and it was not long before he encountered another youthful Rex rider on the Finchley Road.

Davis's and W.O.'s first competitions were just between the two of them, up the unforgiving 1 in 7 incline of a residential side road, Netherhall Gardens, a punishing challenge on their early machines. They'd meet up at Avenue Road for noisy tuning sessions right outside the Bentleys' front door. This was too much for Bentley Sr. First, his son had wasted a fine public-school education by going into the railway sheds. Then he had abandoned the £75 the apprenticeship had cost them and started messing about with motorcycles. The patriarch made his feelings known with a well-aimed projectile – the family bible.

Turning his back on the Great Northern was not only a risky move for W.O., but to all appearances also something of a step down.

On the streets of London in the 1900s one of several dramatic developments was the advancing motorisation of the cab trade. There was money to be made and cut-throat competition sprang up between firms.

To his family's dismay, W.O. took a job with the National Motor Cab Company in Hammersmith, west London, which boasted a fleet of 250 French twin-cylinder Unic landaulets. With the rather unspecific job title of general assistant, he had to master the foibles of these modern machines – and their drivers, who had already devised cunning ways of interfering with the taximeters to fiddle the fares. In this new dog-eat-dog world of motorised transport, margins were cigarette-paper thin, and it was one of W.O.'s jobs to catch them out. He also had to contend with the formidable French foreman Hussein, who came with the Unics. Hussein was a good mechanic, though known for periodic absinthe-fuelled benders, during which he would rampage round the workshop brandishing a spanner, threatening to '*keel you all!*'. The next day he'd come into work, as quiet and courteous as ever.

W.O. took all this in his stride. Your average public-school boy from St John's Wood might have been overwhelmed, but thanks to his stint in the Doncaster engine sheds he was primed. 'It was no good playing the heavy father, taking a holier-than-thou attitude, or treating obstreperous behaviour in a jocular one-of-the-boys manner.'

Dedicated and dogged, he soon rumbled the cabbies' scam. They had drilled tiny holes into the glass of the meters through which a pin could be inserted to alter the fare. W.O. observed that 'labour relations, for want of a better term, can only be learned by experience.' Although he didn't know it at the time, this was invaluable preparation for the far more testing challenges he would face later on.

After life on the footplate of the *Flying Scotsman*, keeping cabs on the road didn't involve much glamour, but there were compensations, starting with an end to the brutally early starts. Also gone were the lonely nights in his digs in Doncaster, where his only company was his gramophone. Now, back in the comfort of the family home, he was earning good money and had the time to enjoy its benefits: the delights of Edwardian London, with Henry Wood's Promenade Concerts at the Queen's Hall, music hall variety bills at the Palace and the Empire, and late suppers at the Piccadilly Grill Room to the accompaniment of David de Groot's orchestra.

Around this time W.O. was introduced to Leonie Gore, the stepsister of Jack Withers, another motorcycling friend, at their house in Maresfield Gardens, not far from his favourite incline. W.O. was smitten, but the way was not clear; the former railway apprentice had to prove himself both to Leonie herself and her family. He would need all his powers of patience and determination.

As it had for W.O., the motorcycle provoked a Damascene moment for Sammy Davis – and a radical change of direction. In 1908, Davis abruptly abandoned his fine-art degree at the Slade for an engineering apprenticeship with Daimler in Coventry.

The company had been founded by Harry Lawson, originally a bicycle pioneer who presciently secured the rights to make Gottlieb Daimler's first petrol engine – and the exclusive use of the name in Britain.

The Red Flag Act had come into law in 1865 with the very first steam-driven vehicles, stating that in front of any 'self-propelled vehicle, a man with a red flag must walk at least sixty yards ahead to warn oncoming horses and foot traffic'.

Concern for safety was only one motive; many parliamentarians held shares in the burgeoning railway companies and were happy to see rival methods of transport given as little support as possible; ideally, in fact, to be strangled at birth.

When in 1896 after much lobbying the Act was repealed, Lawson organised the first London to Brighton run to celebrate the motorcar's emancipation. Though Lawson himself fell from grace after being found guilty of fraud, Daimler became the nation's first commercial motor company. It won a Royal Warrant in 1902, securing half a century of customer loyalty from the British royal family.

For Davis it provided an ideal entree into the nascent motor business. As W.O. had found in Doncaster, the initial ribbing for his supposed public-school airs subsided as he proved himself a spirited worker who threw himself enthusiastically into whatever was required of him.

'When the men went on short time or there was trouble of any kind, I was dispatched to a queer dark cubby hole to help the millwrights, a job of surpassing interest.'

Where others might have been a little nervous of this heavily built fraternity, Davis was in awe of their skills: 'The tobacco chewing fitters of that section seemed able to tackle any job from repairing a big machine to clearing a suds pipe.'

Never bored, he regarded every move as an opportunity to gain valuable experience. 'The subsequent white collar jobs in the drawing office and purchasing office vastly improved my education.' Eventually even his forgotten artistic gifts were deployed, when he was given drawings to do for the advertising department, which led him down another interesting road.

In 1910 he was offered a job as an illustrator on a new car magazine: *The Motor Engineer.* As it happened, this coincided with a crisis at Daimler. In search of greater refinement to meet the demands of its royal clientele, the company had committed to the development of a sleeve valve engine devised by an American, Charles Yale Knight. But Daimler's version was trouble; it refused to start from cold – which was still done by a hand crank, and when it did run the sleeve valves tended to seize. Also, the exhaust it produced was horribly smoky. And that wasn't all. Daimler now had stiff competition in the luxury market from interlopers Rolls-Royce and their imperious Silver Ghost launched in 1906. The future looked decidedly uncertain for Britain's oldest car company.

This time, the artistic route was the common-sense one. Davis said goodbye to the millwrights and purchase clerks and headed back to London, an artist once again.

4

Smiling Through the Dust

The National Motor Cab Company had brought W.O. the means to buy his first car, a 9hp Riley, but there would be limits to his appetite for the rough-and-tumble taxi business. Nor was it something that particularly impressed Leonie's stepfather.

Early in 1912, at the age of twenty-nine, W.O.'s brother Leonard – known as L.H. – had a change of heart about his career choice of farming. Another brother, Horace – H.M. – by now a qualified accountant, decided to help him find a new vocation. Lecoq and Fernie, concessionaires for several French cars based in some old stables in Hanover Court, behind Oxford Circus, were looking for a new director – with money to invest.

Each of the Bentley brothers was due a substantial inheritance from their mother's side of the family. H.M. went along to vet the company and discovered that Lecoq, also a director of Louis Vuitton, knew a good deal more about suitcases than cars. And behind his military bluster Major Fernie didn't know much about anything at all, except that he didn't want the services of an ex-farmer. Instead, they proposed that he – H.M. – take it on. H.M. was intrigued, but knew he wasn't the brother best suited to the role.

Back at Avenue Road there was a family meeting, where it was agreed that the fairest way to decide which Bentley to offer up was by the toss of a coin.

Suddenly W.O. felt his whole future depended on that spinning coin and fate was on his side. He won the toss, handed in his notice at the cab company and joined Lecoq and Fernie as a director, with a £2,000 stake from his bequest.

With its West End address the position at Lecoq and Fernie sounded good – and more palatable at least to Leonie's sceptical stepfather. But having signed away his inheritance, W.O. was dismayed to find precious little business actually going on; the lackadaisical proprietors had only wanted the Bentley money to keep the sinking business afloat. And he soon saw that the major's bullying tone barely masked the man's fundamental incompetence.

'A child of five knows more about selling cars than he does,' he told his brother. After five years in the engine sheds and two more in the cut and thrust of the motorised cab trade, W.O. was not going to be pushed around. He also fastened on the most promising bit of the business: the concession for the little French car: Doriot, Flandrin & Parant, known as D.F.P.

His rapidly developing grasp of automotive engineering told him that this apparently modest machine had real potential. He wasted no time in consulting H.M., then told the other partners his brother would buy them out. With his bold ideas for developing the business he had already made them uncomfortable and, after a few weeks' haggling and the addition of a few items of luxurious Louis Vuitton luggage, the deal was done. Yet another brother, solicitor Alfred – A.H. – drafted the contract and Lecoq & Fernie was no more; from now on it would be known as Bentley & Bentley Ltd.

It was a huge gamble; the brothers, H.M., aged twenty-seven, and W.O., just twenty-four, had sunk a staggering £4,000 – nearly half a million today – into a company that would quite possibly fail.

W.O. rented an old coach house in New Street Mews, off London's Upper Baker Street, and threw himself into the task of developing the D.F.P. – and wooing Leonie at the same time. On 8 June 1912 he entered a D.F.P. in the Aston Clinton Hill climb (the event that would give Aston Martin half its name). There was a lot riding on the day; it was the D.F.P.'s first competition and W.O.'s as well. And he invited Leonie along to watch.

The event, a timed three-quarter-mile sprint up a steep, twisting track, was regarded as a great test of pulling power and precise gear-changing rather than speed. W.O. had done trials like this on motorcycles but was dismayed to find the four-wheel crowd was completely different. He recognised no one and they all seemed to know each other. A modest little runabout in a field of sportier machines, the D.F.P. looked as if it had come to the wrong party.

Feeling all the more awkward for having persuaded Leonie to accompany him, he joined the queue behind the other competitors to await his turn. 'I hadn't the least idea of the way the corners went beyond the general course described by the succession of dust trails that had succeeded me up the hill. I pulled down my goggles and hoped for the best.'

He had already worked out that the D.F.P.'s gearing meant it needed an early shift from first to second and had practised this until he could shave a few seconds off by doing it without the clutch. When his turn came, the car behaved itself. He kept his foot to the floor through the corners, changing to third as the gradient levelled a bit. It was all over in a just a few minutes.

As he pulled to a halt, he was relieved to see that Leonie appeared to have enjoyed it, 'smiling through a mask of grey dust'.

Long seconds ticked by as they waited for the commentator to announce his time. To his amazement he was the fastest in Class 2 and had broken the record time for the 2-litre category, which made him the overall winner of the day. No longer the interloper in the wrong car, W.O. was suddenly the centre of attention.

Emboldened by this success, he decided that competition made for good publicity and that meant coaxing more speed out of the French machine. And Britain now had the ideal venue for his explorations.

Unlike in the rest of the Europe, racing on public roads in mainland Britain was banned.

One of those outraged by this abomination was Hugh Fortescue Locke King, a character who could have stepped straight from the pages of a P.G. Wodehouse novel. Born in 1848, he was pronounced too sickly for school or college, yet in his twenties was somehow called to the bar. But he never got round to practising as a barrister, devoting himself instead to the National Rifle Association. Although on the face of it poor marriage material, the weak and suggestible Locke King found himself in the cross-hairs of the steely Ethel Gore-Browne, who had ideas but lacked the funds to fulfil them. Sighting the ideal means to realise her ambitions, she married him in 1884, the year before he came into an estate worth £500,000 – £62 million today – which she proceeded to help him squander on a series of hare-brained schemes.

These included the purchase of the Mena House Hotel near Cairo, built for the Ottoman ruler Ismail Pasha, which they equipped with log fires so that Hugh could escape the British winters, and Egypt's first swimming pool. Back at Brooklands, the Locke Kings' Surrey estate, Ethel commissioned a fully landscaped 18-hole golf course, motivated by a wager as to whether it could be done on some particularly unsuitable heathland. They topped this with a doomed investment in a new food preservation process, a venture which ended in the law courts as they tried – and failed – to retrieve their money.

Hugh then went to Italy for the 1905 Coppa Florio motor race, which, true to form, he managed to miss in its entirety. Back home again, he brooded on the generally poor British showing in European motor sport. The nation's nascent car industry, he divined, was being constrained by the lack of a venue for high-speed testing. It came to him in a flash. What better use of his estate could there be than to turn it into a permanent racecourse for cars, the world's first?

Ethel shared his new-found passion for cars, so with her encouragement he made a few calculations, which came out at a 'mere' £22,000 – around £2.5 million today – and forged ahead.

The plans showed a track 2.7 miles long and an astonishing 100ft wide. When his engineers insisted on banked corners 30ft high so top speeds could be maintained, he acquiesced. But as the banking grew skywards, so did the costs – and Hugh's anxiety. When it all got too much for him the fearless Ethel took charge. By opening day in June 1907, as she led the inaugural lap of the new Brooklands track at the wheel of her own racing Itala, they were in hock to the tune of £159,000.

The Locke Kings envisaged their events as on a par with Royal Ascot or the Henley Regatta, exclusive gatherings at which to see and be seen. And the Brooklands protocol owed more to horse racing; numbers on cars were not allowed; drivers had to wear *colours* like jockeys and rode *on* rather than *in* their cars. Race days were *meetings*. With entrance even to the public enclosures at high prices, it was more like a members' club. And it struggled to make a profit.

There were more expenses, not least lawsuits from their deafened Weybridge neighbours; poor Hugh was cleaned out. But what seemed his greatest folly turned out to be just the ticket for W.O. and his pioneering automotive peers.

Far more than just a test track, Brooklands would for the next thirty years be the crucible of Britain's racing car and aircraft development. It also became an 'in' place for Edwardian socialites to see and be seen: the perfect place for W.O. to show off his cars.

Despite having sunk all their capital into buying out their predecessors, and with sales only slowly beginning to grow, the

Bentley brothers decided to go all out and head-hunted a specialist mechanic, Jean Leroux, from the D.F.P. factory in France.

The pretext was servicing customers' cars, but the Frenchman's role was primarily to implement W.O.'s engine modifications. They also ordered a bespoke lightweight body with a long, pointed tail from coachbuilders Harrison & Son in Stanhope Street off the Euston Road. With W.O. at the wheel, this stylish machine, tailor-made for Brooklands' high-speed conditions, snatched the 2-litre-class record at a tidy average of 66.78 mph. Bentley & Bentley had taken their first step from selling and servicing cars to re-engineering them. W.O. was on the way to finding his true vocation.

5

The Paperweight

Convinced that there was even more performance to be wrung out of the D.F.P., W.O. took a boat train to Paris to visit the factory on the outskirts of the capital at Courbevoie. He wanted to persuade Auguste Doriot – the D in D.F.P. – to incorporate some of his own modifications. Twice W.O.'s age, Doriot was one of the true automotive pioneers.

In 1891 he had made headlines for the then longest automobile journey in the world, 1,375 miles in a Peugeot, by following the Paris–Brest–Paris bicycle race – following in every sense, since he arrived six days after the winner. He then played a central role in developing Peugeots before going his own way in 1902. Few people anywhere – and none of W.O.'s own countrymen – could in 1913 boast a quarter of a century's worth of top-class automotive experience.

In his office, Doriot listened stonily as the 25-year-old W.O. reeled off the improvements he wanted to see on the D.F.P. engine, chiefly better carburetion and a raised compression ratio. According to his son Georges, Doriot Sr was a hard taskmaster, not to be crossed. 'His cool stare was worse than any punishment.'

While he was in full flow, W.O.'s eye fell on a piston-shaped paperweight on Doriot's desk. 'Pretty, isn't it?' said Doriot. W.O.

picked it up; it was wonderfully light – aluminium. It had been made as a novelty by Corbin, the foundry contracted to cast the D.F.P.'s iron pistons.

At that moment, W.O. was focused on winning Doriot over to his modifications, but on the journey home his thoughts kept returning to the aluminium paperweight. The modest changes to the D.F.P engine which he had requested could only add one or two miles an hour. Pushing any harder was sure to cause the iron pistons to overheat and crack.

Back in London, he confided in his brother H.M. who, lacking W.O.'s engineering nous, urged caution. But W.O.'s curiosity had been fired. He was convinced that what would take the D.F.P. to the next level had been sitting right there on Doriot's desk. Within a few days he was back in Courbevoie.

With the full force of his considerable experience, the Frenchman poured scorn on the idea. 'They will break up and seize before you are doing 2,000 rpm,' he pronounced. 'Aluminium's not suitable for the strains and stresses of that sort of work.'

How on earth could a metal that melted at 659 degrees Centigrade ever work when combustion occurred at 2,000 degrees? W.O. thought he knew better. Though he couldn't begin to match Doriot's years of experience, his time in the engine sheds of Great Northern had given him something that would prove equally valuable: a thorough working knowledge of how different metals behaved when hot and under stress.

Not only was aluminium less than half the weight of iron, its heat conductivity was more than four times as good. And the speed at which it could disperse the heat of combustion made the lower melting point irrelevant. W.O. pressed his point; the stubbornness that had made him such an awkward pupil at school was being repurposed as a useful adjunct to his engineering convictions.

Doriot began to come round, his own position melting in the

heat of W.O.'s passion. He took the young Englishman to Corbin, the foundry that had made the aluminium paperweight.

Corbin agreed to produce an experimental set of pistons to W.O.'s formula: 88 per cent aluminium and 12 per cent copper, the latter for additional strength. A few weeks later they arrived at W.O.'s workshop in New Street Mews.

He and Leroux fitted them to a modified car and put it to the test. The effect was dramatic. The D.F.P.'s top speed was now an incredible 80 mph, unheard of for a 2-litre car, the lighter pistons enabling the engine to reach much higher revs without destroying itself.

W.O. took the modified D.F.P. down to Brooklands and, one by one, broke the 50-mile, 100-mile and one-hour Brooklands records, all previously held by Humber. The British king of the 2-litre class had been abruptly deposed.

At that stage, the secret of the D.F.P.'s success remained just that. It wasn't so much that W.O. went out of his way to hide his cunning innovation; at that time no one imagined such an innovation could work.

But having made his mark at Brooklands, even though his business was really no more than an agency for a French car, W.O. was beginning to develop a reputation as a motor engineer. With the solid but inflexible Victorian values of the engine sheds firmly behind him, the Edwardian era promised opportunity. And 1914 could not have got off to a better start.

6

Le Virage du Mort

Now back in London, Sammy Davis was lodging on the edge of Richmond Park at the home of his boss Arthur Clayden, editor of *Automobile Engineer.* On this new magazine, a more technical companion publication to *The Autocar*, his duties had grown from technical illustration to journalism. His social life improved, too; Clayden's vivacious wife Emmie Kate was an enthusiastic hostess and the personable Davis soon found himself rubbing shoulders with the great and good of Britain's burgeoning motor industry: Herbert Austin, Frederick Lanchester, Lawrence Pomeroy and Louis Coatalen, the Breton expatriate behind the Sunbeam racing machines, all passed through the Clayden drawing room.

It was a good time for motor magazines, with a lucrative two-thirds of their pages devoted to advertising from car and component makers jostling for attention in what was now a booming market. By 1914 there were 113 car makers in Britain. An estimated 90,000 workers produced 34,000 vehicles, but with prices starting at around £300, about £35,000 today, they were still the preserve of the affluent. There was even enough revenue for the entire editorial staff to visit the world's biggest motor exhibition, the Paris Salon d'Auto, showcase of the technological spirit of the Belle Époque. Evening entertainment came at the Moulin Rouge cabaret and nightclub, which included partying with the dancers after the show. Like many well-bred young men of his time, Davis had already been sent by his bon-viveur father to the French capital to be shown the ropes by its famously experienced courtesans, and had no inhibitions about making the most of his assignment.

The French capital hummed with the sound of modernity. Although the motor car was a German invention, and Daimler-designed engines powered many of the world's first vehicles, France in the 1890s was where it acquired vital innovations like the gearbox and steering wheel. It was where it became a viable – and world-changing – commercial proposition. The *Système Panhard*, a front engine driving a rear axle with the passengers seated in between, became the template for the modern automobile. As a result of this early superiority, the majority of motor car terminology was French: *automobile*, *garage*, *chauffeur*, *carburettor*, *chassis*, *piston*, *grille*, *tonneau*, *berline*, *sedan*, *limousine*, *cabriolet*.

Pioneers Panhard, Renault and Peugeot rapidly moved into large-scale production. And although the pneumatic tyre was invented elsewhere, it was the Michelin brothers, Edouard and André, who created the detachable version that did not need to be glued onto its rim, one of the great leaps forward that made the motor car the future of wheeled transport. By the dawn of the twentieth century, France was building nearly half the world's cars.

The French were also ahead in the other key area: aviation. When Louis Blériot's monoplane crossed the English Channel, powered flight ceased to be a passing novelty and promised to shrink the world. This technological breakthrough piqued German sensibilities in particular. Prussian army officers attending an air show outside Reims in 1909, where twenty-eight of the thirty-six aircraft were French-built, were disappointed to report how little Germany had to show in the face of the vastly superior French achievements.

France had also been the birthplace of motor sport, with a race in 1894 between Paris and Rouen, and was home to the very first Grand Prix.

In the summer of 1914 Davis was back in France for the Grand Prix, and his first taste of top-flight international motor racing. The event was held on 4 July outside Lyons on 23 miles of closed public roads that included long straights and perilous sharp turns, one of them dubbed *Le Virage du Mort* – 'the death turn'.

Peugeot's Georges Boillot, winner of the previous year's race, was a national hero. A flamboyant exhibitionist whose skills had been honed on the lethal multi-litre monsters of the early 1900s, he liked to perform an early version of a handbrake turn as he parked outside his favourite Paris bar. He was also part of the Peugeot design team that had created its all-conquering twin-camshaft racing engine with four valves per cylinder.

Davis was in awe of Boillot, and in admiration of his panache and chivalry at the wheel likened him to D'Artagnan from *The Three Musketeers*. The year before, the Grand Prix field had been almost all French. But this year the Germans were there in force, with a team of five Mercedes created especially for the event. The stakes had been raised; it was clear to Davis they meant business.

The atmosphere was already highly charged. Just six days earlier, Austria's Archduke Ferdinand and his wife had been assassinated in Sarajevo. The news plunged Europe into crisis. Never before had national pride counted for so much in a motor race, Davis noted.

'There was something stirring in the difference between the two cars of the rival teams, the Peugeots being big, bluff machines, direct descendants from the finest days of racing. The Mercedes were lower, looked lighter, had a shark-like character and engines more of aircraft type than those of the French cars.' In fact they were a variant of the aero-engines Daimler had been commissioned to build for the Kaiser's war ministry to catch up with France.

At the wheel of the lead Mercedes was Christian Lautenschlager, an unassuming mechanic who had exhibited a flair for steady driving. When the flag fell, his teammate Max Sailer set the pace, with Boillot going flat out to hunt him down – an aggressive manoeuvre which hugely pleased the crowd. To their further delight, Sailer's Mercedes expired after just five laps, putting Boillot's blue Peugeot in a commanding lead.

But Davis noticed the Frenchman was not getting away from the Mercedes as he carved away at the laps. 'There was something remorseless in that formation of German cars.' Boillot clung on, driving right on the limit, while the Mercedes team followed, biding their time like a pack of wolves wearing down their prey.

On the eighteenth lap Lautenschlager pounced, taking the lead, and quickly put a minute between his Mercedes and the Peugeot. Boillot went all out with a tour de force display, pursuing him right up to the last lap. Just before *Le Virage du Mort*, he slowed to a halt; his engine had finally given in. His head dropped to the wheel as the tears flowed.

Lautenschlager and his Mercedes teammates took the first three places. The crowd was stunned. The only applause came from the Mercedes pit.

Not usually a master of understatement, Davis was moved to note that 'curious as it may seem, the effect of that sudden German victory was not as pleasing as it should have been ... there was something more than motor racing in the atmosphere as the crowds made their way dustily from the course.'

On New Year's Day 1914, W.O. and Leonie were married. The bride's stepfather had doubted the suitability of the railway-apprentice-turned-taxi-mechanic; now he approved of the proprietor of a West End motor business and rising star of the fashionable Brooklands set. The happy couple moved into a smart house in Netherhall Gardens, Hampstead, the very hill where W.O. and Sammy Davis had practised on their motorbikes, and the perfect place to embark on family life. Now, finally, W.O.'s future looked set. He had found his vocation, his business was thriving and he was making a name for himself in motor racing. Nineteen fourteen was the high-water mark of British imperial and industrial affluence, and even the moderately affluent were now living the dream. The economist John Maynard Keynes, just a few years older than W.O., wrote that by 1914 for the middle-class Londoner:

> Life offered, at a low cost and with the least trouble, conveniences, comforts and amenities beyond the compass of the richest and most powerful monarchs of other ages. The inhabitant of London could order by telephone, sipping his morning tea in bed, the various products of the whole Earth, in such quantity as he might see fit, and reasonably expect their early delivery upon his doorstep. He would consider himself greatly aggrieved and much surprised at the least interference. But most important of all, he regarded this state of affairs as normal, certain and permanent – except in the direction of further improvement. Any deviation from it would be seen as aberrant, scandalous and avoidable.

Now that they'd discovered the publicity value of record-breaking, the Bentley brothers decided to enter their car in the June 1914 RAC Tourist Trophy. This event on the Isle of Man had acquired international standing and attracted heavyweight foreign competition. But with a car half the size of the rest of the field, they had no expectation of winning.

In fact they came last – in sixth place – but seventeen of the starters had failed to finish. As W.O. noted: 'So long as you stayed the course, the innate British sympathy for the "little man" who bravely battles against the odds ensured the publicity.'

A special Tourist Trophy version of the D.F.P. was planned,

featuring the secret pistons. New catalogues were printed. Bentley & Bentley were now ready to reap the commercial benefit of their racing exploits.

In July 1914, the Bentley newlyweds set off on their delayed honeymoon. They would take a tour of the West Country in one of W.O.'s D.F.P.s, calling in on Leonie's family yacht, which was berthed at Southampton for the Cowes Regatta.

But what focused everyone's attention on the Solent was not the yacht race but the frantic work taking place on Royal Navy destroyers at the Thorneycroft shipyards, which, according to W.O., 'killed stone cold the gaiety of the occasion'. He decided the situation was serious enough to abort his honeymoon. Leaving Leonie with her family, he drove back to London with her brother, Irwin. When they stopped at the Bear in Farnham for lunch they learned that Britain and Germany were at war.

Twenty miles away, Neville Minchin, a keen spectator at Brooklands, was trying to come to terms with the news as it filtered through the crowd. 'While the races were run no one, not even the utmost enthusiast, paid the slightest attention to them. Eyes were turned to watch the trainloads of troops passing every few minutes along the embankment above the railway straight . . . What did it all mean: ultimatums and mobilisation? A continental war in which we were involved was something belonging to history. People quietly melted away and before the meeting was due to finish hardly a soul was left at the track.'

The heady days of racing cars and regattas would be no more. And the Bentley brothers' D.F.P. Tourist Trophy Special never reached the track. It would remain forever only a glossy image in the pages of the specially printed catalogues.

7

A Savage Elation

No one, W.O. included, could have envisaged the scale of destruction that lay ahead, but he knew that Bentley & Bentley, as purveyors of automobiles to the leisured classes, was doomed. Overnight, the demand for cars evaporated.

News of the first casualties soon followed. Within just ten days of the declaration, Jean Leroux, the talented French mechanic who had coaxed the maximum speed out of W.O.'s record-breaking cars, lay dead in the Flanders mud.

Although he was just turning twenty-eight and recently married, doing anything other than enlisting was unthinkable for W.O. And it was more than mere duty. For Davis, now twenty-nine, stories of the German regular army's prowess 'begat a certain savage elation at the prospect of fighting them. That we might lose never crossed my mind.'

H.M. Bentley joined up immediately; W.O. was less successful. He heard about an armoured car brigade being formed but was told to come back in a few months. For the first time in his life, he was at a loss. His money and his future were tied up in a business that suddenly had no reason to exist. And he had just embarked on the next stage of his life, married with a smart new house and perhaps the expectation of junior Bentleys to fill it. What he did know was that this would be the first war in which the internal combustion engine would play a vital role.

One month in, the German army was poised at Meaux preparing its advance on Paris; only a swift counter-attack could save the capital. General Gallieni requisitioned all the taxis in Paris. Six hundred cabs ferried troops to the front and their surprise attack at Nanteuil repulsed the enemy. In November 1914, London 'B'-type buses shipped over to France transported the Royal Warwickshire regiment to the First Battle of Ypres. But W.O. was only half right. This would not be a mobile war on the ground; in the vast, muddy quagmire of the front, the motor vehicle was still no match for the horse. The truly historic change would be in the air. This was where the internal combustion engine would transform twentieth-century warfare.

After Louis Blériot's 1909 Channel crossing, Britain could no longer rely on its sea defences. Its airspace had been penetrated. It was a warning, but one that went unheeded since France was regarded as an ally and Britannia still ruled the waves. But Germany, shocked by French air superiority, had been stung into action.

To mark his birthday in 1912, Kaiser Wilhelm had offered a prize of 50,000 marks for the best aeroplane engine. Forty-four German firms entered designs. Yet by August 1914 there was still not a single British aero-engine in production.

W.O.'s thoughts turned to his own innovation. The aluminium piston had transformed the D.F.P.'s performance. In aircraft engines, weight and top speed was even more critical. Where best could he deploy his secret weapon?

His enquiries brought him to the door of a wooden hut perched on the roof of the recently completed Admiralty Arch on the western side of Trafalgar Square. As First Lord of the Admiralty, Winston Churchill, a champion of the aeroplane's military potential, had instigated the Royal Navy's own 'Air Service', separate from the army's Royal Flying Corps. The wooden hut was the office of Engineer-Commander Wilfrid Briggs, tasked with liaising between the new Service and the nation's builders of aircraft and engines.

Briggs examined the piston and listened while W.O. took him through its advantages. But he was sceptical. What had Bentley got to back up his claims, and why had none of the 'big guns' heard about it?

W.O. reeled off the records he had broken at Brooklands in the transformed D.F.P., the advantages of aluminium's heat conductivity and lightness. As to why his piston had gone uncopied, that could only be attributed to W.O.'s natural diffidence. His preference for leading by example rather than courting headlines meant the secret had remained his.

A youthful thirty-one, only three years older than Bentley, Briggs was also a trained engineer. As he explained his role, W.O. soon divined that it was an 'appallingly difficult post in which he had to deal with jealous, prickly engine-design departments that always knew best and often considered working for a service authority as a favour or as beneath their dignity'.

Impressed by W.O.'s unassuming but clear-sighted engineering pragmatism, Briggs saw a potential ally in his mission to lift Britain into the skies. But what came next filled W.O. with dismay. Finally convinced of the aluminium piston's potential, Briggs decided on the spot that W.O. was the man to take the word round to those difficult engine builders, but warned that it had to be done with 'discretion'.

Meaning? 'We've got to get you into uniform, Bentley.'

In times of war, what mattered was rank. He needed a King's Commission. Surely that took time and training? Two days later, W.O. received a telephone call. 'You're an officer now. Go round to Gieves – and get a uniform with two rings on it.'

For the first time in his life, W.O. had acquired a mentor, who would change the course of his life. Much more than his naval superior, Briggs became '[my] adviser, nursemaid, champion, advocate, pacifier and moderator'.

When he stepped out into South Molton Street in his Royal Naval Volunteer Reserve lieutenant's uniform, he immediately found himself being saluted. His wife Leonie was less deferential. When he appeared on the doorstep she exclaimed, 'What on earth is this?!'

W.O.'s first mission for his new masters was to visit Rolls-Royce in Derby, a daunting prospect given their reputation as makers of 'the best car in the world'. Henry Royce's masterpiece, the Silver Ghost, had set new standards of refinement and reliability. And Royce, a self-made autocrat, was not likely to take orders from anyone.

In 1910 co-founder Charles Stuart Rolls had proposed licensing the Wright brothers' plane for manufacture, and the board had rejected it. Four years later, just days after war had been declared, it imperiously passed a motion that the company 'would not avail itself of the opportunity of making or assembling aero engines for the British Government'.

But, as orders for cars dried up and Rolls-Royce faced the prospect of laying off most of their workers, they reluctantly signed a contract with Briggs to build fifty aero-engines – of a design by Renault. Like the Germans, France had its own aero-engines. Britain had none.

So W.O. had the unedifying task of selling a potentially unwelcome modification to an engine Rolls-Royce didn't want to build in the first place. The hard truth was that since the launch of the Silver Ghost in 1906, engine design had moved on dramatically. The famously silent engine was also heavy and slow-revving, completely unsuitable for use in the air. And Royce was recovering from bowel cancer. In need of round-the-clock nursing, he'd moved his drawing office from Derby to Sussex where the air was less hazardous to the health.

Prepared for a chilly reception, W.O. took himself to Derby, where, in a modest building encircled by a test track, he found their head of development, Ernest Hives. Far from resisting this innovation from outside, Hives, a pragmatist who would in time rise to the very top of Rolls-Royce, showed a keen interest in the aluminium piston and the two men developed a useful rapport.

Soon after his hiring by Briggs, W.O. had received a remarkable piece of intelligence through the motor trade grapevine. Days after their triumph at the French Grand Prix, Mercedes had sold off some of their racers, one of them to a British major, R.M.S. Veal. Hostilities had put paid to the transaction, but W.O. heard a whisper that Veal's car had already been delivered to Milnes-Daimler, the British agents for Mercedes, and was still sitting in the back of their showrooms in Covent Garden. This was one of the team Sammy Davis had watched crushing the Peugeots that fateful 4th of July afternoon. Incredible as it seemed, right there in the heart of London, a prime example of the super high-speed lightweight aero-engine – a key component of the German war machine – had lain unnoticed for months.

W.O. told Briggs immediately and the pair went down to Covent Garden, armed with a search warrant in case of any resistance. But there was none. 'The place was in a fine old mess, but down in the basement, half covered with sacking and old crates, lay the Mercedes.'

Under the bonnet were all the secrets – not just of the Germans' race-winning technology, but also of Paul Daimler's pioneering 1908 aero-engine from which it was developed. With an overhead cam and four valves per cylinder, it was capable of over 3,000rpm, twice that of Royce's car engine and with half the weight.

Briggs and Bentley decided to present their treasure where it could be put to best use, and had it transported to Ernest Hives up at Rolls-Royce. Guardians of Royce's reputation emphatically dismiss any Mercedes influence on the great man. Beyond dispute, however, is that W.O.'s aluminium pistons found their way into the Eagle, Henry Royce's first aero-engine, which bore some resemblance to the Mercedes. For a 28-year-old who had yet to design an engine, W.O. was already making an impact.

8

Sent to Coventry

Like W.O. and his deeply patriotic contemporaries, Sammy Davis rushed to enlist. 'What I wanted was to take a hand in the shooting.' But at twenty-nine, he was told he was too old to be much use as a private soldier.

Devastated, and casting around for a way to be of use, he heard from a fellow reject that the navy was setting up a new department that needed drivers. He made enquiries, and to his huge relief was snapped up by the newly formed Royal Naval Air Squadron's armoured car section.

Initially a support service of touring cars tasked to pick up downed airmen and carry messages and supplies to bases, it rapidly morphed into a separate fighting force. Not to miss out on the fast-emerging land battle, the Admiralty commissioned a squadron of 'land ships', 5-ton lorries clad in 8mm armour plate, each with four Maxim machine guns and a Vickers 3-pounder mounted on a turntable just forward of the rear axle.

By the spring of 1915, elevated – much to his surprise – to the rank of sub-lieutenant, Davis found himself close to the front in charge of one of these vehicles, based in what was left of the village of Neuve Chapelle and was, in his words, 'having kittens'. But he soon found he enjoyed the camaraderie of the crew and, despite his nerves, was at least initially glad to be part of the battle. But this war looked like none he had seen in his Westminster School history books.

All around, as far as the eye could see, was a churned wasteland of mud and tree stumps, flooded shell holes and the rotting carcases of horses. Laden with armour and a crew of seven, his land ship, tottering on its thin, solid tyres, was hopelessly unsuited to the static battle in which the belligerents were now locked.

To fire the Vickers, one side of the armour plate had to be lowered to act as a platform for the gun crew. Davis found they were firing 'most of the time' so collecting up spent cartridges from the mud didn't seem a priority, until he went to stores for fresh ammunition and was threatened with a fine for failing to return them. Furious, he sought out the naval commander in Dunkirk, who listened to his complaint. 'Then he smiled and said: "My boy, you do not know the correct language. Now, I will write a signal and you will send it." The signal read that the cartridges had been "Lost overboard in bad weather".' There was no further talk of a fine.

Parking the armoured lorry amid the ruins of the village, Davis noticed that against the remains of the shattered pale stone buildings, the vehicle's drab olive camouflage was all wrong. Putting his training from the Slade to good use, he designed and painted a *trompe l'œil* canvas screen resembling a bombed-out house and stretched it over the vehicle.

'Fighting is natural to man and is in some ways the finest expression of manhood,' he maintained. But his 'heady exuberance' began to fade as it became clear that much-vaunted 'victories' were in reality no more than 'a matter of eight or nine hundred yards' gained or regained.

His veneration of the high command also began to wear thin. On an errand that took him from the carnage of the front at Ypres to headquarters, he found his superiors in a well-appointed chateau, dining in full evening dress 'with everything which would have been available in England in peace'. The only time he saw a member of the high command he was riding a horse and was followed by a horseman carrying his regimental colours. To Davis it looked like something straight of a G.A. Henty children's book about the Crimea.

On 22 April, the Germans deployed chlorine gas for the first time. Five thousand cylinders were opened, releasing 168 tons of the greenish yellow fog: the apocalypse. On the battlefield, in a trench – or even an armoured vehicle, there was no escape as it blinded and burned, blistering the lungs and throat when inhaled. It soaked into the woollen uniforms with the same effect. Five thousand were killed that day, and countless more injured.

Typical of his generation, the otherwise garrulous Davis determined to remain staunchly tight-lipped about his war, but the brevity of his observations make his story all the more poignant. In May he was sent on leave after 'being gassed'. Since he was not initially hospitalised, he was one of the lucky ones. But nothing could have prepared him for what he found when he reached north London and the comfort of home and hearth. 'Almost all the whole family had gone: father; Hugh, shot down attacking a German squadron, apparently on his own in a berserk mood; and Cyril, killed as a machine gunner in the salient at Ypres. Only Mother and Evelyn were left.'

As well as both of his brothers, the war had also claimed two uncles, two nephews and a cousin. Soon after, he heard that his motorcycling school friend Fatty Bowes-Scott, a second lieutenant in the Indian army, had been killed in Africa. And yet another casualty that year, the Edwin Davis department store in Hull was completely destroyed in a Zeppelin raid.

Despite the magnitude of his losses, Davis's spirit seemed undimmed. When the board assembled to judge his fitness to return to duty, he told them he wanted to fly, and was furious when they flatly refused. His technical knowledge, they said, could be put to better use. He would not see any more action. The board sent him even further away from the fighting – literally to Coventry. But there was a very welcome silver lining. This apparently unpromising posting would take him back into the orbit of his other old motorcycling pal, W.O. Bentley.

9

Dawn Patrol

Briggs's next task for W.O. was to take the aluminium piston gospel to Gwynne's, an industrial pump maker in Chiswick, west London. Like Rolls, Gwynne's had a contract to build French aero-engines under licence for the Royal Navy Air Service. Rotary engines had several advantages over the in-line water-cooled units Henry Royce was designing.

Because the entire crankcase and cylinders rotated with the propeller, this whirling assembly created its own airflow to cool the cylinders even when the aircraft was on the ground. Air-cooling also meant no radiators or water pipes – making the rotary the lightest engine for its power available at the time. The downside was that the gyroscopic effect of the whole engine rotating meant the aircraft could turn very quickly to the right but only slowly to the left, a feature which for many novice pilots proved lethal.

Gwynne's Clerget rotaries were powering Britain's first generation of fighters like the Sopwith Camel. W.O.'s aluminium pistons would boost performance by 20bhp, a dramatic improvement. It was obvious that they should be adopted immediately. But how enthusiastic would Gwynne's be to do his bidding, wondered W.O.

'They're to do what you tell 'em to do,' Briggs told him as he sent him on his way. Company boss Neville Gwynne gave him a cooler reception than Hives had at Rolls-Royce, but from his time in the Great Northern engine sheds and the taxi business, W.O. knew how to win over skilled machinists. However, what he was about to discover would test far more than his shop-floor rapport when a major problem emerged with the engine with its cast-iron cylinders that they were supplying. Rumours were filtering back from the front in northern France that Clergets were seizing up mid-air with alarming frequency and devastating consequences. Naval aviator and future VC Richard Bell Davies was one of the few pilots who made it back with a stricken engine.

'There was a loud bang and an intense vibration started. Throttling back I turned instinctively for home. There was no hope of gliding for fifty miles so I opened up the throttle again ... Gradually we lost height but I had enough in hand to get back. After landing, as the engine slowed and stopped, it sounded as if it was full of crockery. Two of the pistons had seized up and the wrist pins had torn out of the piston skirting, breaking it all up.'

W.O. deduced that, in flight, the forward-facing side of the rotary's cylinders cooled more than the sheltered rearward side, causing the barrels to warp. Clerget had come up with a 'fix' for this; each cylinder was fitted with an 'obdurator ring', a thin bronze washer that was supposed to maintain the seal between piston and the cylinder wall to compensate for the distortion. But the rings were prone to breaking, causing the piston to seize up, almost always fatally. Bentley knew that the high heat conductivity of aluminium would help cure the seizing problem, taking heat from the hot spots on the piston liner and sharing it out more evenly round the cylinder.

Having diagnosed the problem, he pressed them to let him come up with a solution and immediately flew into a wall of resistance. Neville Gwynne's priority was keeping his lucrative partnership with Clerget sweet, not to start telling them to redesign their engine.

W.O. was deeply troubled. Back in the rooftop hut on top of the Admiralty, Briggs could offer little more than commiserations. W.O. had tested his boss's management skills to the limit; the RNAS overlords were deadly rivals of the army's own Royal Flying Corps, who had their own engine contracts, and did not want their navy air service to be shown up. To W.O.'s dismay, far away from the battlefield, his concerns were dismissed as hearsay. But though he was not the kind to make a noise, keeping his head down and toeing the line was not his style either; it was time to take matters into his own hands.

At Portsmouth, he boarded a destroyer, bound for Dunkirk. 'A visit to the squadrons was a drastic and positive cure for any lurking complacency.' More than that, the mission would have 'a profound effect on my outlook, on my attitude to the war and to the men who were fighting it . . . and the very fundamentals of my engineering philosophy'.

In France his reception could not have been more different as pilots and mechanics queued up to tell him their woes. After a day working on a sick Clerget, euphoric at finally getting his hands dirty, he quipped to the CO: 'I wouldn't mind going anywhere in this now.'

'You can go up on the dawn patrol tomorrow if you like,' came the reply.

He had never been in the air before, let alone fired a shot in anger. But it was an instruction he could hardly refuse. Early the next morning, after a quick briefing on the Lewis machine gun, crammed into the rear cockpit, dressed 'like one of Scott's party', he was taken up.

Happily for him, there was only one black-crossed Fokker in the sky and it was out of range. But at 5,000ft above the English Channel, a strong, steady headwind slowing their return, W.O. got a very real sense of how much his life – and all their lives – depended on his remedial work of the day before.

Back on the ground, he stripped the engine to see how it had fared. Three of the piston con rods were blue from overheating: 'Their life could be measured in minutes.' For W.O. this was a defining moment; from here on, reliability and endurance would be everything.

Like Davis, just a few miles along the road at Ypres, W.O. was dismayed by the elaborate formality of mess dinners enjoyed by the commander, Captain Charles Lamb, his faithful Alsatian at his side, oblivious of shellfire from heavy guns blasting just a few miles away. And any lingering sense of romance about this new form of warfare was quickly dispelled as he witnessed five pilots at once all spiralling down in flames to their deaths; parachutes had been developed, but not to the point where they were light and compact enough to be accommodated in the crews' minimal seats. He also saw how the remainder of the squadron reacted: 'with grief, courage and fear thrown together in hectic, drunken parties among the survivors in the evening.'

But Lamb was to prove an ally. Though a cold and severe character in W.O.'s eyes, he gave him a free hand that insulated him from bureaucratic or political interference. This allowed him to immerse himself in the life of the squadron, talking to pilots and mechanics, rolling up his sleeves and getting to grips with the temperamental Clergets. Frightened as W.O. freely admitted he was, he relished this very vital role, like a doctor in the field, saving lives by keeping the aircraft aloft.

His closest shave came on the ground when he had to run for cover from a low-flying Fokker, flown by Manfred von Richthofen – the Red Baron himself – strafing the airfield. The only sanctuary was a canal on the airfield's perimeter where he huddled among the reeds, teeth chattering in the freezing water. He wasn't alone; next to him was Petty Officer R.A. 'Nobby' Clarke. Although neither of them knew it at the time, this encounter was the start of an association that would shape both their lives after the war.

Emboldened, W.O. rushed back to Chiswick with a clear idea of the modifications needed to sort out the Gwynne Clergets.

The cylinder heating problem could be resolved by creating an aluminium cylinder with a cast-iron liner shrunk into it which would resolve the unbalanced temperature issue. The weeks of battle that ensued over this at Gwynne's were almost more taxing than anything he had experienced in France, and took every ounce of patience to resolve.

Returning home to Leonie in Netherhall Gardens, drained and frustrated, he was acutely aware of what poor company he was for his young wife and wondered when their married life would ever properly begin. Gwynne's, W.O. realised, would rather ignore him than compromise their lucrative relationship with Clerget. Ever the diplomat, Briggs suggested that W.O. persevere with Gwynne's, make a piston and cylinder to his own specification and fit it to a Clerget to prove his case. But he knew it was a losing battle, and probably so did Briggs, because on his next visit to the rooftop hut, his boss had a new idea that left him almost speechless.

Like so many of Coventry's car makers, Humber had started out building bicycles. But by 1914, they were W.O.'s chief rivals at Brooklands. Their designer, Fred Burgess, had modelled his TT race-winning 3-litre on the Peugeots that had been so humiliated in that year's French Grand Prix. But Humber was not having a good war. With contracts only to build army bicycles and mobile canteens, its machine shops and talent lay seriously underused. And Briggs had the solution: W.O. was to go to Humber and build an engine of his own design.

Given the stifling internal politics of the navy, it was an astonishingly audacious move; though his growing reputation spoke for him, W.O. had still not yet designed an engine. How would Humber react?

10

THE MORNING DESTROYER

For W.O., Humber was the opposite of Gwynne's in almost every way. The chairman was the 2nd Earl Russell, brother of Bertrand Russell, and a man of considerable notoriety. Romantically connected to several young men in his youth, he had also been married three times, tried for bigamy in the House of Lords in 1901 and known ever after in Edwardian society as 'the Wicked Earl'. Also a Fabian, he was the first peer of the realm to declare his support for the newly formed Labour Party and would serve in Ramsay MacDonald's government as Parliamentary Secretary for Transport. Finally, as a keen motorist, he was immensely proud to have been the recipient of London's first registration plate in December 1903: A1.

More importantly for W.O., Russell was a passionate supporter of what would become Bentley's own aero-engine, and drove the project with relentless energy. By now well-practised at inserting himself into established workshops, at 'The Humber' W.O. was welcomed as a saviour, not least by their chief designer, Fred Burgess.

All rivalry from their Brooklands record-breaking days cast aside, W.O. was delighted at how Burgess threw himself into the job. 'He had the most facile pencil of any man I have known, a pencil that flashed across the board in deft strokes, expressing in lines our ideas as quickly as the words were spoken. It was a wonderful sight and the magic of it never failed to impress me.'

W.O. even found praise for Arthur Niblett, the sceptical works manager, who tempered their flights of fancy, and his assistant Meason with his 'live-wire enthusiasm'.

Billeted in Coventry's King's Head hotel, W.O. seldom slept a whole night as work continued day and night. All the lessons of the flawed Clerget combined with reports from where it mattered most – the pilots and mechanics in France – were poured into the project.

Unleashed, W.O. developed not one but two engines. The first was a direct replacement for the problematic Clerget, similar in size but with twenty more brake horsepower, giving the Sopwith Camel a further 4,000ft of ceiling. The aluminium cylinders with cast-iron liners, which he had tried and failed to have fitted to the Gwynne's Clergets, were a key feature, which enabled him to dispense with the self-destructing obdurator ring. The second, a larger engine but using common parts, the B.R.2, promised 230bhp from its 24.9 litres.

Developing two engines seemed like a smart move – too smart though, even for his protector at the Admiralty, who warned W.O. not to run before he could show that he could walk. Having gambled a lot of his capital persuading his superiors to sanction the development of the navy's 'own' engine, Briggs had received only grudging approval. One engine at a time; W.O. needed to rein himself in.

By the summer of 1916, the new engine was ready for inspection. This was not Briggs' role; he was too senior for that. By now the Admiralty had its own man for the job: the recently appointed Lieutenant S.C.H. Davis.

How qualified Davis actually was to approve the work of W.O., at the cutting edge of aero-engineering, is questionable.

Having abandoned his Daimler apprenticeship for Fleet Street, he was more an enthusiast than a practised engineering authority. Possibly he was put in there merely to rubber-stamp the progress.

But for W.O. it must have come as a relief that the Admiralty had sent a kindred spirit. And if he minded having his 'homework' marked by an apprentice-turned-journalist, he didn't show it. Davis's sunny demeanour, seemingly undimmed by his recent experiences at Ypres or his dreadful family losses, contributed to the positive atmosphere in which W.O. was at last working.

The Admiralty had given Davis one further task which he thought ridiculous. He was asked to persuade Bentley to salute visiting senior officers.

W.O. had by now developed a healthy contempt for authority in all its forms. But Davis had nothing but admiration for his old friend's ability to stay on task in the face of bureaucratic interference. 'We always turned W.O. on to the official concerned for no man can shake W.O. when he is certain of what he wants and intends to have it.'

And whether his inspecting really mattered to the authorities or not, Davis – and W.O. – knew that the real test of the new engine would be in the air. W.O. insisted on seeing it being flown in anger. To his delight, fitted to the Sopwith Camel, his creation boosted its 'ceiling' way up to 20,000ft, 5,000ft more than those powered by the Gwynne's Clergets. But there were teething troubles.

He was back in France at 4 Squadron's airfield in Dunkirk when four of the aircraft fitted with his new engine force-landed with engine failure, one of them on the beach. W.O. dashed to the scene, interrogated the dazed pilot and examined the engine: the valve springs were too stiff and had broken under pressure. This was a catastrophic humiliation; there was only one thing for it. That afternoon he crossed the Channel. Back in Coventry, he worked through the night, took a train back to Dover, boarded a 'morning destroyer' and had aircraft flying with the new springs by the end of the day.

But rather than receiving congratulations or a medal for his prompt action, W.O. was in more trouble. The Admiralty's accounts department complained that the invoice lacked an 'authority reference' of the Admiralty inspector. And on whose authority had Bentley used the destroyer?

Throughout the war, W.O. had struggled to get home to Leonie, often returning exhausted and preoccupied and then departing early. He was glad that her mother lived nearby and that she had not been alone when there was a threat of a Zeppelin raid. These early bombardments of London created more fear than damage. Now, with the war finally turning in the Allies' favour, that threat was gone and they could at last finally pick up their life from where it had left off, on their curtailed honeymoon in the summer of 1914.

Particularly pleasing to Briggs, who had gambled his reputation on W.O. delivering, was that at £605 each his engines were only two-thirds the price of the Gwynne's Clergets. Not only that, but no other engine could match the Bentleys for power, weight and reliability, putting them in such demand that Humber was unable to cope alone; other factories, including Davis's old firm Daimler, were enlisted. The squadrons loved it, and 'BR' – Bentley Rotary – equipped Sopwith Camels were in high demand. The 'Red Baron' von Richtofen even complained that they were so much faster than his Fokkers that German pilots didn't want to fight any more. There was also some righteous satisfaction when the Luftwaffe's air ace, who had pursued W.O. into that freezing canal, was himself shot down by a BR-engined aircraft. In all, 5,000 BR rotaries were produced, some of which saw service well into the 1920s.

Inspecting W.O.'s work should have been the happiest part of Davis's war. He had an unswerving admiration for his old friend and his impatience with any obstacle that got in the way of his work, and was highly amused by the Humber staff run ragged by his exacting demands. The bond forged back in their motorcycling days grew deeper. Davis was in awe of W.O. and his emerging talents, the fruits of which would have a dramatic impact on his life later on. But the partnership at Humber wasn't to last. In his first of three memoirs, *Racing Motorist*, Davis mentions with uncharacteristic brevity and bluntness that he 'cracked up entirely and went to live in hospital.' In a later version he downgrades his condition as 'general worry'. But this, combined with gallstones and an appendectomy, put him out of action for the rest of the war.

Like many shell-shocked soldiers, Davis was sent back into service – albeit not at the front – when he was still far from well. Guilt at having survived when so many had not weighed heavily on him and his peers. Tellingly, he also recorded a peculiarity of the First World War veterans: the 'feeling that older people at home looked at one oddly because one was still alive and so many were not'.

11

The Invisible Foe

Three thousand miles from Coventry, in an olive grove not far from Cairo, Captain Joseph Dudley Benjafield MD of the Royal Army Medical Corps, who would one day be Davis's co-driver, was fighting another kind of war.

Although he sprang from a similarly affluent north London background to that of Davis and W.O., medicine rather than machinery would determine his direction. It was a family tradition. His father's lucrative practice in Edmonton and his mother's legacy from the family timber business in Shoreditch financed the household. After Marlborough and University College Hospital Medical School, he was awarded his MD in 1912. His first position was as house surgeon at the Evelina Hospital for Sick Children, founded by Ferdinand de Rothschild in memory of his wife, who had died in childbirth. But in 1913, Benjafield's interest was caught by a relatively new field: bacteriology. His choice would take him not only to war – but the front line of the most devastating peacetime killer of that century.

In 1914, Benjafield was already an established physician, dividing his time between his home and consulting rooms in Wimpole Street – just the other side of Oxford Street from the Bentley brothers – and the Grand Hotel, Folkestone, a favourite retreat of the late King Edward VII and his various mistresses. The hotel manager, Gustav Gelardi, was the father of Vera, who that summer became Benjafield's wife.

But poor Vera would see even less of her husband than Leonie Bentley saw of W.O. Straight away the RAMC plunged him into multiple theatres of war – in the Aegean, Mesopotamia, the Dardanelles, and Mudros in Greece, the Allies' main Mediterranean HQ. Their son Patrick was born in December 1916, but he missed the birth and his christening; not until he was back on leave that June did father and son meet. But then came Benjafield's most challenging assignment.

The 37th Mobile Bacteriological Laboratory was a donation from Henry Wellcome, the pharmaceutical entrepreneur, kitted out with state-of-the-art instruments by Baird & Tatlock. With a crew of five, Benjafield and his lab were shipped out by boat and train to Lydda in Palestine to meet up with the Egyptian Expeditionary Force. Under General Allenby's command, they encountered a very different war from the sort Davis saw through the gunsight in his armoured truck at Ypres. With a combination of mechanised forces, air power and the deployment of irregulars led by Lawrence of Arabia in his Rolls-Royce armoured car, this was a highly mobile campaign.

In the grounds of the No. 6 Egyptian Stationary Hospital, under a giant shade he constructed out of rushes against the brutal and stifling heat, Benjafield went into battle.

Allenby's army was already one giant Petri dish. As well as diagnosing multiple cases of cholera, dysentery, typhus and VD, Benjafield reported that 90 per cent of the men were infected with malaria. There were relatively well-established treatments for these conditions, but they were not life savers, and nothing in his biochemical arsenal was effective against the other killer working its remorseless way through the camps.

The new strain of flu swept across the world at a breathtaking rate, even faster than the news of its spread, taking the medical world completely by surprise. Previously fit victims could die within hours of showing symptoms, their skin turning blue, their lungs filling with fluid that drowned them from inside. Their immune systems already devastated by one or more of the maladies acquired in their camps, Benjafield's patients were dropping like flies. The conventional medical wisdom was that it was caused by a bacterium. And there was no vaccine.

Benjafield's orders betrayed little sense of urgency. He was merely asked to investigate, 'with a view to suggesting some therapeutic and prophylactic measures'. Initially deducing that strepto-diplococcus could be the organism responsible, he set about producing his own vaccine from strains he isolated post-mortem.

The first results were promising; among a sample group of sixty-three patients the mortality rate fell from 35 to 20 per cent. So he produced more, which he distributed to the other hospitals and casualty clearing stations. For four chronic cases with broncho-pneumonial complications, he then developed autogenous vaccines by isolating micro-organisms from the patients' own saliva, disarming them and injecting them back into the patient to cause an auto-immune reaction; they all recovered.

He wrote up his findings for the *British Medical Journal* of 9 August 1919 speculating that an 'ultramicroscopic filterable virus' was the primary aetiological agent (the probable cause) of influenza, which then rendered the lungs more susceptible to bacterial infection. It would be another thirteen years before the invention of the electron microscope would confirm his hypothesis.

In all likelihood he probably wished he could have tried even harder. His account closes with the modest hope that his findings would 'dissipate – in part at any rate – the diffidence felt by many medical men to the employment of vaccine'. Autogenous vaccines, rather like W.O.'s aluminium piston, were apt to encounter establishment resistance. Here, albeit couched in the cautious language of the time, it's possible to detect a lingering frustration with the medical establishment, just as W.O. experienced with the bureaucrats of the War Office. Back home, Benjafield re-established his practice and immersed himself in his work. But it wasn't enough. He was restless, and despite the pandemic still raging around him, he set about pursuing new adventures away from his wife and baby son Patrick, born in his absence.

In London, the official line was an early version of 'Keep Calm and Carry On'. *The Times* suggested the illness was probably a result of 'the general weakness of nerve-power known as war-weariness'. The *British Medical Journal* judged overcrowding on transport to workplaces as necessary for the war effort and the Royal College of Physicians pronounced the malady no more threatening than the Russian Flu, which had killed a million worldwide in 1889–94. Even when the pandemic was at its height in the closing months of 1918, the Armistice Day parades were allowed to continue, with devastating consequences.

The pandemic claimed nearly a quarter of a million lives in Britain alone, approximately 60 million worldwide. Young adults succumbed the fastest, especially pregnant women. And in December 1918, barely a month into her long-postponed peace-time married life, Leonie Bentley became a casualty, aged just thirty-two.

12

Out of the Firestorm

On the surface, the Britain of 1919 looked much the same as it had in the summer of 1914. Horse-drawn traffic still mingled with increasing numbers of motor buses, lorries and taxis. Most homes were still lit by gas, and telephones were rare. Stiff collars and spats were still worn by men of substance and the radical development in women's fashion was the exposure of ankles.

What had changed most was inside the minds of men. The unquestioning fervour of duty to King and Country, which had driven so many to enlist in 1914, had been severely tested by the pure horror those men witnessed daily in the trenches of northern France, and death on a scale which left almost no family untouched. The Armistice brought no feelings of triumph, merely a weary sense of relief. The jubilation of those at home was short-lived, tempered by the return of servicemen haunted by what they could never erase from their shaken minds.

Although class divisions would prevail for decades to come, cracks deep in the subterranean foundations which previously held them firmly in their place were spreading, as men saw for the first time the folly of their superiors. And in the filthy intimacy of the trenches, officers and 'tommies' who would never have been on equal terms in civvy street were levelled by the basic demands of survival.

For Davis, the Armistice came not as a moment of joy but a shock, 'leaving one numb and unable quite to imagine how on earth one was to face civilian life once more'.

There was no going back to the carefree days before August 1914; the shadow cast by the war would stretch long into the future. 'Things were somehow very different. Like everyone else, I had lost too many friends to feel the same.'

Another shock was the fate of aeroplane builders. Between 1914 and 1918, Britain, a latecomer to the skies, had turned out 55,000 aircraft, taking the industry from the hobby of a few eccentrics to the world's biggest manufacturer of aeroplanes, employing 350,000, a third of them women. W.O. Bentley could legitimately consider himself at the forefront – well placed to pursue a promising career in this burgeoning endeavour.

But on Friday 13 November 1918, just two days after the guns in France fell silent, newly recruited apprentices watched in dismay at Airco on the edge of north London as finished aircraft received their final adjustments, were checked by inspectors, passed, stamped, signed for, wheeled out to the back of the factory, and, now redundant, burned on a giant bonfire. The pall of smoke hung over Colindale for several days.

Overnight, the RAF's order for 20,000 B.R.2 engines was cancelled. Humber, Daimler and the other car plants pressed into building them were directed to return to peacetime production. Large and advanced as it was, Britain's aircraft industry had only one client – the government. Within a year, half those businesses would be gone.

And recognition for W.O.'s contribution to the war effort would be tainted. In uniform, he had been a 'two-ringer', having to get by on a relatively lowly naval lieutenant's pay, promoted to captain only at the end of the war. The grateful Briggs had managed to find him a £1,000 gratuity to help him out. And in 1919 a Royal Commission for Awards was set up to consider applications for remuneration from 'inventors or owners' whose unpatented efforts had contributed to winning the war.

To support his claim, W.O. lined up Briggs and a formidable squadron of RAF top brass led by Air Chief Marshal Brooke-Popham and including a number of much-decorated pilots. He also retained a King's Counsel, Douglas Hogg, the future Lord Hailsham, who argued for an award of £107,000. He met with considerable resistance.

One witness for the Treasury, a Captain Fairbairn, disputed that W.O.'s engines contributed to Britain's air supremacy in the war. Surely, the Commission contended, as a serving officer he was merely carrying out his duties. Meanwhile, Gwynne's also put in a claim, arguing that the 'original' design for the BR.1 was merely an evolution of their Clerget rotary and originated on *their* premises.

Eventually W.O. was granted a consideration of £8,000 (£360,000 today), which Hogg considered so measly that he reduced his fee, which would otherwise have eaten up nearly half of W.O.'s award. To rub his face in it, Gwynne's put in a claim for £150,000 and was awarded £110,000. And to add further insult to injury, the Inland Revenue attempted to argue that W.O.'s award was taxable, though they backed down when Hogg threatened to mount a test case against them. Nevertheless, it was a Pyrrhic victory which left the recently bereaved W.O. in little mood to celebrate.

But unlike Davis, struggling to see his way in the post-war landscape, W.O., his vision sharpened by grief, had emerged from the war with a very clear idea of what he wanted to do.

13

Best in Class

On 20 January 1919, barely a month after Leonie's death, W.O. sat down to plan the first original Bentley car. He rented an office on the top floor of 16 Conduit Street – opposite the Rolls-Royce showroom – which may have seemed extravagant, but his empty home was not conducive to creative thought. And Mayfair, the heart of London's clubland, might help shape his inspiration. It was an extraordinarily audacious move.

He had never built a car before; his only experience of manufacturing was developing his aero-engine at Humber. He had no factory, no machinery and no drawing office to call on. He was not a draughtsman and was never going to pick up a slide rule. His engineering experience was hands-on, going back to the dismantling of his first clockwork train, and then with his motorcycles, the D.F.P.s and the Gwynne's Clergets, modifying – transforming even – other people's designs. He had never designed anything from scratch.

His role model was his first idol, locomotive designer Nigel Gresley, with whom he shared a strong distaste for maths. 'Working out a design mathematically at first drove him mad with impatience as it has always exasperated me. With your head close to the drawing board you can't see anything else at all; it is all detail work and the overall principle of design is liable to be lost.'

What W.O. had was a vision – a very clear one – of the car he wanted to make: 'A fast car, a good car, the best in its class, a car that could be driven hard without minding.' This in a time, he noted, when reliability was still a doubtful factor in a touring car. And the really fast cars – racing machines – were famously fearsome, temperamental things, only for the initiated with nerves of steel and money to burn.

W.O.'s excursion into building aero-engines, where the consequence of mechanical failure was frequently fatal, had drilled into him the fundamental importance of reliability. He knew the key was to design an engine to work well within the limits of its capability. To that end, he specified four valves for each cylinder, each with two spark plugs and plenty of water cooling around them. At a time when most car journeys were short, and Britain's road network had yet to emerge from the era of the horse, he also wanted 'a sensibly high top gear'.

His vision was not puttering along on the winding, hoof-pitted tracks of his home country, but fast cruising on the long, straight continental roads that he had become acquainted with on his visits to the D.F.P. factory at Courbevoie. But even these were inferior. 'Their surface was often appalling and at the same time there was a great temptation to drive fast. What we were aiming at was a car that could be pushed all day long at 60 mph or more over almost any sort of road surface.' This had never been done before in a car this size.

To put his vision on paper he turned to a man who had helped him with his aero-engine at Humber: the blunt, forthright Frederick Tasker 'Monkey' Burgess (so named on account of his supposedly simian facial features). Burgess's last car had been the 1914 TT Humber racer, which bore striking similarities to Ernest Henry's Grand Prix Peugeot.

W.O. regarded him as 'a sound designer but not an adventurous one', and did not think he would produce a very interesting design under his own direction. 'But he was a magnificent draughtsman, the quickest I have ever known.'

From Vauxhall, another contender in that 1914 TT, he took on Harry Varley, who had worked under Lawrence Pomeroy, a star among Britain's very first generation of automotive engineers, whose Vauxhall 30-98 was one of very few machines that would bare comparison with W.O.'s car. Varley, who had been runner-up in a worldwide draughtsmanship competition, more than made up for what W.O. lacked in theoretical knowledge, and, though meticulous, frequently clashed with the quick and impatient Burgess. The equally strong wills of the two talents made for a combustible atmosphere, soothed by W.O.'s quiet, focused determination.

In Britain's blossoming post-Great War motor industry, both men could have stepped into far more secure, better paying positions. Burgess even confided that he had 'thrown up a damn good job to join this outfit', but there were other inducements. Even then, with the industry barely two decades old, few designers got to dream up entirely new products; much of their work was compromised by having to improve or make over existing machines. W.O.'s proposition was a very enticing carte blanche.

As a matter of principle, and unlike many of his peers, W.O. was unwilling to take credit for anything that was not his. He saw no merit in originality for its own sake, but chose instead to 'take the best of what other people had done before us'.

This was actually only what others like Henry Royce were already doing, the only difference being that W.O. was honest enough to admit it. Where leading designers like Royce or Ettore Bugatti in Alsace were figureheads with teams of nameless skilled technicians working away in their shadow, W.O. was the opposite. He made no secret of the fact that, while he was responsible for the design, he did not consider himself 'the designer'; it was emphatically a team effort.

For the engine, a major source of inspiration was Burgess's 1914 twin-camshaft TT Humber – the near-copy of Swiss engineer Ernest Henry's racing Peugeot, which in turn had been closely based on a Hispano Suiza designed by Henry's former employer, Marc Birkigt.

Although they enhanced performance, Bentley rejected twin camshafts on grounds of the noise generated by the chain required to operate them. The single overhead cam with bevel drive, which he adopted, came from another source of inspiration, Paul Daimler. His was the engine that had powered the 1914 French Grand Prix-winning Mercedes team cars, one of which W.O. had liberated from the basement in Covent Garden and passed on to Rolls-Royce. The valves driven directly by the camshaft above them enabled the engine to achieve much higher revs than with the more conventional side valve system. Without the men and facilities enjoyed by Daimler or Humber, W.O. and his tiny team had their work cut out. But with nothing else in his life to distract him, W.O. poured every waking hour into his new creation – and expected no less of his men.

Outwardly, W.O. could be an intimidating figure – taciturn, dogged and poker-faced, his considerable reputation enhanced by his game-changing contributions to Britain's aircraft during the war. Ensconced in Conduit Street, he put in rare and brief appearances at Bentley & Bentley in Hanover Court, which was increasingly overseen by the more affable H.M. and a willing young recruit named Hillstead.

14

Market Fever

Arthur Finch Clitheroe Hillstead had arrived at Bentley & Bentley during the war, having been ruled out of military service by a back injury. He too came from much the same affluent background as W.O., Benjafield and Davis.

Passionate about cars from an early age, by fourteen he was chauffeuring his GP father on house calls round Putney, south-west London in his De Dion. He then talked his way into Brooklands, carrying fuselages from Weybridge Station to help A.V. Roe put together his first aeroplanes.

Whenever he could Hillstead blagged a ride or a drive on whatever machinery was circling the Brooklands track. It was here that he first heard about W.O. and his remarkable feats with the D.F.P. But after an altercation with Roe, in 1913 he went off in search of further adventures and ended up driving lorries across the uncharted Patagonian Desert, where he sustained the injury that would render him unfit for military service.

Confident, personable, mechanically handy and a capable driver of a variety of vehicles, Hillstead was an asset to Bentley & Bentley, keeping the wartime business ticking over, servicing cars and selling the odd second-hand machine. With both Bentley brothers taken up with war work, the day-to-day management had been delegated to A.H.M. Ward, husband of their sister Edith. The other family presence in Hanover Court was that of their father, Alfred, of bible-hurling fame. Evidently his view of his son's experiments with the internal combustion engine had softened, as Hillstead frequently found Bentley Sr in the showroom keen to lend a hand. 'This usually consisted of a tidying-up process. Surplus catalogues were parcelled and put away . . . I even found him wearing a top hat with black coat and striped trousers, adjusting the ball-valve in the W.C. He would do anything for anyone and one of his greatest pleasures was to talk about his son's achievements.'

But within weeks of the Armistice, as quickly as the aeroplane business collapsed, a new trade arose. With a dearth of available new cars, the second-hand market was booming, particularly at the top end. By early 1919 the enthusiastic spectator and component maker Neville Minchin was witnessing hectic lunches at the Royal Aero Club in Clifford Street not far from the Bentleys' premises, where the leading lights of London's motor trade gathered to wheel and deal. 'Someone whilst taking his soup might be a possessor of say a 1911 Rolls-Royce but by the time he was eating his meat he had sold it, yet whilst partaking of coffee it might again be his property.' Minchin recalled a 1913 Rolls-Royce selling in 1919 for an astonishing £7,200, double the price when new.

Over at Bentley & Bentley, demobbed from the Air Ministry where he had risen to the rank of colonel, H.M. instructed Hillstead to buy up every second-hand D.F.P. he could find, which they rapidly sold on for a tidy profit. As market fever gripped, Hillstead recalled on one occasion buying and selling the same car twice in the same week.

When D.F.P. resumed peacetime production, demand in Britain was such that Hillstead soon found himself reprising his Patagonian adventures, organising a relay of drivers, heavily swaddled and with nothing but a frame to sit on, to ferry unbodied chassis from the factory in Courbevoie to the Channel ports. That year, Bentley & Bentley would bank a heady £20,000, the seed money for development of W.O.'s own car. With demand outstripping supply, never before had there been such a good time to start a motor company, so it seemed. In the two years after the war, forty-six new firms were born. While W.O.'s design was still on the drawing board, the brothers agreed that his brand new car needed a brand new company, with Hillstead charged with helping to launch the venture.

Hillstead got on famously with the genial H.M. but was dismayed that W.O. could be his brother, reaching for an appropriately automotive metaphor to illustrate their contrasting characters.

'In build, complexion and manner, he was as different as a chain drive is from the conventional bevel and crown wheel. Whereas H.M. was of average height, well-built, neither dark nor fair, cheerful, ready to crack a joke and possessed of a decided twinkle in his brown myopic eyes; W.O. was short, stocky, dark, inclining to ocular fierceness, deliberate, monosyllabic and decidedly dour.' Nevertheless, keen as mustard to be part of the new venture, Hillstead threw himself into finding investors, even putting in some savings of his own. In the spring of 1919, they held a lunch party at Verrey's restaurant in nearby Regent Street, a venerable establishment that had counted Dickens and Tennyson among its clientele. On the guest list were wealthy friends and friends of friends, who might be persuaded to part with some funds.

These included H.M.'s wartime acquaintances General Whittington and Colonel Wolfe Barry. Martin Roberts, one of Hillstead's D.F.P. customers, and proprietor of an engineering business, hoped an investment might bring his firm some Bentley contracts in return. Hardy, the solicitor brother, was present to deal with any formalities, ideally before the warm glow of food and wine wore off.

With the audience 'suitably mellowed', W.O. got up to speak. Hillstead, aware of the designer's famous aversion to uttering more than three words at a time, was apprehensive. He need not have been. W.O. rose to the occasion. Letting himself go 'with what was undoubtedly the longest speech of his life', he ranged across the state of the post-war car market and the chronic shortage of cars, set out the vision for his own car and 'wound up with vigorous peroration on the value of racing to the industry as a whole'.

Hillstead had already grasped that H.M. and brother-in-law Ward did not share W.O.'s passion for racing, a pursuit that hardly promised the prospective investors round the table a clear return. And he found it dispiriting that all the questions were about profit rather than the product itself, but evidently W.O. had worked some magic, as the response from the potential backers seemed unanimously positive.

Hardy was instructed to proceed with the formation of Bentley Motors. To keep things in the family, the directors were W.O., H.M. and Ward. The first £30,000 of shares were issued to W.O. and H.M. in consideration of the existing design work already done. That left a nominal capital of £20,000 to cover the remaining development, prototypes, factory, machinery, staff and marketing, none of which could be recouped until the first cars were sold. Like so many start-ups, Bentley Motors was founded on little more than a heady cocktail of inspiration and optimism.

And the booming car market of 1919 was double-edged. While it offered encouragement to amateur speculators, it also created an expectation of quick returns – which Bentley Motors, with nothing to show but some drawings, was in no position to offer. The goodwill soon evaporated as the shareholders realised that much more investment would be needed before they'd see any dividends.

W.O. soon learned that as beggars they could not be choosers. 'We were not in a position to pick and choose our directors, and some whom we persuaded to invest in our motor car were totally out of touch with the car business in general and our sort of car business with its emphasis on reputation and long term customer goodwill.'

As Burgess and Varley completed their drawings, another pressing question had to be addressed. Without a factory, who was going to make the parts they were designing and where would they be put together? Motor manufacturing was still in its infancy, fraught with trial and error, with a heavy bias towards error. For any investor it was a leap of faith. The methodology of making cars *and* money was still being worked out.

Because of Henry Royce's fanaticism about quality control, Rolls-Royce made almost all its components in-house and even had its own foundry, but this was not typical. At Cowley outside Oxford, William Morris bought in as many off-the-shelf parts as he could, and regarded himself as an assembler not a maker. But with the motor components industry still just a string of small workshops scattered around the country, their order books mostly chock full, a tiny new company like Bentley with a list of parts to be made to order, all to W.O.'s exacting standards, would have to join a long queue.

The only components W.O. would be able to buy off the shelf were wire wheels from Rudge Whitworth, the electrics and the steering wheel. The rest would have to be individually cast, forged or machined to Burgess and Varley's drawings by whichever of these small suppliers happened to have a bit of spare capacity. Although itching to produce the parts himself, W.O. had neither the means nor the premises in which to create his own machine shop. Still, he pressed on with the design.

On 17 May 1919, the first report of a new Bentley appeared in *The Autocar*. There was no photograph as there was no car to photograph, but there was an appetite-whetting artist's impression by the magazine's in-house illustrator Frederick Gordon Crosby of a sporting touring car at speed.

It detailed the specification: four cylinders with a bore and stroke of 80 × 149mm (2933.80cc), four valves per cylinder, a four-speed gearbox, wire wheels, and two-wheel brakes. The price of £750 included running boards, front wings, spare wheel and tyre, revolution counter, speedometer and tool kit. When W.O. saw Crosby's visual rendering he was delighted. It absolutely caught the spirit of what he was about, so much so that it became the face of Bentley, with Crosby's distinctive domed radiator shell realised in solid nickel silver. W.O. also commissioned the artist to create a logo: the timeless 'winged B' which has lasted a more than a century.

As the technical drawings neared completion, another challenge emerged: Burgess's first costing came out at £950, including gearbox, back axle, brakes and tyres, a rather problematic £200 over the projected sale price.

That wasn't good, but W.O. was more concerned about where he placed the orders for bespoke components. He had to have people with a track record in precision engineering, whom he could respect and trust. And he wasn't convinced that Roberts, who'd put his workshop forward at the Verrey's lunch, was up to scratch. The fact that he was a shareholder would not sway W.O.

Roberts took it badly and demanded his investment back. So did two others who'd attended the lunch. Without a single car even built, Bentley Motors was already in a predicament. As W.O. ruefully noted: 'To design and build a motor car in 1919 without substantial capital was like being cast on to a desert island with a penknife and orders to build a house.'

To make things more difficult, he was fast developing a visceral hatred of board meetings. He loathed having all his best-laid plans queried by increasingly unsympathetic people with no grasp of the business or the kind of reputation he wished to establish.

> All my ambitions were contained in that car, and the designing, building and perfecting of it were my whole life, occupying all

my waking thoughts and every minute of my days. In those critical formative years of the company, when the loss of my wife still lay heavily on me and there was no gentle cushion of domesticity to support me and absorb the shock of the reaction after a hard day's work, I am sure I was not easy company. I was taciturn, unresponsive and over-sensitive to criticism, and in the intimacy of the boardroom these characteristics became more marked and I was at my worst.

15

Bentley Boys Assemble

In the summer of 1919, as the plans for the engine started to take shape, W.O. faced another problem: not in the boardroom but close to his heart, in the design team.

Between them, Burgess and Varley covered most bases, but none of them, W.O. decided, had enough experience of overhead camshafts. A further sign of W.O.'s perfectionism, to get this one part right, he recruited the one man in Britain who he knew was up to the task. As a lieutenant colonel in the Royal Flying Corps 56 Squadron, Clive Gallop had experienced W.O.'s aero-engines. But what marked him out was that, before the war, he had completed an apprenticeship with Peugeot in Suresnes. There, under Ernest Henry, he had been exposed to the mysteries of overhead camshafts in their Grand Prix winner.

Gallop's association with cars went back even further, to his school days at Harrow. Already a car owner in his teens, he was once caught skating in Holland Park during the school day by his housemaster. Ordered back to school forthwith, he offered the master a lift. The master accepted, but after being driven the 9 miles at speed told Gallop to stop well before the school gates. They arrived separately, and no more was said.

With so little capital at his disposal, W.O. only took on more staff as and when he needed to, and made the best use of the space they already had. As the first parts began to arrive, at the D.F.P. service garage in New Street Mews, the old hayloft above became the engine shop. Now there was another question: who would put the first engine together?

Back in Dunkirk, sheltering from von Richthofen's bullets in a freezing canal, W.O. had chanced upon Petty Officer Reginald A. 'Nobby' Clarke, a mechanical engineer. By 1919, demobbed from RAF Waddington and back at his old job at Margate Corporation, Clarke was bored. After dodging bullets on French airfields, he had little appetite for civvy street and was craving a challenge. W.O. had left a deep impression on Clarke, of a public-school man who nevertheless showed a deep respect for the mechanics on the front line, a refreshing can-do attitude and a healthy impatience with airs and graces.

Clarke contacted his old CO for W.O.'s whereabouts and, spurred on by boredom at his desk in Margate Town Hall, plucked up the courage to write to him. His timing could not have been better. He had impressed W.O. with his cool-headed speed, diligence and unflappability when servicing No. 4 Squadron's rotaries, suggesting this was a man with all the right qualities to assemble the first Bentley engine.

Clarke got a summons to Conduit Street by return of post. The interview was more like a reunion. 'W.O. was still the same W.O. that I met on the Western Front, the same man that when we were short of oil pump springs borrowed transport and got some coppered springs over to us to keep us going.'

He listened avidly while W.O. expounded on the sort of car he envisaged: 'A type unknown in this country, a docile yet virile sports car capable of fulfilling a long-felt want, a car for the open road and yet docile enough to be used in town, as distinct from the pre-World War I racing machines with their attendant difficulties when used for touring purposes.'

Also, having toiled under canvas for four years, repairing and rebuilding aero-engines while dogfights thundered overhead, he was not going to be bothered by the primitive facilities in the former hayloft. In fact, he couldn't wait to roll up his sleeves. 'Bentley Motors more or less became my life from that day on.'

Downstairs, seventeen-year-old Leslie Pennal, from Forest Gate in east London, dreamed of one day being a mechanic. He had been taken on to do odd jobs. When he was sweeping the D.F.P. showroom he liked to gaze at the photograph hanging on the wall of W.O. descending Snaefell in the 1914 RAC TT, with his riding mechanic Leroux in goggles, scarves flying in the wind. 'I used to look at this picture and dream – how wonderful it would be – if ever it came to that.'

Since he was handy with tools, it wasn't long before Pennal was put to work on service jobs. He soon noticed the new man going up to the hayloft and parts arriving for him from outside suppliers. 'There was a large hole cut in the floor, protected by a handrail. Nobby used to shout through this hole occasionally, something about the weather, chat of that sort.' Soon a healthy banter developed between the two, which grew into horseplay. 'I suppose I was the average bad lad. Things got to such a state one day that I actually got the hose and turned it on and squirted it up through the hole.'

Once he found out exactly what Clarke was doing up there, his attitude changed. 'Of course it was everyone's wish to get on W.O.'s own motor car, he'd done so well with the D.F.P. and made it a much faster car.'

Although the parts had been made according to Burgess's and Varley's blueprints, they only had preliminary machining and wanted hand-finishing before they could be put together. Clarke needed help and called down to Pennal to abandon his broom. 'He came up here one day and didn't go back; he'd got promise so I kept him.'

It was a hard grind – literally, recalled Pennal. 'At first my chief job was treadling the grindstone and working the bench drill.'

These were the only pieces of machinery up there – and there was no power. Together they finessed and polished the parts which became the first engine.

'When Nobby wanted to grind something I was the means of power. That was all we had; all the holes and brackets and those sorts of things had to be made with them.' For polishing, they created a primitive polisher by adding a layer of emery cloth on top of the drill flywheel. 'I used to turn the handle while Nobby held the pieces he wanted polished on the emery cloth. There was a lot of the first Bentley polished like that.'

Since the Armistice the public's interest in cars had grown dramatically. Thousands of men – and women – had been introduced to driving during the war, where the motor vehicle had proved itself much more than a toy. Although still well beyond most pockets, it was no longer seen as exclusive to the wealthiest. The pent-up desire for all things new and fresh and exciting was heightened yet further when it was announced that the much-anticipated first post-war motor show would open at Olympia that November.

Two hundred and sixty-four makes would be exhibited – 134 of them from overseas. Every square inch of the hall was let, with models on show in every corner of the halls and even the passages. Three hundred and eighty thousand tickets were sold.

On the face of it, W.O.'s timing couldn't have been better. *The Autocar* had already announced that he was building a car; he just needed something to show. The pressure was on. It is a tribute to W.O.'s focus and determination that the Bentley made it there at all. Just nine months after conception, it made its entrance with a bodyless chassis and an engine with a crankcase mocked up out of wood. Yet the response from the onlookers was intense, bordering on the fanatical. Hillstead, in charge of manning the stand, was swept off his podium by the surging crowd. Pennal, sent along to keep the impressive nickel silver radiator shell and engine fittings looking spick and span, was thrilled. 'It looked like a beautiful job. All the parts were polished, crankcase, cam chest and even the sump.'

Still polishing, Pennal listened hard as Hillstead and W.O. fielded a barrage of enquiries, soaking it all up so that by the end of the week the teenager was answering questions himself – something W.O. did not overlook. 'I got a pound more in my wages for that – a wonderful rise for those days.'

In its special report *The Autocar* went all out. The Bentley was 'an automobile comparative to ordinary motors as a first class hunter is to a cab horse'.

The public agreed. Even in its bodyless state, it had an irresistible appeal. As Hillstead observed: 'Orders from agents were as easy to collect as postage stamps, while deposit cheques could be had for the asking.'

But somehow there was a sense of unreality to it all. W.O. was pleased with the reaction: an encouraging list of prospective owners happy to leave a £10 deposit on the promise of a car that would be delivered by the following June. This from a company that 'did not possess one single machine tool or the money to buy them with'.

As he faced increasingly negative discussions with the board, this response galvanised W.O. When the impatient investors demanded that Bentley outsource the whole assembly operation, he refused even to consider it. After the Gwynne's experience, and even at the more amenable Humber, he had had enough of making things in other people's factories. He wanted his own plant with his own hand-picked staff.

Hillstead agreed. 'Bentley was a hand-built car and that involved inspection of the highest order. This would inevitably lead to criticism, which men are apt to resent when coming from someone who is not their actual employer.'

He observed that the board soon split into two warring camps, the meetings 'more acrimonious than fruitful'. And the car itself had yet to turn a wheel.

16

A Lovely Sound to Die to

There were eight of them in the hayloft that morning in October 1919. The engine stood, gleaming, on a wooden trestle without an exhaust manifold and just a small tank for fuel and a battery. Pennal, banished once more to the ground floor to look after H.M.'s dog, could only peer up through the hole in the ceiling. W.O. likened the gathering to 'some sect drawn together to witness an ancient rite'.

Knowing W.O.'s abhorrence of exhibitionism, Hillstead was dismayed to find so many present to witness the birth. 'W.O. pressed the starter switch, the bendix pinion engaged with the toothed ring on the flywheel, the starter motor came into action, and the psychological moment had arrived.'

Nothing happened. No one spoke. Keeping his usual cool head, Nobby Clarke tested the valve timing and adjusted the carburettor.

W.O. pressed a second time: still nothing.

After an agonising silence that none of the gathering dared break, he barked: 'Benzole! Get me some benzole!' A by-product of coal, even more explosively inflammable than petroleum, benzole had been widely used in munitions during the war.

Pennal tied the dog lead to the banister and ventured up a few steps to get a better look. A can of benzole was found and added to the tank. And W.O. pressed the starter a third time. 'Almost at once there was a sharp explosion accompanied by a vivid yellow flash, and – after a moment's hesitation – the air was filled with a pleasing roar.' Pennal agreed. 'It was a really beautiful sound.'

Not pleasing to everyone, however, as a minute later a nurse from the adjoining convalescent home appeared with a message: the matron was about to call the police. 'What a lovely sound to die to,' observed Gallop, as the nurse moved out of earshot.

Over the next weeks, W.O.'s vision gradually began to take shape. The engine was carefully lowered from the hayloft by block and tackle onto the waiting chassis below in the service workshop. A basic open body from an old D.F.P. demonstrator was grafted on.

Gallop came into the works and was thrilled to see the assembly, wheels and radiator fitted, almost ready to be driven. In W.O.'s absence, they couldn't resist. Pennal attached the body with three clamps – holes for bolts had yet to be drilled. They laid a board across the chassis rails and added a cushion. Gallop took the wheel, Clarke climbed in beside him and told Pennal and Jackson, another D.F.P. hand W.O. had brought in from his taxi firm, to get in the back.

'Then Gallop started it up, put it in first gear and drove it out of the garage and we turned left into the mews. We turned round at the end and started coming back. Everything was going all right – Gallop had just tried the brakes and said how lovely it felt – when all at once he began to sort of submerge down into the chassis.'

His coat, trailing beneath him, had wrapped itself round the drive shaft and ripped all the way up the back. They stopped and unwound him, then reversed the car back into its position. After lunch W.O. appeared and saw the car with the body on. Pennal was convinced he could feel his eyes boring into him. 'I felt very guilty to think that he wasn't the first to drive that very first car.' But nothing was said. Thirty years would pass before W.O. learned the truth.

What followed were several days and nights of fine-tuning and adjustment to get the machine running as well as W.O. expected. It was a few weeks before Hillstead got his first ride in the EXP, as the first Bentley was now known, with W.O. at the wheel. Since he would be the one selling the car, he was anxious to see how it would perform. He had driven Burgess's TT Humber, which had provided inspiration for the Bentley, but was noisy and highly strung. To his relief W.O.'s creation was a very different animal.

He marvelled at its dual personality, happily dawdling along in slow traffic while in fourth gear 'giving the impression of a large car running well within its capabilities', and then on the open road turning into 'an out-and-out racing machine with astonishing ability to rev'.

For the rest of the year, W.O. devoted himself to further testing and refining the car, smoothing out the sharper edges of its racing car roots. The dry sump was abandoned; the two pumps which had pushed the oil around made almost as much noise as the engine. Straight-cut racing style gears were swapped for quieter, helical-toothed alternatives, and the crankshaft, out of alignment by 'one or two thou', was finessed.

The product Hillstead would sell was coming on in leaps and bounds. It just lacked a place to sell it from. Less than a year before its launch onto the market, Bentley Motors had no showroom.

No. 3 Hanover Court, across a yard from the D.F.P. premises, had been a dress shop. There were no offices inside, just a partition which had made the changing room, and a lot of beige carpet. Hillstead and H.M. decorated it with a watercolour of the still-in-development car at speed, while a cylinder from a Bentley rotary mounted on a wooden base graced the front window, along with a copy of the descriptive article from *The Autocar*, reporting no actual car yet but 'an abundance of optimism'.

Meanwhile, as soon as he was pronounced fit enough from his wartime convalescence, Sammy Davis had made his way back to his employers, the publishers Iliffe, where the lengthy discussion about his return felt to him as if he was having to apply for his job all over again. Grilled about what he had done in the war, it was as if he was having to justify serving his country. It was only when he turned to his aircraft inspection role that someone said: 'Well that's of some use to us anyhow.'

Smarting at the belittling tone of ignorant men too old to have seen any action, he nearly walked out. Haunting him was the 'feeling that an unbridgeable gap separated those who had been in the war from those who had not ... it seemed impossible to get through the barrier; we were neither talking nor thinking the same way.' A yawning gap had opened up between the generation who had fought and those who had not and therefore still subscribed to Edwardian notions of deference. Davis and his peers were impatient to make up for years taken up with a war that ended without fanfare and, having lost so many comrades, had developed a sharpened sense of what it meant to be alive.

Iliffe's old family atmosphere had gone, but in its place he found something unexpected and appealing: a new sense of urgency and competitive rivalry. This was just the sort of excitement he craved, and he moved rapidly through the Iliffe stable of titles from *Automotive Engineer* to *The Light Car* before graduating to their 'veteran' title *The Autocar.*

He also married Rosamond Pollard, the younger sister of a Westminster school friend, 'with all the glamour of war, arch of swords, St George's Hanover Square and the rest'. Though eleven years his junior, Rosamond had known him long enough not to be taken unawares by his enthusiasms. 'Perhaps the fact that her brother and I set fire to her mother's curtains during an experiment in flame throwing, she being a witness, made it easier for her to understand that neither of us ever grew up properly.'

Desperate to get involved in motor sports, Davis seized every chance that came his way, mainly speed trials and hill-climbs. It was a rich man's sport; ordinary cars – let alone racers – were beyond the reach of jobbing journalists. So he made what use he could of his mechanical knowledge – and the promise of column inches in the magazine.

This did not suit his bosses, worried about the reaction from their advertisers if a member of *The Autocar*'s staff was injured or killed in one of their cars, or worse – seen racing the machine of a competitor. But he befriended Claude Wallace, head of the advertising department, and was soon helping him out on his fearsome 1914 Grand Prix Piccard-Pictet – 'whose huge engine could only be started by shoving a glove in the air intake then rushing round to the exhaust pipe end to retrieve it when the engine did start.'

The car attracted adventure. On the way to the 1919 Southend Speed Trials it was damaged in a collision with a cow but still entered. And when Wallace was promoted to managing director, all resistance to Davis's racing aspirations came to an end. *The Autocar*'s man behind the wheel was now seen as a publicity asset. And he was about to get the assignment of his dreams.

17

The Song of Roland

In January 1920, almost exactly a year after W.O. had sat down with Burgess and Varley and the blank sheet, the first road test of the Bentley appeared in *The Autocar.*

To have delivered a finished motor car from scratch in twelve months was a heroic achievement. And who better to test it – and get it into print – than Sammy Davis?

Davis's report did not hold back, beginning with an obligatory dig at the prevailing British speed limit. 'Although frowned on by the authorities, limited by law and penalised when discovered, speed is the greatest attribute of a car, and from the car alone it is possible to realise to the full that peculiar feeling of greatness soaring almost to poetic heights, consequent on high-speed travelling.'

Hardly a pampered press demonstrator, EX 1, the only Bentley in existence, was delivered to Davis 'untuned, unaltered and hand built, with a rough four-seated body carrying the mud of previous runs, lacking a hood, with a narrow windscreen – in fact having bare accommodation for four people ... just a suggestion, perhaps, at all events, something which showed its breed through the external work-a-day disguise'.

Davis praised the 'more than ordinary tractability, the power of either brake being altogether extraordinary and impossible to believe, save from the evidence of actual experience'. But once on the open road – in an unspecified location – Davis's foot was pressed to the floor and his pen ascended to even dizzier heights:

> Instantly the exhaust changed its note from a purr to a most menacing roar, the white ribbon of road streamed towards the car, while the backs of the seats pressed hard upon one's shoulder blades. As the speed increased over 70m.p.h. the landscape leaped at us, wind shrieked past the screen, while the flanking trees and other objects seemed, not definitely and sharply contoured, but a blurred streak hurtling past as the roar of the exhaust rose to its full song. To such an accompaniment the pulse beats quicker, there comes an almost irresistible desire to burst into some wild war song, greater even than The Song of Roland – in defiance of the demons that howl invisible without.

He did manage to come back to earth with a few criticisms, drawing attention to the noisy oil pump drive, and an intermittent 'penetrating grate' from the engine, but conceded that these were understandable in the first chassis of a new design and easily overcome. But it was clear to even the most sceptical reader that the new Bentley 3 Litre was something special.

W.O., the polar opposite of Davis when it came to self-expression, was thrilled at this ringing endorsement from Britain's foremost automotive journal (so much so that he included the entire text in the appendix of one of his memoirs thirty years later). There was only one problem: the first delivery of actual cars was eighteen months away.

And already the market was changing; Hillstead could see what was coming round the bend. 'It was too good to last, and one felt that sooner or later the pendulum must swing the other way, bringing in its wake a spate of cancelled orders and a clamorous cry for the return of moneys paid under the spell of false optimism.'

But even in his gloomiest moments Hillstead could not have imagined just how far the pendulum would swing. The motor industry was about to be plunged into its first major crisis. First, the pent-up demand which had burst forth after the war began to level off. Then the iron foundry moulders went on strike. From September 1919, four months of industrial action deprived the industry of castings and put 100,000 people out of work.

Herbert Austin, still in the throes of returning his vast Longbridge factory to peacetime production, was among the first to suffer the full force of it. Having seen what Ford had achieved with the beginnings of mass production in Detroit, he had borrowed heavily to embark on the wholesale modernisation of his plant. But he also decided to follow Ford's 'one model' policy and concentrate production on a single large 3.6-litre, 20hp model, just at the point when the market was moving in favour of cars which were smaller, lighter and cheaper.

The entire industry was heading into a perfect storm. By January 1920 Austin was £1 million in the red, with a further million owed to suppliers; by the end of April, the receivers had been called in and the company was rescued by banks.

Even William Morris, whose 1.5-litre model was much more marketable, saw sales of 50,000 in 1920 shrink to 32,000 the following year. In the aftermath of the boom, prices of labour and materials shot up. And now the government, burdened with war debt, announced a rise in income tax.

Even Rolls-Royce was not immune; by November 1920, almost half the order book had been cancelled. Napier, its main British competitor at the top end of the market, gave up car making altogether. And Wolseley Motors, who had just opened their spectacular Italianate Piccadilly showroom next door to the Ritz, would soon go bankrupt.

In this economic climate, W.O.'s projections now looked ridiculously optimistic. His shareholders had been promised that five chassis a week would be produced from June 1921, each with a projected profit of £200. But well before that date, it was clear that the further expenditure required to put the car into production would wipe out any possibility of a dividend. This was not the news they wanted to hear.

To his extreme irritation, W.O. now found that he had to justify every new piece of equipment for the works case by case, with every purchase questioned. This slowed progress towards production. Once he had cars to actually sell, investment would flood in, he argued, if they would only let him get on and build them.

He still needed somewhere to do that. Many car builders had evolved from established firms with factories, like the former bicycle builders of Coventry. Morris's plant outside Oxford had been a military college, while Austin's factory was originally a tin-printing works. Even Ford, arriving in Britain in 1910, adapted a former tramcar plant in Old Trafford. Lagonda, a company closer in scale and ambition to Bentley, was the exception. Founder Wilbur Gunn, an American opera singer who settled in Staines, fancied a motorcycle. He built one in the most convenient space available to him at the time, his greenhouse. Then he wanted to try four wheels, so the garden was gradually roofed over and eventually the whole house was also given up to building cars.

With all his attention on the car, W.O. had left the search for a premises to H.M. and Hillstead, who appeared to have had no clear idea of what they were looking for. In a rash moment they began negotiations with the Air Ministry for the purchase of Tangmere Aerodrome, imagining they could sell off or sublet the excess capacity. But it soon dawned on them they would be taking on a liability of 'gigantic proportions'.

And other more mundane questions belatedly occurred: 'Where

was the labour coming from? What arrangements could we make for its housing? Where would the womenfolk do their shopping?'

Given that they would be dependent at least initially on outside suppliers, common sense suggested that they should have looked to the Midlands, but W.O. put his foot down. He wasn't moving anywhere; the works had to be in the London area. Then, towards the end of 1919, he revealed that he had found a plot of land in Cricklewood, on the edge of north London, still a separate village. Today it is close to where the North Circular meets the start of the M1; then it was open fields.

They took out a mortgage to pay for it and set about building their own works, initially a brick structure, where the next two experimental cars were assembled, and then a larger assembly hall with a steel frame clad in breeze blocks. Because of the straitened financial conditions, development was piecemeal. Only after W.O.'s car got stuck in mud were railway sleepers laid to make a primitive road.

With the first building now completed, W.O. focused on getting the next two prototypes built. However, there was no state-of-the art machinery. Clarke and Pennal made do with the bench drill and grindstone they had brought from the hayloft. Ever positive, Pennal got stuck in.

'We managed. We just had to. In any case the work was so interesting ... we worked all hours, late nights, even Sundays sometimes. Many a time I caught the workmen's train out of Liverpool Street to Forest Gate where I lived. I went home and had some breakfast, a wash and about one and a half hour's sleep, then caught the last workmen's out of Forest Gate to go back again.'

It was a long and arduous journey, right across London and out the other side. From the far side of east London he caught a train to Liverpool Street, then the Underground to Baker Street, an 'electric train' to Brondesbury and then a bus. Still the most junior member of the team, he had to fetch and carry, 'taking tyres to be vulcanised, collecting welded parts from Willesden, all by bus or tram. Often I had to plead with the conductor to let me on, especially with a tram car ... There was one occasion when I rolled two tyres all the way down the Edgware Road, because I couldn't get on the tram.'

Once he collected an exhaust pipe from a welder's in Willesden. 'It was much taller than me and I had an awful time trying to get on a tram. Finally one conductor took pity on me and told me to go upstairs with it ... I had to swing the pipe round to lay it across the seats, and all the passengers ducked.'

Wally Saunders, another Bentley mechanic who had joined in his teens, had the job of shaping the pipes, packing them with sand, heating the section to be shaped and bending them round a nearby tree with a handy forked branch. 'We used to get the pipe all hot, run outside, get the pipe in the fork, bend it round a bit, run back and put it up against the line [sketched out on the workshop floor] – run out again, come back in – and so on until it was finished.'

When an old army hut was erected beside the workshop, W.O. and Burgess left their office in Conduit Street and moved in. As more staff were taken on during the following months the works began to develop its own atmosphere. Pennal, for whom W.O. had been an elusive, monosyllabic presence, now began to see another side to his boss. Even when they were working through the night W.O. would be there, not interfering but watching closely. When he did intervene, more often than not it was to lend a hand on even the most menial jobs. Pennal recalled him helping to 'strain gallons of petrol through a chamois leather, which was a perishing rotten job on a cold night'.

Pennal's tendency to be late, which he blamed on his tortuous journey across the capital, also did not go unnoticed by W.O. 'You know, Pennal, when I was a stoker for the Scottish express I used to have to start out at half past five in the morning to get to the engine sheds. You know I hated it; I hated the early start and I hated the sight of coal – but I was never late.' Only afterwards did Pennal realise he was being ticked off.

Though not given to effusive praise, W.O. did find ways to show how much he valued his workers. When he learned that Pennal's fiancée was seriously ill, he arranged for her to be seen by a specialist at his expense, and then lent him his own Bentley so he could take her to hospital, while W.O. drove himself home on an unbodied chassis. Pennal was overwhelmed. 'It was done in such a quiet, gracious way – the sort of thing you would never forget.'

With the works up and running, Bentley Motors' prospectus still promised the production of five chassis a week, delivery to start in June 1921, with a margin of £200 profit per chassis yielding a projected £50,000 per annum, enough for the business to pay a decent dividend. But, as W.O. had been warned already, the figures were a fantasy. In 1919 the company had already run up a deficit of £16,000, and by 1921 was a further £7,400 in the red. And without a properly equipped works, five chassis a week would remain a pipe dream.

By August 1921, *The Autocar* was noting that 'motorists to whom the chassis had appealed especially have been wondering what was happening, why no cars had succeeded the original experimental chassis', and questioned whether the Bentley 'would ever be a production job'. They needed to get cars to customers, fast.

18

Endangered Species

Gradually, the first production cars took shape. But the heady days of the Olympia Show in 1919, when Hillstead found himself collecting orders 'like postage stamps', were long gone. The question was no longer how and where to build them, but who would be in the market for a luxury sports car costing the same as a three-bedroom house?

The obvious candidates would have been those carefree young blades immortalised by P.G. Wodehouse. But the Bertie Wooster type, the rich and unattached young man with enough inherited wealth to protect him from ever having to do a day's work, was a product of the Edwardian era; by the 1920s he was an endangered species.

Between 1914 and 1925, the number of people with an annual income exceeding £10,000, about £450,000 today, had fallen from approximately 4,000 to 1,300. A more sombre statistic is the disproportionate number of potential future Bentley customers who were killed leading their men out of the trenches into the hail of enemy fire. It is a crude measure but nonetheless telling, that some 35,000 ex-public-school boys were killed during the First World War, 18 per cent of those who enlisted, compared with a national average of 11 per cent.

Even if W.O. had had this information to hand at the time, it is unlikely it would have deflected him from his path. Although famously not a social animal, he had already exhibited sound judgement when it came to assembling his team. Now he used the same instincts to select the right candidate to be the first Bentley owner, who would be an ambassador for the marque, and who would not be deterred when he heard that the price quoted as £750 at Olympia two years before had now climbed to £1,150.

Noel van Raalte fitted the bill perfectly. His mother had owned Brownsea Island in Poole Harbour, but, though independently wealthy, he was not a feckless, moneyed, spoilt child burning through his inheritance. More like Bulldog Drummond than Bertie Wooster, van Raalte, 'tough, smart, short-set', was technically literate and had a strong spirit of adventure.

Like W.O., he was a keen engineer; he had converted the living room of his home in Bursledon on the Hamble into a machine shop complete with a universal grinder. He had even competed in the 1915 Indianapolis 500, one of the first and only Brits ever to do so, managing tenth place despite losing his engine cover.

In W.O's words he was 'something of a social butterfly who would mix in the right social strata and spread the good word far and wide'. He also had a rather alluring reckless streak. While at Cambridge he had been arrested for challenging a fellow student to a car race round the town – in reverse – the loser to pay all fines. Van Raalte, in an 8-litre Minerva, had won. In court the loser, William Rhodes-Moorhouse, was described by the judge as a useless good-for-nothing. Five years later, he became the first airman to be awarded the Victoria Cross.

One morning early in September 1921, van Raalte arrived at Cricklewood to collect his car and become the very first Bentley customer. 'Let us know if anything goes wrong,' W.O. told him. 'You've got a five-year guarantee, don't forget.'

'He looked the car carefully all over, raised the bonnet and cast an experienced eye over the engine, got in ... and drove away. Our first customer had taken delivery of our first production car.'

Van Raalte took him at his word. Leslie Pennal, still very much a junior, was charged with returning van Raalte's car to him in Bursledon after it had been back to Cricklewood for modifications, and saw how well the 3 Litre suited their first customer's particular spirit. 'He had a yacht maroon [distress flare] fitted to the side of his car because he got so fed up trying to get past lorries. He used to fire this thing, and the lorry driver would immediately pull over, thinking the back tyre had gone. He was a great character, Van Raalte, and he thought the world of Bentley.'

The choice of customer worked like a dream. Within weeks of taking delivery, van Raalte was broadcasting his satisfaction with his new machine in the letters pages of *The Autocar*. 'The reason I bought a Bentley was because of its exceptional performance in all respects on the road, and the care and attention which I believed had been given to its production. Such features as steering, suspension, holding the road, brakes, change of speed, and engine efficiency leave nothing to be desired and are in my opinion, to be found to a higher degree in this make of car than any other of the many makes I have owned or use ... I admire the Rolls-Royce intensely and have owned two of them and must say that, as regards the features I have mentioned, the Bentley is far in advance of it.'

To get such a public vote of confidence from a thoroughly satisfied – and wealthy – customer was the endorsement for which W.O. had been hoping. A brand new car from a brand new company being so publicly compared with the exalted Rolls sent shock waves that were felt all the way along the coast to the West Wittering design office of Henry Royce.

19

The Serpent of Speed

Rolls-Royce was in trouble. The customer base it had established before the war was shrinking. Compared to the devastation of Russian and German nobility, Britain's ruling classes had got off lightly, but they were depleted. A keen detector of shifts in the tectonic plates of society, Evelyn Waugh observed how the certainties of the Edwardian era were crumbling. In his short story 'Winner Takes All', Mrs Kent-Cumberland, her husband killed leading his men in Flanders, shuts a wing of her house, lets several servants go and allows sheep to graze her lawns.

Rolls was in danger of pricing itself out of an already dwindling market. Before the war, a Silver Ghost chassis was £506. By 1920 the rising cost of materials and wages had sent it rocketing to £2,250. Henry Royce's solution was a more modest model to sell alongside the old-school Ghost. The six-cylinder 'Twenty' – codenamed 'Goshawk' – had a 3.6-litre engine, not much bigger than the Bentley's, and at £1,100 would sell at a similar price. But heavier and with only a three-speed gearbox, it was criticised for its lack of performance. The younger engineers at Rolls-Royce in Derby, who were more in tune with the expectations of the growing numbers of owner drivers, were unimpressed. Rolls engineer Bill Morton called it a 'gutless wonder', especially when laden with the heavy closed coachwork. Others labelled it the 'Shytehawk'.

This kind of talk infuriated Royce's managing director Claude Johnson. In a memo following a board meeting in July 1922, he made his feelings clear. 'The serpent of speed has entered into this company and is likely to poison its existence ... Anyone encouraging in any way the making or selling of high compression cars will be regarded as an unfaithful servant of the company and his services will be dispensed with.'

Johnson believed Rolls-Royce's unique selling points were its silkiness and silence, not the acceleration or top speed. On the face of it, the Twenty and the Bentley 3 Litre were aiming for the same customer base: wealthy professionals. But Royce and Johnson, both approaching their sixtieth birthdays, were hardly attuned to the tastes and preferences of that group. Some simply wanted to travel in comfort as befitted their status. Others were feeling a different pull, the pent-up desire for adventure.

For Osbert Sitwell, son of a wealthy baronet, survivor of both Eton and Ypres and just four years younger than W.O., the motor car promised something entirely new:

> Mine was the first generation in which the young men were allowed to take their sweethearts for drives ... They would sit together, the two of them, the man at the wheel, the girl beside him, their hair blown back from their temples, their features sculptured by the wind ... There was the awareness of speed itself, and the rapid thinking that must accompany it, a new alertness, and the typical effects, the sense it might be of the racing of every machine as dusk approaches ... All these physical impressions, so small in themselves, went to form a sum of feeling new in its kind and never before experienced ... No other generation had been able to speed into the sunset.

The Bentley 3 Litre was essentially a grand touring car before its time, built for speed but also highly durable. Although the roads were comparatively empty, they were full of hazards. Neville Minchin, the Brooklands regular and Rolls-Royce-owner-turned-Bentley-enthusiast, had first-hand experience of what the Bentley was capable of tackling.

Hurrying back to Boulogne en route home from a motor race, driving at a steady 75 mph along the *route nationale*, he saw to his horror that 'the road ahead was one vast area of big unrolled stones. These were elevated about six inches above the tarred black surface. Without slowing at all, the front wheels mounted this "step" with a crash, the car leaping in the air and plunging on over the rough surface. With its high geared steering and stiff springs, the Bentley remained wonderfully steady and nothing was broken.'

But there were teething problems. Hillstead, in charge of sales, was the first to hear about them. Chartered accountant Arthur Pelham Ford reported to him that oil from his 3 Litre's engine had 'crept up the speedometer cable and dripped onto his wife's stockings', and that she was 'not exactly pleased'. Pelham Ford then experienced 'the wholesale spattering of his right trouser leg with the same lubricant – this time from the gearbox'. Summoned for what he expected would be a dressing down, Hillstead found himself being given the full story over lunch at the palatial Cecil Hotel with lobster and champagne, followed by a fat cigar.

Hillstead found his clients enjoyed this exciting new adventure W.O. was leading them on, and they were behaving rather like members of a select club. Encouraged, he courted further members assiduously. 'When one did come along we played him with a care equal to that of a trout fisherman who has hooked a lively one.'

Invariably some of this playing involved lunch at the Berkeley or the Mayfair. And with the Bentley board in no mood to agree expenses, it was Hillstead himself who picked up the bill. But he, too, was part of this exclusive new club. 'I was a shareholder, intensely interested in racing and speed model development, and had known every member of the Bentley family.'

And W.O. thought him 'an excellent salesman who could drive so beautifully that he could have sold a lorry as a limousine to a duchess'.

20

The Tourist Trophy

W.O., the taciturn, focused perfectionist, was in many ways a model of prudence, but when it came to motor racing he was a gambler. His brother H.M. was wary of motor racing for its tendency to use up valuable time and money, and the shareholders were entirely opposed, but there was never any doubt that the new Bentley 3 Litre would soon find its way to the track.

At Cricklewood, W.O. opened a discreetly named 'Experimental Department' – in reality just a corner of the workshop. To look after it, he hired Frank Clement, who he had talent-spotted at the 1914 TT. A cool-headed and meticulous engineer, Clement had also raced for several firms before the war. He would become the only Bentley driver to be paid to do the job; all the rest would be self-funding amateurs. His first task was to quietly prepare the second car, EXP 2, for W.O. to take to Brooklands for the event on Easter Monday 1921, on the justification that racing improved the breed. He won the last race of the day. 'No one ever attempted to dispute that competition success was the cheapest way of selling cars,' he pronounced – the critical word in that sentence being 'success' . . .

Later that year, the RAC announced that it was reviving the Isle of Man Tourist Trophy race for cars in June 1922. W.O.'s performance in the 1914 TT had been such a vote of confidence in the D.F.P. he had to go back, this time with a team of his own cars.

Less logical, in fact bordering on the irrational, was his decision also to enter the 1922 Indianapolis 500, only weeks before the TT. Not only did Bentley lack a presence in America – still being at the beginning of building a customer base in Britain – no one there had even been across the Atlantic. The only explanation is that van Raalte, who had raced there, talked W.O. into it. Certainly he was the only one who could claim any familiarity with the idiosyncrasies of the banked and shatteringly bumpy 'brickyard' speed bowl. W.O.'s only rationale was a vague desire 'to show the Americans what we were doing'.

Brooklands regular Douglas Hawkes, his riding mechanic Bertie Browning and the crated-up Bentley were shipped across the Atlantic. Hawkes, who also had never been to America before, found himself up against an almost entirely home field of specially designed machines with drivers who knew every brick on the circuit.

His first sight of the track was when he and Browning arrived for qualifying on the morning of Elimination Day. 'We were at panic stations. No time to look around, just knock the crate to bits, put on the wheels, fit the battery, which I had been nursing, press the starter – and pray.'

They not only got through but qualified nineteenth out of twenty-seven. The Americans were impressed by the performance of the Bentley – literally straight out of its box. Hawkes drove a steady race and finished thirteenth – last, but quite an achievement for a new and untried road car to go the full 500 miles when more than half the field retired. W.O.'s 3 Litre had staying power all right, but it was an expensive way to find out.

Back in Britain, no one noticed. Much more sensible, if just as costly, was W.O.'s return to the TT. If Bentley was to make its mark on the British automotive landscape, this was the event at which to do it. But it carried huge reputational risk.

His cars would be up against two of the most seasoned British competitors, Vauxhall and Sunbeam. Both firms dated back to the previous century. Vauxhall was an established engineering concern before it turned to cars in 1903 and Sunbeam had begun as a bicycle maker. Both were aiming at the same affluent end of the market as Bentley, but with considerably more resources as well as long experience in racing. Sunbeam's chief designer, the extrovert Breton Louis Coatalen, was a daunting rival. Nine years older than W.O., he'd learned his craft in the 1890s at the drawing boards of France's automotive pioneers Panhard and De Dion. Lured to Coventry in 1900, he put his skills to use first at Humber, Hillman – where he married the founder's daughter – and then at Sunbeam.

W.O. had first encountered him in Douglas for the 1914 TT where he teased him by referring to his winning Sunbeams as 'Peugeots' because of the similarities. Like W.O., Coatalen, according to Sammy Davis, also found racing caused friction in his company. Just before the war, having banned him from making any more six-cylinder racing engines, 'his directors became apoplectic at the sight of a six-cylinder engine on test. Coatalen was requested to explain this at once. With the cheerful face of one completely innocent but unjustly accused he bent forward to examine the engine. Slowly, he counted the cylinders, "one, two, three, four . . . five . . . six", a pause, then "Why so I 'ave!"'

As it turned out the engine became the basis for Sunbeam's own wartime aircraft engine that Coatalen would build for the Admiralty. His TT cars for 1922 had eight-cylinder pure racing engines.

Vauxhall, whose road-going 30/98 model would become the Bentley 3 Litre's closest competitor through the 1920s, arrived on the Isle of Man with equally specialised racing engines featuring three spark plugs per cylinder and seven timing gears which had first to be correctly meshed then locked with dowel pins.

Beside these machines, the Bentleys were merely modified road cars. Under Clement's supervision, each engine received high-compression pistons, a racing carburettor, and an exhaust pipe which sprang from the bonnet and snaked down the nearside of a lightweight body, its streamlined tail concealing a spare wheel. Special steering wheels were made with steel spokes to soak up vibration, bound with cord for extra grip. Petrol tanks of solid copper were located amidships to bring their weight within the wheelbase, with a brass filler cap under the mechanic's seat.

Six mechanics were detailed to prepare the cars, and three would ride in the race. Just three years after gazing up at the TT picture while he swept the showroom floor, Pennal's dream was about to come true: he would be riding with W.O. himself.

As he was to discover, a riding mechanic had his work cut out; the main task was manually controlling the oil and fuel pressure pumps.

> First of all you had two to two and a half pounds of pressure in the petrol tank; that would keep you going for quite some time as soon as the level of the petrol got a little low. But then after about four laps, you had to put pressure in the spare oil-tank underneath the floorboards of the chassis and then turn a two way tap over so that the oil would pass into the engine. That had to be on so long – you had to guess it – or work it out from one corner, say Ramsay, until we got over Snaefell and down the other side. Then you had to turn the oil off, and switch your air back on to the petrol tank. The risk was if you left your oil flowing too long you'd lose pressure in your petrol tank. Or you'd have to switch off from your oil and blow the pressure up in the tank and then quickly back to the oil, to keep the oil in the sump at a safe level.

All this Pennal rehearsed until he could have done it in his sleep.

> At the same time you had to watch revs and be ready for any eventuality, also look behind to see if anybody had caught you up and give your driver information. If there was another car there by the rules of the race, you had to let it pass, because it was the faster car, and having left so many minutes later. The pressure business alone was really enough to watch, as well as hang on and enjoy the drivers' performance – that was the best of all.

But his first outing was nearly his last; testing at Brooklands, W.O. was just coming off the banking when the wooden board holding the seat cushions split and dropped onto the furiously spinning prop shaft where it met the gearbox. Pennal could hear the machinery chewing through the splintered wood beneath them as they struggled to a halt.

As late as the day before the race the cars could still be modified, and W.O. calculated that if they could find a way to carry a further eleven gallons of fuel they could go the whole distance non-stop. He sent a telegram to Cricklewood ordering second tanks to be built and dispatched to Liverpool where another Bentley mechanic, Wally Hassan, would collect them, bring them to the island and fit them, just hours before the start. That night, a last-minute coat of 'bath enamel' paint was applied to smarten up the cars, but it refused to dry. There was nothing for it but to rinse it all off with petrol and go over the whole thing again with quick-drying white undercoat.

That was the least of it. On the day, the conditions were appalling. Among those braving the elements was former Brooklands stalwart Neville Minchin, now Bentley's battery supplier. Always one to travel in style, he had also brought over his Silver Ghost, and a pair of Brooklands veterans, Algernon Guinness and Eric Horniman, who before the war had excited crowds with his monster 15-litre Benz.

With Sunbeam, Vauxhall and Bentley the only teams for the main race, it seemed a very British affair. But Sunbeam's driver was Jean Chassagne, a Frenchman of exceptional pedigree. Born in 1881, he was competing in major races when W.O. was still a railway apprentice. But his origins were far humbler than those of most drivers of the day. At the turn of the century he enlisted in the French navy and served on submarines, after which he was variously a mechanic, driver, pilot and instructor. Then in the First World War, aged thirty-three, he joined the French army artillery. Coatalen, with the help of the Admiralty in London, managed to spring him and bring him to Wolverhampton to work on his Sunbeam aero-engines.

By the time of the TT, with his regular riding mechanic Robert Laly he had competed in three French Grand Prix, four Indianapolis 500s and two Targa Florios. It would have been hard to find a more formidable opponent.

Their other adversary was the weather. Heavy rain had left the track, a mixture of tarmacadam and moorland stone, as an obstacle course of potholes and puddles; even the few smoother sections were slimy with moisture, and the higher parts were shrouded in low-hanging cloud.

In practice, Pennal had a shock. The circuit was a collection of rough, narrow roads, and hump-backed bridges between dry stone walls. And in the early morning mist, he discovered that Keppel Gate wasn't merely the name of a turn but a real gate, which was closed by the farmers at night.

'You couldn't see if the gate was open until you got right close to it.' But it was a thrill to sweep down from the mountains 'sometimes breaking out of the cloud like a diving aeroplane'.

On the day, he was in the car first. W.O. arrived holding a small bottle of brandy and a bandage, which he placed under his cushion, 'looking at me with a smile as if to say "Let's hope we don't have to use them".'

The cars were flagged off at five-minute intervals in the driving rain, the density of the downpour such that their goggles steamed up immediately. Seeing W.O. trying to shield his eyes, Pennal attempted to put his cap on his boss's head, but it was too small. Then there was an ominous crack. The floorboard cut to fit the last-minute second petrol tank had snapped. 'One of the bolts had come out and directly that happened there was only one thing to do – rip the remnants out so W.O. could get at the pedals and take the can between my knees.'

In spite of this, W.O.'s driving was a model of smoothness with very little sliding, even where the track was rough and slippery; their first lap was the fastest of the team. They were up against faster, more powerful Vauxhalls and Sunbeams, both with pneumatic four-wheel brakes (making all four brakes come on at the same time with the same force was still proving to be a technological challenge). But the three Bentleys, despite having brakes only on the rear, and in spite of the punishing conditions, averaged between 60 and 70 mph.

Standing guard in the pits among the tools and spares, Hillstead pitied the mechanics on board. With only one mudguard on the driver's side, they were drenched in sticky wet mud flying up from the road and the rain stinging into them from above. Even as the weather lifted, the cars still 'proceeded in the centre of a nimbus of muddy spray'.

Then W.O.'s exhaust pipe broke off, leaving the gaping hole of the manifold just a couple of feet from Pennal's face. The sound was blistering and it smothered him in a cloud of soot and muck. And each time W.O. changed down, a tongue of flame leaped up from the broken pipe. 'I kept thinking of the can of fuel I was nursing.'

Despite this, they stayed the course and came home fourth. Clement's Bentley was second, and Hawkes in the third car, fresh from Indianapolis – despite losing a radiator plug and all his water – finished fifth. The winner was Sunbeam's French veteran,

Jean Chassagne. But despite being full-blown racing cars from companies with vast resources, only one each of the Sunbeams and Vauxhalls made it to the end. The Bentleys, adapted production touring cars with only two-wheel brakes and less power, all reached the finish. This was what W.O. wanted, even more than a win.

But there was no team prize. Minchin protested to Sir Julian Orde, secretary of the organisers, the Royal Automobile Club. He agreed they deserved recognition, but they didn't have a trophy to present. As dusk approached, Minchin and Horniman set off in the Rolls and scoured the island until in a shop window in Ramsay they spotted a large silver cup, a prize in a forthcoming agricultural show. The shop was closed, so they hunted down the proprietor, who refused to part with it. Minchin assured him he could get a substitute from the mainland and pressed a cheque onto him so generous that he couldn't refuse. They dashed back to Douglas in the still pouring rain, and delivered the trophy into Sir Julian's hands just as the ceremony was about to begin.

The Bentley team were jubilant, all except W.O. who, to everyone else's dismay, retreated into his shell, although, ever the master of understatement, he did manage to pronounce the result 'very pleasing'.

Even Hillstead got his reward; shivering and soaked in the pits, he was buttonholed by a stranger who introduced himself as George Porter of Blackpool. Porter announced that he wished to be the Bentley agent for Lancashire, telling him, 'that car of yours is going to be a world-beater', and on the spot, placed an order for six.

The improvised team prize got just the sort of press W.O. wanted for his cars. The *Sunday Times* noted that, compared to the competition, 'for all practical purposes they were standard stock cars as sold to the general public'.

Hillstead had special brochures made, proclaiming the result 'to show potential customers that in the 3 Litre they had a car that could be as docile as a limousine and yet could also compete on equal terms with the fastest stripped racing cars of the day'.

Anyone reading all this would have assumed that a young company with a dazzling new product had arrived. But W.O.'s shareholders didn't see it that way. They were aghast at the extravagance of both the TT venture and the shiny brochures. Furthermore, they expected this success would negate the need for any further racing. It was a sign, thought Hillstead, of 'how little they understood W.O. and his forceful character'.

Days later Hillstead was in Blackpool, following up Porter's proposition, when he received an urgent telegram from H.M. telling him to try to sell off one of the ex-TT cars for £1,200. Another cashflow crisis had hit.

Racing car buyers were very few and far between and in any case the machine was in London. But Porter said he knew just the man, if they could find him. It was midnight when they tracked him down to the bar in the Metropole and, as Hillstead observed, 'happy and well contented with life. By the time we had consumed two bottles of champagne I was in the same mood.'

An hour later Hillstead was struggling to remember the way to his bed, armed with a cheque for £1,200. 'Had he not been decidedly happy at the time I doubt if I would have pulled it off. I must have consumed at least one bottle of champagne and, considering I was unable to show the car – let alone give a demonstration run – I was lucky to come away with a cheque in full settlement.'

W.O. agreed that this somewhat desperate measure to recoup the racing expenditure went some way to placate the board. But they were now becoming the bane of his life. He dreaded the meetings and 'resented the loss of time from what I considered the real work.' Financial crises, he was starting to discover, were 'cropping up like festering boils all through this Bentley Motors period'.

Hillstead made no secret of his dislike of 'having anything to do with money, except to know there was a reasonable balance at my bank', and found it particularly difficult to raise the vexed matter of his expenses with H.M. Aware of the unspoken understanding that he was expected to meet them out of his own pocket, he had been doing just that. And he was an assiduous and brilliant salesman with a gift for responding to a deadline. During a subsequent, particularly gloomy, month as another board meeting loomed, he was due to meet a coachbuilder who had expressed interest in an order for six chassis. He arranged to see him the same day that the board were to meet, closed the deal and had the cheque for the deposit delivered to H.M. personally just as the directors sat down. This ploy worked and a further period of grace was ensured.

The challenge for Bentley Motors was that, although the 3 Litre was perfectly suited to wealthy, independently minded men like van Raalte, and the oil-stained Pelham Ford, they were too rare a breed.

And of the chassis that *were* sold, W.O. was dismayed to find that many of the customers of his fast tourer were, as he saw it, ruining the performance by ordering closed saloon coachwork with all the aerodynamic advantages of a garden shed. And the thrilling news that Prince George had joined the Bentley 'club' was tainted for W.O. when he learned that the future monarch had also chosen the sort of 'clumsy and elaborate saloon bodywork of the time'.

Yet the business was growing. By the end of 1922 around 150 chassis had been sold, which a year later increased to 200. For a young company with a new and expensive product, surely this was a sign of success? It did not look that way to the board, impatient to see a return on their investment. Hillstead despaired of them.

In his assessment, it was 'because they were undercapitalised, W.O. and H.M. could not be choosy, and had to resort to sharp men with improbable backgrounds'. For his part, W.O. dismissed them as riffraff who did not appreciate that what he was building was their long-term reputation, not something that would produce a quick buck.

On 23 June Bentley borrowed £40,000 from the London Life Association, an enormous sum. The money, notionally for expansion, was also to help keep the company ticking over. The day before the deal was sealed, with a board meeting looming, W.O. and Hillstead embarked on a trip to the French Grand Prix. Their absence was a desperate measure to 'circumvent a carefully planned coup by a certain group to secure control of the company at the expense of the original shareholders. Apart from that hideous embarrassment we were still woefully short of money.'

The security against the loan included all the land and buildings, in Cricklewood and Hanover Court, all plant machinery, designs and – a rash and desperate move – the patents and stock. Bentley was mortgaged to the hilt.

21

Leading from the Front

War hero, steeplechaser, stuntman, fencing ace, record breaker – to say John Duff liked a challenge would be a feeble understatement. There was no template for him.

Part Lawrence of Arabia, part George Mallory, he was a product of the Empire who embraced new worlds, a restless soul whose thirst for adventure would take him all the way to Hollywood. Tall, with a beaked nose, furrowed brows, and a pair of goggles semi-permanently perched on his forehead keeping at bay a thick lawn of dark hair, he was a regular among the restless veterans who populated Brooklands in the early 1920s.

Born in 1885 to Canadian missionary parents, Duff threw himself into every new adventure with zeal, except the quest by his mother and father to convert the indigenous inhabitants of Kiukiang in China. Instead of bible-bashing, he learned to ride wild horses and hunt wild boar. Packed off to school in Ontario, he absconded, jumped a train and disappeared. He re-emerged after some weeks an accomplished cowhand and poker player, whereupon he was expelled.

Back in China, when the Great War started and desperate not to miss the show, he set off overland via the Trans-Siberian Railway; when he eventually reached England the recruiting sergeant took some convincing that he was not a spy. He joined the Royal Berkshire Rifles and was rapidly promoted to captain. At a time when it was still the done thing for officers to lead from the front, he was hit by friendly fire at Ypres.

As soon as the war was over, his thirst for adventure undimmed, Duff learned to drive, and rapidly made a name for himself as a practitioner of prodigious determination. Having discovered Brooklands, he bought a monstrous pre-war 18-litre FIAT named *Mephistopheles*, out of which he tried to coax even more power. The engine exploded and the bonnet flew off, nearly decapitating him as he was showered with boiling shrapnel.

Undaunted, he borrowed another pre-war dinosaur, a 21-litre *Blitzen* Benz, to try to beat the Brooklands circuit record, and was averaging nearly 115 mph when he failed to slow sufficiently at the end of the finishing straight. The Benz climbed the banking and hit a telegraph pole at the top, which sent it over the edge and down through the trees on the other side. Lying beside the wreck, his indignant passenger was only silenced when the petrol tank – which had lodged in a tree – fell on his head. Duff is reputed to have said: 'There, now you will have something to complain about!' He himself had sustained a burst lung, a crushed ankle and a broken knee. Brooklands was awash with rich young things keen to try their luck on the banking. Duff was different; although a relative newcomer, he quickly distinguished himself by displaying an appetite for challenge, physical courage and dogged determination. For him, breaking records was the automotive equivalent of conquering mountains.

From then on his obsession with going further and faster was focused on more manageable machinery. Among the first to try the 3 Litre Bentley, he was so impressed with its all-round performance he campaigned for his dealership, Duff and Aldington in London's St Martin's Lane, to become an official Bentley agency. From then on, he would pursue his passion for record breaking exclusively in W.O.'s machines. The Brooklands Double Twelve became his next goal, two twelve-hour stints in one weekend.

As if to prove his absurd level of toughness, Duff had the car fitted with an unpadded metal 'bucket' seat which he had made himself. Teenage mechanic Wally Hassan, who had brought the extra petrol tanks to the TT, was in his pit crew. He recalled: 'After the first twelve hours he more or less had to be lifted out of the car and practically carried up to the Hand and Spear in Weybridge where we were all staying.'

Leslie Pennal, also on hand, had to help Duff into the bath, 'but he was right as rain in the morning'.

Towards the end of the second day, however, Duff stopped and disappeared behind a hut. When after some minutes he had still not reappeared, Pennal went to check, and found him looking uncharacteristically sheepish, his fingers too frozen to undo his fly-buttons. Pennal obliged, and, at an average 86.52 mph over 2,082 miles, Duff went on to break thirty-eight class records from the three hour to the 1,000 miles.

It was a faultless run, as great a tribute to Duff's own grit and determination as the staying power of the Bentley. Through the entire twenty-four hours, which consumed six tyres, the only malfunction was a single loose screw.

The *Sporting Times* of 6 October said: 'Duff's double-twelve on a standard Bentley four-seater is a performance that puts everything else of a similar nature clean into the shade.'

The *Investors Chronicle* of 4 October 1922 wrote: 'Such a test gives remarkable evidence of the sound construction and workmanship of Bentley cars.'

Yet this Herculean achievement did not satisfy Duff for long. No sooner had he climbed one mountain than he had to find something higher. For him, it was not so much a matter of beating his opponents, or being faster through a corner, as going further and lasting longer. Endurance was what mattered. And he had enormous confidence in W.O. Bentley's creation – more, it seemed, than even W.O. himself.

Early in the spring of 1923, Hillstead bumped into Duff in Oxford Circus, round the corner from the Bentley showroom. Duff was very excited; he had just heard of a plan by the French to run a continuous twenty-four-hour race exclusively for production cars just outside the city of Le Mans. He said that if W.O. would lend him a mechanic to prepare it, he would buy a new Bentley and enter it in the race. Hillstead could see he was deadly serious. The idea of driving through the night thrilled him. And what better test for a car plucked straight from the showroom?

Duff had found his next challenge and was impatient for an answer. Hillstead was torn; this was potentially another much-needed sale, it being one of those times when 'ready money was as scarce as water in the Sahara'. But he knew all too well that W.O. had already rejected two owners who wanted to race their cars with free Bentley support. Hillstead scoured the motoring press in search of more information on the reckless-sounding French event before telephoning W.O.

'Will he pay for it?' asked W.O.

'Yes, he'll pay for the car.'

'I mean for all the extra work, you idiot.'

When W.O. read up on the race details, he was aghast. 'I think the whole thing's crazy. Nobody'll finish. Cars aren't designed to stand that sort of strain for twenty-four hours.' Furthermore, he noted that 'no other British manufacturer was supporting the event and I thought they were probably very wise'.

But Hillstead, himself a Brooklands regular who had witnessed Duff's exploits, knew that there'd be no stopping him; he was set on going with or without Bentley's backing. Since they lived not too far apart, Hillstead had developed the habit of calling in on W.O. at home after hours. He was often alone, and with his formidable guard down, glad to have someone with whom to enjoy a drink.

For his part, Hillstead valued the chance to hear what was going on behind the scenes. 'And when the conversation turned to sales (particularly the lack of them) more than ever was I grateful for a generous measure of whisky, to say nothing of the majestic proportions of the tumbler into which it was poured.'

Hillstead worked the conversation round to Le Mans. W.O. agreed that Duff was different from the other keen amateur racers. By his own efforts at the Double Twelve, he had already brought a measure of glory to Bentley. This would bring them another sale, plus Duff would pay his own way. As the whisky flowed, W.O. grudgingly came around. He would give Duff his blessing, even though he still viewed the whole venture 'with the gravest suspicion'.

A few weeks later, on 21 May 1923, a lone 3 Litre set off from Cricklewood bound for the coast with John Duff at the wheel. Beside him was Bentley works driver Frank Clement, and, crammed in the back, mechanics Arthur Saunders and Jack Besant. Under their feet and strapped to the running boards were all the tools and spares they could carry.

The road to Le Mans would bring joy and pain in equal measure and change the fortunes of Bentley in ways even the visionary W.O. could not have imagined.

22

The Road to the Sarthe

For several years after the Armistice, European motor racing had been a pale shadow of its pre-war self. In the hubristic, gladiatorial combat of the 1914 French Grand Prix, national virility was at stake. Now, in the wake of such previously unimagined carnage, the appetite for pitting men and machines against each other again had waned.

At the dawn of the century, motor sport had exploded into action. Continental Europe saw a series of multi-car, breakneck chases on the public highways that linked the major capitals of Europe. And France, having been the first nation to embrace the motor car, was at the forefront of the thrilling new sport.

By 1903 and the 800-mile Paris–Madrid race, excitement had reached fever pitch. On 24 May, 100,000 spectators descended on Versailles to witness the 3.30 a.m. start as the first of eighty-two entrants, the Englishman Charles Jarrott, in a De Dietrich from Alsace, was flagged off.

Such were the crowds that he could only see his route out of the city when they parted at the last minute. Another two million lined the route, most of whom had never even seen an automobile before, let alone anything travelling at a hundred or more kilometres per hour. Jarrott remembered 'fleeting glimpses of towns and dense masses of people, mad people, insane and reckless ... to be ploughed and maimed to extinction, evading the inevitable at the last moment in frantic haste'.

By noon the field was churning up a continuous tunnel of choking dust, that cloaked the route for a hundred miles. The nineteenth-century highways of Europe were built according to a method pioneered by Scottish turnpike surveyor John Loudon McAdam. His recipe, a trench filled with coarse stones and topped with finer ones then doused with water and steam-rollered, worked well enough for slow-moving horse-drawn transport; for speeding motor cars it was a disaster. The area of low air pressure created under fast-moving vehicles sucked dust up from the surface, creating a dense cloud and reducing visibility to zero. In addition, high-speed cornering and furious braking gouged treacherously deep ruts.

By the afternoon, several spectators and two drivers were dead, among them Marcel Renault, co-founder of the eponymous marque, when he missed a corner south of Poitiers. Panicked by the news, French Prime Minister Émile Combes ordered the race to be stopped at Bordeaux and the cars towed to the railway station by carthorses for the return trip to Paris. When Jarrott surveyed the devastation along the route, he was surprised that, given the terrible condition of the road and the absence of any spectator control, more had not died.

But road racing survived, and with a new twist that would pit nation against nation.

James Gordon Bennett, yachtsman, balloonist, adventurer and hell-raiser, is perhaps best remembered as the origin of the once-popular expression of incredulity 'Gordon Bennett!', apparently inspired by an incident at the mansion of his fiancée's parents when he arrived late and drunk and urinated into a grand piano. In another of his exploits, as proprietor of the *New York Herald*, he had funded journalist Henry Morton Stanley's famed venture into the African interior in search of the lost explorer David Livingstone.

In 1900 he launched a series of motor races with an unusual twist. Instead of individual cars and drivers, the Gordon Bennett Cup fielded national teams of no more than three cars each, painted in national colours: blue for France, white for Germany, yellow for Belgium, green for Britain. Everything including the tyres had to be manufactured in the country of each entrant, with the winning nation obliged to stage the subsequent race. It was a success: each year more nations came to compete. But France, with far more car makers than the rest, saw it as a slight; as top nation, it deserved its own race to showcase its superior technical prowess. And its official body, the *Automobile Club de France*, was determined to make it happen.

The city of Le Mans was known for two things. First, its network of narrow, cobbled streets and half-timbered houses had once been the power base of the Plantagenets, who ruled England for 300 years. And secondly, by the end of the nineteenth century it had already gained a reputation as a centre for the latest technology: self-propelled vehicles.

In 1873, a full decade before Daimler and Benz unveiled their creations, master bell-founder Amédée Bollée produced a vehicle which 'could move without horses, at a rapid walking pace'.

Optimistically christened *L'Obéissante* – the Obedient One – his twelve-seater steam carriage managed the 130 miles to Paris in an astonishing eighteen hours. His son Léon – Bollée – put Le Mans even more firmly on the map with a petrol tricycle *voiturette*. The driver sat behind the front passenger, who was completely unprotected, which earned it the nickname *Tue Belle-mère*: the mother-in-law killer.

It looked like an invalid carriage, yet it won several races, bringing it to international attention (Sammy Davis later bought one, which he named Beelzebub). On these nimble machines, Léon and his brother Camille came first and second in the original London to Brighton run in 1896. Several hundred were made, and Le Mans became a centre for the manufacture of automobiles.

By then the city was blessed with another citizen whose passion would secure the city its place in the future of motor racing. Georges Durand was a former highway official of the *Corps des Ingénieurs des Ponts et Chaussées* – the Bridges and Roads Authority. Following the Paris–Madrid debacle, he applied his expertise to envisaging a motor race on a closed circuit of public roads, which could be sufficiently well-surfaced and policed to satisfy the now far more safety-conscious authorities.

He approached the Bollées to help promote Le Mans as a centre for self-propulsion. Such was the pace of the town's growing reputation that in 1908 Wilbur and Orville Wright would bring their aircraft to Le Mans for its maiden European flight at the Hunaudières racecourse just outside the city.

Meanwhile, the city had been blessed with another stroke of luck. The *Automobile Club de France* fell out with Gordon Bennett over the vexed matter of entry being limited to one team per nation and boycotted his races.

Durand was ready. He marshalled the city councillors and hoteliers to collaborate on a bid to stage the greatest race in the world, with an enormous prize: 45,000 francs – more than £180,000 today: the first ever Grand Prix.

Durand had planned out a roughly triangular-shaped 64-mile-long circuit just outside the city. But the public roads still posed a challenge. Although the long straights would allow speeds up to an ambitious 90 mph, some of the sharpest bends had to be taken at as little as 3 mph: walking pace.

And parts of the route were treacherous. The road through the town of Saint-Calais was nothing more than a rough track; a control point with an enforced speed reduction might be needed. So he commissioned a bypass – of wooden planks – through the neighbouring fields. Then he laid another across the boggy marshland at Vibraye. And in the aftermath of the spectator deaths and injuries at the Paris–Madrid event, he ordered 65km of palisade barrier to keep the public off the track.

The race was to be run in two parts on consecutive days: 26 and 27 June, each with six 64-mile laps making 384 miles – 768 miles in all.

By early morning, thousands were gathered at the start and finish point – the village of Pont-de-Gennes, named for its picturesque ancient bridge. Many had camped overnight, some in the wooden grandstands on either side of the road. Seating capacity was a generous 35,000, but by the start of the race the crowd had swelled to around 180,000. Of the twelve teams entered, nine were French, as were twenty-four of the thirty-three cars, with six from Italy and only three German.

The cars were flagged off from 6 a.m. at intervals of ninety seconds. As the temperature climbed, the tar laid over some of the course in an effort to keep the dust at bay began to give off fumes. Soon it would melt.

Although pits didn't really exist yet, and pit crews were in their infancy, any extra help was nonetheless forbidden. Only drivers and their riding mechanics could work on the cars; if anything went wrong, the others could only stand by and watch. In addition, they weren't allowed to contribute so much as a spanner; repairs could only be made using the spares carried in or on the car. One driver whose goggles were smashed by a flying stone was forbidden to use a new pair on the grounds that equipment could not be replaced mid-race.

As the friction from the speeding cars threw up sticky particles of tar, drivers and some spectators suffered chemical burns and eye irritations. The plank bypasses also proved a liability. Two cars skidded off, one into a wall. Incredibly, both drivers were unhurt. Of the thirty-two starters, seventeen finished.

Despite a collapsed rear suspension 30 miles from the finish, Hungarian-born locksmith-turned-auto engineer Ferenc Szisz was the winner in a Renault.

The decisive factor was not the car itself, nor even the surface of the roads, but Renault's new tyre technology from Michelin. Until now, tyres were glued onto the wheel rims, and punctured rubber had to be cut away with a knife, then the new tyre wedged on, a laborious process that could take eight minutes. The *jante amovible* – detachable rim – system enabled both tyre and rim to be unbolted and swapped – reducing the eight minutes to two.

The first French Grand Prix was judged a great success and more were planned. But it was a movable feast, which didn't return to Le Mans until well after the war in 1921. While hostilities raged across Europe, motor racing gravitated to America, where European cars won five Indianapolis 500s. For 1921, the *Automobile Club de France* astutely adopted the Indianapolis 3-litre formula, which widened its appeal, particularly to Americans. The circuit on the edge of Le Mans was reduced to a more manageable 10.7 miles and the race limited to thirty laps. Without such long waits between cars, the spectators would see them more frequently. But the surface was still a challenge. Chassagne's riding mechanic Robert Laly vividly described his driver's struggle to avoid a competitor, as he braked hard at the end of the long Hunaudières straight. 'Driving on those awful stones, we went hurtling across the road from left to right and right to left, in and out of the ditches on either side, seven or eight times. Chassagne put up a great fight with the wheel, never taking his foot from the accelerator so we got back on the right path eventually, but it was a close call.'

The race became a titanic duel between Chassagne and the American Jimmy Murphy in a Duesenberg he had rolled in practice while avoiding an unexpected farm wagon. Still in hospital two hours before the race, he insisted on driving and had to be lifted into his car. He was nearly knocked out when a stone smashed into his radiator, but he pressed on, steam spewing from his engine as the water boiled away. He had to change a wheel and then damaged another before struggling across the line to finish a spectacular first. Chassagne suffered a split petrol tank and retired after seventeen laps.

The incident-packed race delighted spectators; it looked like the dawn of a new era of trans-Atlantic competition, but the Americans favoured Indianapolis-style speed-bowl tracks. Jimmy Murphy and his Duesenberg would be the last all-American team ever to win a Grand Prix. But everyone agreed the event had been a great test of driver and machine. The scene was set for a new form of motor racing.

23

The Birth of Endurance

Even at the start of the 1920s, motoring any distance was still the preserve of the intrepid. Punctures, overheating, oil loss and brake failure were all part of the normal driving experience. Weather-proofing was still a challenge and the great invention of Mary Anderson of Alabama – the windscreen wiper – had yet to find its way across the Atlantic. But France even before the Great War had been encouraging the first generation of motorists to go far and wide. From 1900, the enterprising Michelin brothers distributed free copies of their Red Guide to France's restaurants and hotels. Also listed were sources of petrol and, perhaps most helpfully, instructions on how to change a tyre. There were other advantages to motoring in France, in particular the comprehensive network of *routes nationales*, commissioned by Napoleon a hundred years before the British Automobile Association's 1920s guide *France For the Motorist* enthused: 'No country enjoys in like measure to France the luxury of possessing a vast series of trunk roads radiating from the capital . . . outlined by a directness that though primarily intended for rapid marching of armies in pre-military days, is now a completely suitable for automobile locomotion as if it has been created in the twentieth century for that purpose alone.'

But for their members with the means to explore those longer, straighter roads, there was the small matter of the Channel crossing. The primitive conditions are vividly recalled by intrepid motoring enthusiast Neville Minchin, en route to the French Grand Prix, when he rashly decided to sail via Guernsey and Saint-Malo. 'By clearing a space on deck there was just enough room for the car . . . There was practically no passenger accommodation on this ship, built in 1872, but on deck was a large coil of rope. I climbed into this and there, well protected from the wind, fell into a sleep of exhaustion.'

Once across the Channel, his four spare tyres were all immediately eaten up by the awful roads. The light was fading when a garage refused to take a sterling cheque so, in desperation, they went in search of the local bank. Needless to say, it was closed, but, *heureusement*, the manager lived over the shop.

'I cannot let the bank depart from its rules,' he explained. 'But although it is a sum I could not possibly afford to lose, I will cash your cheque for you myself. For four years I fought alongside the English and from my experience I don't think you would let me down.'

In the aftermath of the war, Georges Durand, now secretary of the *Automobile Club de l'Ouest*, had come to feel that the interests of motor racers and motorists had diverged. Where road users needed staying power and reliability, Grand Prix racing cars were highly strung, becoming temperamental beasts requiring specialised attention. In light of this, he began to imagine a different kind of event.

In October 1922, he travelled to Paris for the annual motor show, where he hoped to solicit a second opinion from someone with their finger on the pulse of what preoccupied motorists. While there, he made an appointment to see the editor of one of France's leading motor magazines, *La Vie Auto*, Charles Faroux.

Born in 1872 in Amiens, the son of a sheep trader, Faroux

displayed an early appreciation of mechanics. He studied mechanical engineering at the prestigious École Polytechnique, and won the prestigious *Prix Scientifique Fourneyron*, which came with a generous 25,000-franc award. He spent it on getting to North America, where he worked for a time for a tramway company.

But, just as Sammy Davis discovered during his apprenticeship at Daimler, Faroux realised his true vocation was journalism. On his return to France, he joined the cycling and automotive magazine *L'Auto*, which catered for all wheeled vehicles, deadly rival of the much more successful *Le Vélo*.

In 1902 its editor, fitness freak and fanatical patriot Henri Desgrange, was still preoccupied by his country's humiliating defeat in the Franco-Prussian War. He believed the French were 'tired, without muscle, without character and without will-power', and decided that robust physical activity would restore national virility.

But his paper was in crisis; circulation was a fraction of that of *Le Vélo*. His backers, which included one of the enterprising Michelin brothers, were not happy. Desgrange called a crisis meeting with his editorial team and demanded ideas. Last to speak was the most junior member of staff, Géo Lefèvre, who had not expected to be asked to contribute. At a loss, he blurted out the first idea that came into his head – a multi-day race, not on a track like most bicycle races but round the country. Desgrange seized on the idea and in 1903 'Le Tour de France' was born. It transformed *L'Auto*'s circulation from 20,000 to a quarter of a million readers by 1908.

Faroux didn't stay long at *L'Auto*, but it was enough to arouse his interest in competition. In 1909 he founded *La Vie Auto* and by 1913 he was writing about the virtues of his very own Rolls-Royce. *La Vie Auto* took him to all the great races of Europe and back to America for the 1913 Indianapolis, where his wife became the first woman ever to circulate the 'brickyard'.

In 1914, though over forty, he managed to enlist and fought at Verdun, before – like Sammy Davis – getting a technical role in aircraft engine supply.

At his meeting with Faroux in October 1922, Durand laid out his proposal for a touring car endurance event. Faroux immediately saw the potential – both for his paper and for himself. No circuit race for production cars existed and it might be of far broader appeal to his readers than the increasingly rarefied world of Grand Prix racing.

He introduced Durand to Emile Coquille, the French agent for British company Rudge Whitworth, pioneers of the centre lock wire wheel. Following the Michelin brothers' removable rim, Rudge Whitworth had made the next great leap forward in tyre changing with the development of a splined axle, which held the whole wheel in place with a single wing nut.

Durand's original proposal was for an eight-hour event, but when Coquille heard the idea he went one further. Why not make it a full twenty-four hours, twice round the clock? Racing through the night would be new and exciting, he argued, a formidable challenge for modern electrics and lights. Faroux was doubtful they would get permission, but Durand, the driving force behind the original French Grand Prix, had the ear of the authorities at Le Mans and was confident he could see off any opposition. Coquille promised to put up a trophy, the Rudge Whitworth Cup and a prize of 100,000 francs, the proviso being that the race truly captured the public imagination.

While Durand focused on the permissions and the lighting of at least the most challenging corners, Faroux drafted the regulations. The event was designed to replicate as faithfully as possible the conditions of everyday touring, so the cars had to be genuine production models. His original way to ensure this, for entrants to present ten similar cars so that scrutineers could select one at random, was agreed to be too cumbersome and likely to deter private entrants. Instead, evidence had to be presented that the cars conformed to manufacturers' specifications with full road trim: mudguards, running boards and hoods. And, except for the smaller entrants under 1100cc, all had to have touring bodywork and four seats. There would be no riding mechanics; a pair of drivers for each car would take turns at the wheel. And the cars had to carry the equivalent weight of a full complement of passengers at 75kg each using either a bag of sand or an ingot of lead. All spare parts and tools required for any repair had to be carried on board. Once the race was underway, only the drivers could carry out any maintenance or repairs.

There was more. On-board electric starters had to be used after pit stops – no hand cranking or push starts – only ordinary fuel supplied by the organisers was allowed and refuelling was only allowed at specified intervals to penalise heavy consumption. Between pit stops the radiator, oil filler and fuel filler caps were sealed with lead by race officials known as *plombiers* (*plomb* being French for lead). The winner would be the car that travelled furthest.

24

Twice Round the Clock

Although W.O. was not in favour of free factory support for private racers, he made an exception for John Duff. As a fearless record breaker and assiduous promoter of the Bentley brand, he was a special case. Although he was entering as a private individual, Duff's car was prepared at Cricklewood under the watchful eye of Frank Clement, who would also be his co-driver.

'We went in the car we raced with. I drove the whole way from Dieppe with everything in it we needed, mechanics and all. The whole thing was extraordinarily light-hearted and casual.'

Although as an employee he kept his own counsel at the time, Clement shared W.O.'s scepticism. 'When it came to the race itself, of course nobody knew what would happen – nobody had tried to race cars for twenty-four hours before – not on roads anyway. They had no idea what thirty-odd cars going round a dirt road for twenty-four hours on end would do, either to the road or the cars.'

The event was held on 26 and 27 May, with thirty-three cars on the grid. Apart from Duff's privately entered Bentley and a pair of Belgian Excelsiors, the field was entirely French. The line-up reads now like a roll call of fallen French automotive icons: Chenard-Walcker, Bignan, Excelsior, Brasier, Delage, Salmson, Rolland-Pilain, Amilcar, Lorraine-Dietrich, Berliet,

Vinot-Deguingand, Corre La Licorne, Irat and Sara. Of the whole field, only Bentley and Bugatti would prevail.

Duff and Clement had allowed plenty of time to reach Le Mans and get to know the circuit, which was just as well. The road surface was already rutted, muddy and covered in loose stones. Clement was horrified. 'It was simply dreadful. I mean to say we had holes a foot deep. And the stones they seemed to be a foot deep too, they were so bad.'

The route, outside the town of Le Mans, wove its way through the nearby villages and hamlets. At the hairpin in the centre of the village of Pontlieu, locals would be pinned in their houses by thundering *bolides*. Facilities were primitive; the pits where they prepared their car in the run-up to the race weekend were just timber-framed canvas tents.

~

Back in Cricklewood, W.O. was struggling with himself; for all his doubts, it wasn't his style to stay away from the action. 'By Friday morning I was already in a fever of anxiety and suffering from a very bad conscience, and in the afternoon could stand it no longer. In spite of the promise I had made myself, I drove over from the works to Hanover Street where I found Hillstead. "Come on, we've got to go and see this stupid race. We'll take the night boat."'

Hillstead was delighted, but, by the time they reached Paris, W.O. was in a foul mood. 'He refused to take part in any conversation either with porters or taxi drivers and, when I jibbed at having to air my ignorance of the French language, I was treated to a flow of invective that put a stop to any interchange of opinions for some considerable time. Somehow we reached the Gare Montparnasse and, more by luck than judgement, found ourselves in a train scheduled to arrive at Le Mans in the early afternoon.

There was no dining car, we were without sandwiches, nor had we eaten anything since the previous evening.'

They reached Le Mans at midday, just four hours before the flag. 'Never again,' grunted W.O. 'Next time we'll take the car.'

They were in time for the 'weighing in', where Hillstead was perturbed to see how thin the line was between the French idea of a standard touring model and an out-and-out racer. On Saturday afternoon the cars lined up on the track two by two, numbered in order of engine size – the Bentley was no. 8.

Durand and Faroux had opted for May in the hope of avoiding the searing heat that broiled the tarmac in late June, 1906. But in trying to avoid one problem they'd unwittingly created another. At 4 p.m., when Faroux, as clerk of the course, dropped the flag, the whole area was engulfed in a hailstorm, followed by four hours of torrential rain.

When Duff came in at 8 p.m. to hand over, he warned Clement that the road surface was beginning to break up. Despite having decided to go at the last minute, W.O. had already taken charge of proceedings. Hillstead, who'd hoped to watch the race under the canvas cover of Duff's pit, was banished to a sandbank 20 yards up the road with a pair of stopwatches and a manifold book and told to stay at his post, counting laps, for the full twenty-four hours.

As dusk settled over the route the rain lifted, but now they were contending with the dark. Giant floodlights provided by the French army illuminated some of the corners and the pit area, but out on the long straights drivers depended on just their headlights. W.F. Bradley, reporting on the event for *The Autocar*, noted that the challenge of racing through the night proved to be the test of lighting systems the organisers envisaged.

'After a couple of hours' running one third of the cars had lost time by reason of the failure of electric or acetylene sets. Just before darkness a stone went right though one of the Bentley headlights.

The Chenard-Walcker team sportingly offered them another lamp, but the change would have taken too much time. The car forged onward with one headlight working and the other intermittently.'

In the pits, W.O.'s deep misgivings about the event were starting to wear off. 'Before darkness fell and the acetylene arc lamps at the corners were turned on, Le Mans was beginning to get into my blood. By midnight, with the cars pounding past the stand with their lights on, my first sight of racing in the dark – I was quite certain that this was the best race I'd ever seen.'

Squinting into the murk, Duff and Clement raced on through the night. They clung onto second place behind a Chenard-Walcker, but were losing ground. At dawn, they were more than 20 miles behind the leader.

Then Duff started to gain, set a lap record of 64.7 mph, which he then broke several times over. With brakes only on the rear wheels, he had to resort several times to the escape road at the end of the straight. But he clawed away at the leader until finally the Bentley took the lead.

But it wasn't to last. Just before noon, he failed to appear. Word reached the pits that the Bentley was stranded 3 miles down the track. A stone had pierced the fuel tank right at the back of the car, three inches above the exhaust pipe. Duff the sportsman did what came naturally: he sprinted all the way back to the pits.

After conferring, the officials allowed Clement to set off on a bicycle borrowed from a nearby soldier, pedalling against the race traffic, a pair of *bidons* of fuel slung over his shoulders. With the track barely more than two cars' width in places, his life was now at greater risk than it had been behind the wheel. 'All the cars were coming towards me and as they were using all the road on the corners there wasn't much room for me. I was petrified with fear and in the end walked in the ditch and pushed the bicycle.'

At the roadside, he widened the gash in the tank until it would accept a wooden bung and poured in some fuel, then threw the bicycle in the back and raced to the pits, where he made a slightly more permanent repair with cork and soap. It was touch and go as the hole was right above the exhaust – a fire risk that would have immediately disqualified them in later years. They had lost a full three hours, but they were back in the race.

Duff's worst moment came as he was about to overtake a Bignan when it burst a rear tyre, producing a wall of blue smoke. The driver, in a panic, slammed on his very efficient four-wheel brakes and Duff, temporarily blinded, very nearly rammed the stricken machine.

Despite the extreme weather and the deterioration of the track, it would turn out to be one of the least dramatic Le Mans races. The two Chenard-Walckers led from start to the finish, twenty-four hours later, with the Bignan third. Even with the delay to fix the petrol tank, Duff and Clement managed a creditable equal fourth at an average speed of 50.05 mph. They also set the fastest lap, in 9 minutes and 39 seconds, at 66.69 mph. But spectators agreed that the lone Bentley provided the most excitement, with repeated attacks on the front runners, and the race through day and night was judged a success.

Though he had difficulty showing it, W.O. was a convert. 'I was never more surprised and delighted than when we came in fourth in that first casual and slap-happy effort.'

The post-race dinner was somewhat derailed by the quantities imbibed of Amer Picon, a vicious orange-flavoured aperitif, Hillstead recalled. 'There was much humour, some bickering and an unlooked for climax when one of our guests, wishing to depart in a hurry, tried to make his exit via a cupboard door.'

A few days later, W.O. and Hillstead drove on to Tours, where they were among the few Brits to witness Henry Segrave win the French Grand Prix in his Sunbeam. With Bentley's achievement at Le Mans and Segrave's triumph, they would have been forgiven for thinking that a new dawn of British motor competition was on the horizon.

25

Chasing the Phantom

In April 1920, fifteen months after Leonie's death, W.O. married again. Audrey Morten Chester Hutchinson was seven years his junior, the daughter of a respected barrister, who moved in society circles and enjoyed entertaining. She seemed just the right woman to provide that cushion of domesticity he longed for, and even to bring him out of his shell.

But it soon emerged that, unlike Leonie, who gamely accompanied him to his first competitive events, Audrey had no interest in cars. And as the workaholic W.O., who hated small talk, did not want to end the day with frivolous partying, it was almost inevitable that the couple soon began to live separate lives. Le Mans had introduced W.O. to the joy of driving in France, but his increasingly frequent road trips over there were with colleagues rather than his spouse.

His previous experience of France had been limited to his sorties to Dunkirk to see to the warplanes powered by his engines. Now, his peacetime drives over long, straight, poplar-lined *routes nationales* awoke a spirit that eluded him back home in his unhappy marriage in London. 'The only relaxation I ever had during the entire Bentley Motors period that remotely resembled a holiday was on Continental tests of the cars. In these extended runs all over France, up and down the passes to test the cooling and at high speeds for a hundred miles at a stretch I could combine my love for travelling over great distances with something that was useful.'

The diffident, formal W.O. felt that France liberated him with its 'friendly classless people ... My idea of heaven has always been to take a car across the channel and drive along those incomparable roads to the south – and the Mediterranean sun.'

Just as the motorcycle's promise of independent travel had turned him away from the railway, the 3 Litre fuelled that dream of independence, agility and speed. Before the end of the decade, he would claim to have driven from Dieppe to the Côte d'Azur in a day, cruising in places at over 85 mph, without switching on his lights.

W.O. had never thought of the 3 Litre as anything other than an open car, certainly not a 'town car', and was initially dismayed when customers ordered 'performance killing', heavy, closed bodywork in the interests of comfort and escape from the elements. But the 3 Litre was not a quiet car, and the downside of its good road-holding was quite a stiff ride. Coachbuilders who supplied car bodies were working to the same customs and practices as they had the previous century for horse-drawn carriages. Mounted on a car, these bodies may have kept the weather at bay around town, but at any decent speed over rough surfaces they were transformed into squeaky, creaking echo chambers.

The solution was one of the first examples of aircraft practice to be applied to the car. When John Duff made his Montlhéry record attempt, he had a lightweight body built in Paris by Charles Weymann. Born to a Haitian mother and an American father, Weymann had been a pioneer aviator before turning his attention to cars. He eliminated the squeaks in the wooden frame by putting metal between the joints, added thick layers of cotton batting to deaden sound and covered the exterior with waterproof fabric or sheet aluminium. It was so effective that other coachbuilders queued up to license the technique, and, until the advent of the all-steel body in the 1930s, Weymann *méthode* bodies would be de rigueur. W.O. was impressed, enough to soften his prejudice against closed coachwork. With this in mind, he began to formulate his next car.

He was about to venture further into Rolls-Royce territory with a six-cylinder car, a refined, quiet cruiser but with the powerful acceleration and top speed of his 3 Litre. This would be a far cry from the smaller model Hillstead had campaigned for and which W.O. had promised the shareholders.

In such an economically febrile time, it seemed to make no sense to develop a new car for an even narrower clientele. Hillstead thought taking on Rolls-Royce was the height of folly, 'at a time when the company couldn't buy a packet of cigarettes without increasing its overdraft'. But W.O. simply did not have the resources to produce a smaller, higher volume car. The 3 Litre could be the basis for a larger model, which would command a higher margin. In 1924 400 Bentleys were delivered – a healthy total. But a manufacturing profit of £13,529 was cancelled out by an operating loss of £57,700 on development and other expenditures to improving the works. This was the harsh reality of trying to grow a company on limited investment. More than once the message came from Cricklewood to Hanover Court to sell more cars: 'Nothing to pay the wages next Friday – go out and get some money!'

26

Neck and Neck

For the second Le Mans in 1924, Durand and Faroux made some changes. In search of better weather they pushed the date back three weeks to mid-June – and were rewarded with road-melting temperatures.

They also added another real-world challenge as a further element of entertainment. After the first five laps, drivers had to pull in, put up their hoods and drive with them up for the next twenty laps. They were pleased to see the field increase to forty entrants, but it was still very much a domestic affair. This year, Bentley was the sole foreign competitor.

W.O. tasked Leslie Pennal, just twenty-two, with preparing Duff's car. As well as completely rebuilding the engine and suspension, he added wire mesh stone guards to the headlights and lagged the fuel tank with a protective layer of coconut matting, held in place with leather straps. Fuel pipes were duplicated in case one got damaged and encased in rubber hose. But by far the most significant improvement was the timely addition of front wheel brakes.

At a time when most recruits toiled for years before being given even the smallest responsibility, it was a huge vote of confidence in the young man, who only a few years before had been sweeping the showroom. And as the one who knew the car most intimately, he would be with it at the race – a thrill but also a baptism of fire.

This year W.O. travelled there in the six-cylinder prototype he was developing, disguised with a monstrous and doubtless very squeaky limousine body built by Freestone & Webb, and an ungainly hexagonal radiator. Low-pressure 'balloon' tyres were fitted to soak up rough surfaces. With him came Hillstead, Richard Winchell, whom W.O. had known since his Clifton schooldays and had appointed works manager, and Bertie Kensington-Moir from the service department. Moir had raced an Aston Martin in the TT and in the bar on the ferry back from the Isle of Man he had convinced W.O. to give him a job. A larger-than-life character in every sense, he also doubled as self-appointed jester in W.O.'s court.

Knowing sleep would be at a premium, W.O. had booked a four-berth cabin for them, but Moir, never one to miss an opportunity for a party, was in no mood to let the others rest. As Hillstead recalled, W.O. having retreated to a top bunk 'found himself precipitated into the bunk below and then onto the floor. Thereafter followed a general mix up that very quickly turned the cabin into a shambles. Moir could be very troublesome on occasions, and that was one of them.'

The mood was still ugly in the morning when the prototype was craned onto the quayside at Dieppe. Since the disguised radiator bore no badge except a mysterious 'sun' design, a long debate ensued with the suspicious customs officers as to the car's provenance. Matters were resolved when W.O. offered to pay duty on his cigarettes.

At the circuit, Pennal was involved in his own drama with officialdom. 'The scrutineer who of course was a Frenchman, seemed much stricter with us than the others, and was very severe on every detail. First of all, we had to drive the car over a tray of sawdust. If you blew any large amount out of the tray, then the exhaust pipe was pointing downwards too much and would, we were told, blow up a lot of dust on the track – into the faces of the French drivers.'

The Bentley just about got through that test, only for the officials to pronounce the front mudguards too narrow – by 3/16ths of an inch. Pennal extended them by grafting on thin steel strips, working all through the night. During the early hours he realised he was not alone. A few feet away, W.O. was watching him. Pennal, used to his boss's habit of appearing at all hours, simply got on with the job. But then he heard him mutter something. At first he thought, in his tired state, that his ears were playing tricks on him. Was W.O. considering withdrawing the car from the race?

Pennal was flabbergasted. This was the man to whom he owed his career, whose word was law at Bentley Motors, a decorated naval captain, public-school bred. Despite this, Pennal, a cockney lad barely out of his teens, couldn't help himself. 'What will the fellows say back at the works?' he exploded. 'We bring this car all this way and I couldn't even get it up to the line?'

What Pennal had just witnessed wasn't personal. W.O. was letting slip the self-doubt that haunted this otherwise dogged and determined individual. There was a pause before he answered very quietly: 'Well, we'll think about it.'

Nothing more was said. W.O. had got the message. Much later, he admitted: 'I had obtained the confirmation I needed – both about the man and the machine.'

In the morning Duff appeared at the pits dressed for action, in plus fours, tweed jacket and a blue beret, carrying 'a huge sheet tied up like a navvy's handkerchief, full of fresh lettuce, a whole bag of fresh eggs, and a jar of honey'. During breaks from driving he would take a spoonful of honey, crack open an egg and swallow the contents with a few lettuce leaves. A passionate vegetarian, he lectured Pennal on the vice of eating meat. Clement, a good few inches shorter than Duff, arrived with a cushion tucked under his arm, 'like a schoolboy with his books'.

At four o'clock in the afternoon, Faroux dropped the flag. A slow start put Duff into ninth position as the pack hurtled down to the Pontlieue hairpin. With their thunderous new 4-litre straight-eight engines, Chenard-Walcker looked to be dominant. But when it came to the hood stop five laps in, Duff, who had rehearsed this repeatedly and seen to it that the mechanism was thoroughly oiled, broke his record: done in just 38.5 seconds without even leaving his seat.

As he disappeared up the road, André Lagache – the previous year's winner – was left fumbling with the telescopic tubes of his Chenard's primitive hood. But he made up for it, put his huge performance advantage to good use and raised the lap record to 69.076 mph. It seemed Chenard might win again.

Back at his post on the sandbank, armed with his stopwatches, Hillstead witnessed the first drama, a thick column of black smoke rising some distance away. The Bentley was due, as was the leading Chenard.

Several long seconds ticked by as he peered into the distance. He had seen a racing car on fire before, 'but when the actual conflagration is out of sight the inevitable suspense is magnified a thousand fold. Whose car was it?'

Then he saw Clement tearing towards him – and no Chenard.

The three Lorraines now emerged as the team to beat, proudly sporting the emotive double-barred Cross of Lorraine on their radiators, lest anyone forget the recent liberation of that region from German control. The lone Bentley was fifth. After six hours, only twenty-four of the original forty-three starters were still in the race, the casualties crippled by fire, mechanical failure and wear and tear from the punishing road surfaces.

Just after Duff handed over to Clement at 8 p.m., a Bignan lost its radiator plug and was forced to retire. The Bentley was now lying second, but somewhere in the night the rear friction dampers, first one and then the other, fractured, making the car a handful at speed, as it bucked and bounced all over the pitted track. The windscreen shook itself to pieces, the remains to spend the rest of the race on the back seat, and, just before dawn, Duff roared into the pits complaining that he couldn't get into third gear. With the pit crew forbidden to touch the car during the race, all Pennal could do was hand him a torch.

Duff spent forty minutes stretched face down across the seat, probing the gate at the base of the gear lever. A coachbuilder's steel staple used to secure the fabric to the inside of the body had worked loose and dropped into the mechanism and was jammed in fast by the repeated gear changes. Duff eventually winkled it out with a screwdriver.

For the rest of the night, the Bentley bore down on the leading Lorraine. All through the long hours of darkness, Hillstead stayed awake, recording the laps and times of the front runners as they passed his post. At dawn W.O. paid him a visit and examined his notes, glaring. 'You're wrong according to the official scoring board. Why don't you pay attention to what you're doing?'

Furious, Hillstead insisted he hadn't missed a single lap. 'My figures are correct and you can bet your life they are trying to do us out of a lap because we have a chance of winning.'

W.O. took the carbon copy of Hillstead's scores and marched back to the pits. After what *The Motor* reported as a 'long and bitter wrangle', the scoreboard was corrected.

At noon on the Sunday, Stalter's Lorraine expired. Clement was now in first position, with a stunning 95-mile lead over the second-placed car. With an hour and a half to go, Duff took the wheel again. But the battle was not over yet.

Having decided as a precaution to pit for a change of rear tyres, they found one of the wheels stuck fast on its hub and spent a heart-stopping forty minutes working it free. Incredible as it seemed, a needle file had been jammed in the splines. How? Was it sabotage? Desperate not to lose his lead, Duff drove flat out to the finish.

Even as the flag fell, there was yet more drama. Duff's final 90-mile dash was discounted; his time in the pits had dragged his distance below the minimum allowed between stops.

Had they won – or not?

The team collectively held its breath while they waited for the result. His official total for the full twenty-four hours was 1,290 miles. To their inexpressible relief, the runner-up Lorraine had covered only 1,280 miles. Duff and Clement were still the winners – by just 10 miles. And of the original field of forty, only fifteen survived the full twenty-four hours.

It was an incredible vote of confidence for this lone foreign car. The Bentley team was ecstatic, yet not for the first time Hillstead would find himself mystified by his boss. What more reassurance could W.O. have needed, in this brutal war of attrition, than to see his creation deliver once again?

'The evening which should have been a feast of celebration fell extremely flat. W.O. was in one of his silent moods, and it was not until Moir ordered a bottle of champagne off his own bat that anyone thought about drinking a toast. Afterwards we visited a café on the opposite side of the road and – under the mellowing influence of excellent brandy – I had every hope of a speedy retirement to bed.'

No such luck. W.O. announced they were driving back to Dieppe that night. Hillstead's turn at the wheel came at 1 a.m. With everyone else fast asleep, he fought to stay awake, haunted by the memory that somewhere along the route was a village where an open drain ran right across the road. He saw it just in time to slow, but not enough to avoid waking his passengers, who complained bitterly.

Then Winchell the works manager took over and got lost. An

obliging Frenchman offered to show them the way as it was on his route home, only for Hillstead to realise after he had left them that it was not the Dieppe road at all. A thick mist then descended, after which they had a puncture. The jack would not fit under the car with its deflated balloon tyre, so all hands had to lift it while the change was made.

Still in Le Mans, Pennal was rewarded for his efforts – no thanks to Bentley. Having stayed behind at the track to pack up the pit, he found Duff's goggles and decided to drop them off at his hotel. 'I was very dirty, I was very tired, and I was terribly hungry and feeling although very happy that we'd won the race – well, rather flat.'

In the lobby he was accosted by an American who, on hearing that he was the winner's mechanic, insisted on buying him a drink. When the American discovered that Pennal was berthed not in Duff's hotel but over a nearby café, he was shocked. 'Do you know what you'd do if you were an American mechanic?' he exclaimed. 'You'd come here and you'd have a bath and then a jolly good meal, and you'd say "Put that on Duff's account." That's what you'd do!'

Pennal replied that he wouldn't dare do such a thing, whereupon the American, after a swift exchange with the front desk, marched him upstairs where a maid was waiting with towels. 'So I did have a lovely bath, and when I went down there was a little table laid and a delicious meal all ready for me ... I was scared stiff what would happen but Duff never said a word.'

Though their victory was a huge milestone for Bentley, few in Britain had even heard of Le Mans. The event was only in its second year, and all the other competitors were French manufacturers unknown in Britain. There were no headlines; the hard-won triumph was unlikely to translate into those desperately needed orders.

But W.O. was not to be discouraged; he pressed ahead with his new six-cylinder model, deaf to questions as to how it could be financed. Without significant investment, Cricklewood couldn't expand. They were running to stand still.

Production was stepped up, but instead of bringing joy, the increased overheads produced greater anxiety about the acute shortage of working capital. In Hillstead's view the situation was 'chaotic'. With nothing to pay the week's wages, he was sent out to bring in some cash, 'a job I loathed more than anything'.

His method after he had exhausted potential new shareholders was to persuade other Bentley agents to give him a cheque on the promise of advancing a delivery date. But since this frequently didn't work, he resorted to selling a chassis at a greater discount. And when *that* didn't work, H.M. would write a cheque for a hundred pounds 'just to carry us over a weekend'. On two occasions Hillstead himself did the same.

Increasingly, Hillstead and H.M. found their weekends taken up with 'chasing capital' – namely selling the company rather than the cars, in effect going around with a very substantial begging bowl.

On one occasion they called at a particularly attractive Georgian house on the Sussex Downs. It was the home of Rowland Rank of the flour and bakery empire, younger brother of J. Arthur, who would go on to found the film studios. Despite being in the role of supplicant, Hillstead enjoyed these excursions. 'My interest in old furniture and houses had been greatly enhanced through getting about the country visiting other people's properties,' he recalled. At the Rank residence he found himself in awe. 'Nothing was out of place, and the mellow dignity of age contrasted sharply with the sordid nature of our visit.'

Their opening gambit betrays all the hallmarks of a thinly veiled contempt for the whole business of finance. 'What we really need', said H.M. airily, 'is someone to look after the financial side of the company. So we are all free to get on with our respective jobs.' This was not so much a sales pitch to invest in an exciting, go-ahead company, more like a plea for help from a distressed acquaintance. Rank listened very politely, plied them with alcohol and repartee, and showed no interest whatever in their proposal.

Meanwhile, W.O. was back in France pounding the *routes nationales* in his big six-cylinder prototype with a car full of Bentley men. Once he spotted another large car, on a parallel road. It was trailing a cloud of dust as it travelled very fast towards a fork in the road up ahead. Could it be what he thought it was?

W.O. put his foot to the floor. The other party followed suit and both cars arrived at the junction together. Neither gave way as they sped along side by side. Although disguised like the Bentley, W.O. knew the mystery machine could only be a Rolls-Royce prototype. Right in the heart of the vast land mass of France, he was neck and neck with the much-anticipated replacement for the aged Silver Ghost – the future Phantom.

W.O. kept his foot down. From cruising at 65 mph, they were now in the high eighties, neither giving an inch. 'I suppose we would have continued like this all the way to the Channel coast if the cap of one of the Rolls' crew hadn't blown off and gone spinning away in the dust cloud in our wake.'

Back at Cricklewood, W.O. held a council of war with Bertie Kensington-Moir and Fred Burgess the designer. W.O.'s instincts told him that – having found themselves unable to shake him off, Rolls would be tempted to raise their game. So Bentley would do the same.

Their six-cylinder development car was currently a mere 4¼ litres. 'Because the Rolls-Royce would almost certainly be increasing its power in order to claim superiority over us . . . we had better keep two steps ahead and increase our capacity to 6½ litres.'

The battle was on.

27

A Presumably Respectable Doctor

Unlike Sammy Davis or W.O., Dudley Benjafield did not grow up with petrol running in his veins. Like his father and brother he had devoted himself to medicine. But after the war, though well established in his profession, he was restless. Away when his son Patrick was born, and not unusually for men of the time on long, drawn-out postings, he never bonded with him. Back in Wimpole Street he was restless for distraction.

Once, during the war, encamped near a creek in Mesopotamia with nothing to do, he had made a primitive boat. He took a sheet of corrugated iron, laboriously hammered it flat, folded it in half and nailed each end to a baulk of wood to form a bow and stern. It alleviated the boredom but was less than seaworthy; it sank so often he had to attach an empty petrol tin on a length of rope to act as a buoy 'to proclaim its whereabouts'.

He replaced it with a dugout – 'a vast improvement'. But it was heavy, hard work to paddle and apt to get blown into the dense clumps of date palms that bordered the creek. So he traded up to a clinker-built dinghy to which he fitted a small lug sail and centreboard. In the midst of treating the sick and injured, boating provided a welcome respite.

He found he missed those adventures. 'Turning these things over in my mind I drifted into my club and picked up a weekly magazine called *The Motor Boat*.' In the classified ads, he happened on the *Lumiere*, a motor launch with a 30hp Daimler engine, on sale at £150. And it was moored conveniently nearby, on the Grosvenor Canal behind Victoria Station. Benjafield bought it on the spot, 'with a view to taking her round to Folkestone where I proposed to keep her for sea fishing'.

It did the job, though not without histrionics, which Benjafield perversely seemed to relish. He found a mechanic, Jackman, to help him with the engine, but the man suffered terrible seasickness. And the association was cut short when 'a few months later, while he was working under a lorry which had been jacked up, the jack slipped and the back axle came to rest on his head'.

So Benjafield befriended 'a waterside loafer named Flynn who provided me with endless amusement', regaling him with stories of 'waterfront opium dens, murders, and corpses being disposed of in the river. I always knew he was an unmitigated scoundrel . . . but I considered him very good value.'

Each setback seemed to offer a fresh challenge. When the *Lumiere* shed its propeller in the canal, Benjafield managed to have the section drained and spent several hours contentedly probing the sludge with a bamboo cane until he found it.

When the day came to head down the Thames and round to Folkestone for the fishing, Flynn – who he'd entrusted with the keys to the cabin – vanished, having taken everything of value that wasn't nailed down. Relentlessly cheerful, Benjafield reflected: 'I do not bear him the slightest malice and should be delighted to buy him some more beers in exchange for some more stories.'

Once finally berthed in Folkestone, the *Lumiere* did provide Benjafield with many pleasurable sea-fishing trips, but in January

1924 disaster struck. While she was moored in the harbour, an easterly gale caused two fishing smacks to break loose. 'Poor *Lumiere* was sunk. And not even decently sunk at that, with one good hole that might have been repaired, but sunk by repeated broadside buffetings which had sprung every seam. The hull was sold to a timber yard for £5 as scrap, and I never will forget the dreary sight of its procession through Folkestone on a large trolley, dragged by six horses.'

To fend off the feeling of aimlessness, he now devoted his spare time to finishing the second medical degree that the war had forced him to postpone. But he was also becoming increasingly enamoured of a new love in his life: his recently acquired Bentley.

In 1923 he bought a long-chassis 3 Litre and had Harrisons coachbuilders clothe it with a saloon body, which he used for the weekend excursions to Folkestone. It wasn't just the freedom and independence he enjoyed; the actual physical experience of driving the car was great fun, for it fed his appetite for adventure and challenge. 'I soon learned the trick of dropping to third at speed with a quick double de-clutch and foot hard down all the time and I began to rather fancy myself.'

Early in 1924, bereft from the loss of the *Lumiere*, he took the car to Bentley's service depot in Cricklewood, where he encountered Bertie Kensington-Moir. 'I was rather in fear and trepidation of him as a well-known and skilful handler of fast cars . . . a big fat man with a unique and cheerful laugh which was very infectious.'

Benjafield soon found himself engaged in lively banter. Never averse to mischief, he warned Moir that he fancied something faster and more powerful – and was thinking of looking elsewhere. Moir rose to the bait, but not in the way Benjafield expected. 'So you like going fast?'

Moir took Benjafield's arm and marched him to the back of the workshop where four mechanics were working on a 'dirty little dark red coloured car'. 'I'm taking her down to Brooklands tomorrow afternoon on test. Perhaps you'd like to come?'

Benjafield felt he couldn't very well back down. 'Having accepted and arranged to meet him there at two o clock, I left hurriedly to resume my work.'

Arriving at Brooklands the following day, he found Moir in the paddock with the red car, tightening the shock absorbers and changing the plugs. He handed Benjafield a pair of goggles and invited him to get into the passenger seat while he climbed behind the wheel. The engine exploded into life.

> He let in the clutch with a screech. The car started with such a jerk that my head and shoulders felt as if they were left astern. For the next eight minutes or so, all hell let loose. We darted out through the gate and joined the main circuit at the top of the finishing straight. Half way round the home banking down went his foot and by the time of the end of the railway straight was reached the rev counter was showing just under 3,700. The din was terrific and the bumping prodigious. The rush of air tore the goggles off my face and somehow the strap had slipped down and was round my throat and was nearly throttling me. This diabolical state of affairs seemed to last for hours, but having completed the two laps he slowed down, turned into the finishing straight and then returned to the paddock. Engine switched off and peace reigned again. Trembling like an aspen and feeling rather sick I got out of the beastly thing; never had I been so terrified.
>
> With a dirty cackle Moir turned to me and said: 'How do you like that, Doc?' My knees were still feeling like limp jelly; I managed to articulate one word – 'fine.'

Before Benjafield could compose himself, Moir threw down another gauntlet. '"Why don't you buy the car, Doc?" said my tormentor.

'"Why not?" say I against all my better inclinations. Then in a feeble attempt to maintain face, "What's the price?" say I, all control being completely lost.'

The car in question was a one-off, its chassis shortened by 9 inches and drilled for further lightness, its radiator narrowed to improve aerodynamics and a tuned engine fitted with three carburettors. It now began to dawn on Benjafield where Moir's talents out of the car really lay – getting customers to part with money against their better judgement.

Moir told him the price, which Benjafield could not recall, 'with a sneer, implying: "You're too blooming soft – no guts – you daren't." What a psychologist he would have made – he employed the only technique that would make me fall. Had he approached reasonably at a normal time, I should have reacted reasonably and normally, but having established an ascendancy he maintained it and gave me no time to recover.

'To my horror, I heard myself say: "Okay, I'll buy it."

'That evening, having recovered normal sanity, I was filled with misgiving at what I had done. Here was I, a presumably respectable doctor, with amongst other things a job on the staff of a teaching medical school, committed to the control of a mechanical monster. Even the idea of being a passenger again terrified me. How much worse it would be to try and drive this juggernaut. And that's just where I was wrong. To go as a passenger in a racing car is still utterly repugnant to me, but to sit at the wheel thereof is an entirely different matter, as I very soon discovered.'

Brooklands was tailor-made for a man of his means and inclination to let rip. To Benjafield it was a revelation. 'For the sum of five guineas per annum you could join the Brooklands Automobile Racing Club and receive three badges in gilt and enamel which gave you and two ladies the entrée to Brooklands that season for all meetings and gave you the use of the track itself on non-race days. Thus it was possible for the beginner to drive round the track as much as he liked and by practising in this manner, with one of the older hands to advise him, get used to driving at high speed yet with safety. It was possible to make mistakes at Brooklands and thanks to the banking and plenty of room, get away with it, whereas a similar mistake made elsewhere might well be a good deal more expensive.'

Under Moir's tutelage, Benjafield gradually got the measure of the red 3 Litre – and the track.

'Many of the uninitiated consider that track driving consists merely of putting your foot down on the floorboards and steering. This is by no means true of any track and least of all Brooklands. For it is not a symmetrical circle or oval but of an irregular pyriform shape. The result of this is that the correct line for any given car is determined by its speed and not only does this apply to one's position on the banking which is obvious but also to the correct position in the straight.'

He entered his first race, a modest 9-mile dash, and came fourth. Emboldened, he put himself down for two more on the Whitsun Bank Holiday. But in practice, forty-eight hours before, a valve broke and smashed through the piston, which in turn collapsed and punched a hole in the sump.

Moir had the car towed back to Cricklewood and summoned a couple of the mechanics, Browning and Freddie Settrington. 'I concentrated on keeping them well fed and cheerful and with this in view repaired to my house and collected some bottles of champagne and masses of sandwiches.' The block and crankshaft had survived and by working through both the Saturday and Sunday nights they had it ready by dawn on the Monday morning.

Moir instructed Benjafield to drive it for 150 miles to run the engine in at a maximum 2,000 revs for the first hundred. He headed to Folkestone and after breakfast at his father-in-law's hotel, he was back at Brooklands by 11.30, just in time for the first race.

'I engaged first gear, speeding up the engine in short bursts to two thou or so, at the same time holding her on the handbrake. With a second to go I accelerated up to three thou and as the flag fell, let in the clutch and with a shriek off we went, foot hard down. From that moment until we crossed the finishing line, all out pressure on the accelerator pedal was maintained. As soon as the revs reached 3,000, in first, crash change into second, to third and top soon we are bowling along showing 3,600 on the rev counter.'

Benjafield was a natural. Despite his inexperience – and the two days without sleep – Benjafield and the engine managed to pass several other cars. 'If only she lasts, judging by the number of cars we have already caught, we must be in the picture at the finish,' he reckoned.

With only one lap to go there was still one car ahead. A hundred yards before the line he passed it. He was declared the winner at an average speed of 91 mph. In the second race he came third, the event marred by a fatality when a car went over the banking. He was physically and mentally exhausted. 'After, I retired to bed with a temperature of 103 and a full week elapsed before I was back to my normal self.'

But for the bacteriologist of Wimpole Street, life would never be quite the same again.

28

Sound and Fury

Early in the 1925 season, Benjafield won a 50-mile race at Brooklands, witnessed by W.O. A few days later he got a telephone call from Bertie Kensington-Moir. For the first time, they would be entering a 'works' car in Le Mans, and Bentley would like to offer him a drive.

Benjafield was flabbergasted. He had barely a season's racing under his belt and all of it on the great wide swathes of the banked Brooklands track. A road race was a very different game, embracing, as he put it, 'most hazards likely to be met on a long tour'.

And in spite of his own success, he was still very much in awe of Moir's driving, considering him 'a great artist, the gear changes being so sweet that it was only by the change in the exhaust note that one realised the car had a gear box and I had felt at peace with all the world'.

Travelling with them was W.O. After the cars were unloaded at Dieppe they motored into France and stopped for an omelette. Benjafield's joy was soon shattered when Moir asked him to take the wheel. True, he had won a few races but had never chauffeured the boss. 'I slid into the seat offering up a short prayer, debating whether to show the great man what I could do or carry on quietly. Fortunately I decided on the latter.'

Their first stop once at Le Mans was the Hôtel de Paris, where all the teams gathered, and Benjafield was introduced: 'Telling lies and listening to bigger lies, the idea being to lead the opposition up the garden path', while trying to find out about any of their weak spots.

For the first time, Bentley had competition from home: Sunbeam, with Jean Chassagne who had beaten them in the TT, and an unexpected surprise. Driving with him was none other than W.O.'s friend and cheerleader Sammy Davis, with Britain's sole Grand Prix winner Henry Segrave in the second car.

Cars and mechanics were berthed at the Hôtel Moderne on the rue du Borg Béle, Bentley's headquarters from before. They were welcomed back by Monsieur David, the proprietor. David's elderly father, a confirmed Anglophile, was interested in Nobby Clarke's time in France during the war and had a prophetic warning. 'The Boche have come twice in my lifetime,' he told Nobby, 'once in 1870 and again in 1914. They will come again in your lifetime.'

Benjafield the newcomer now strove to study the intricacies of the 10.6-mile circuit; he learned the more challenging parts by walking round it. Practice was from 5 a.m. to 8 a.m., then 9 a.m. until midday. And there was a new twist to the start.

The cars all had to be parked facing out onto the track, angled towards the direction of travel, their drivers standing facing them on the opposite side. When Faroux dropped the flag, they had to sprint across the track to their cars, raise their hoods and complete twenty laps before they could fold them away.

The Bentley drivers followed Duff's lead, practising until they could do it blindfolded. Because of the fuel tank being at the extreme rear, the weight of the petrol on board could affect the cornering, so they calculated the minimum they would need to carry before the first stop.

Just before 4 p.m. the cars lined up and Benjafield watched as his co-driver Moir took up his position. Faroux stood in the middle of the track, his huge flag raised aloft.

'*Soixante secondes avant le départ!*' blared the loudspeakers.

As the flag fell there was a short silence broken only by the scuffling of feet as the drivers dashed across the track to their cars and quickly – but carefully – erected their hoods. Then the air was full of sound and fury as forty engines barked into life and sped away. Those who had not practised, or whose cars had less straightforward hoods, provided the spectators with extra amusement.

The two Bentleys got away first, but by the end of the first lap Segrave in his Sunbeam snatched the lead. Although there were twenty-four punishing hours to go, Moir drove like a demon to catch the Sunbeam and for several laps he and Segrave thrilled the crowd, storming past the grandstand, wheel to wheel at full speed, their hoods flapping madly. It was a mistake.

On his fifteenth lap, just as Benjy was preparing to take over for his first ever racing laps at Le Mans, Moir failed to appear. After a few agonisingly long minutes a message reached the pits – the Bentley was stationary at the roadside near Pontlieue, a mile down the track. He had run out of petrol. W.O. took the blame. 'Bertie at his most determined was very determined indeed and I should of course have slowed him down.'

Moir started his agonising walk back to the pits, leaving a car with nothing wrong with it but an empty tank. It wasn't his fault. The calculation for the quantity of fuel required for the first twenty laps had been made when the hood was *down*. Up, the hood became a parachute, slowing the car and making it burn through more fuel. It had run out a full 15 miles before the permitted stop for replenishment. Benjafield's race was over before he had even got in the car.

Minutes later, on the opposite side of the track, Duff stopped with the same problem. Undeterred, he set off across country and ran all the way back to the pits where he demanded a bottle of fuel.

W.O. refused: the rules now forbade *any* refuelling of a car out

Walter Owen Bentley, born in 1888, the youngest of nine. He hated his first name and preferred W.O.

June 1907, opening of the world's first purpose-built racing circuit at Brooklands, Surrey, the inaugural cavalcade dwarfed by the thirty-two-foot high banking.

W.O. in his mews workshop behind London's Baker Street, 1912.

W.O. puts the French D.F.P. through its paces at the 1912 Aston Clinton Hill Climb. Beside him is Leonie Gore, his future wife. She died in the Spanish Flu epidemic in 1918.

Origin of the species. W.O. at the wheel of the very first Bentley 3 Litre, 1919.

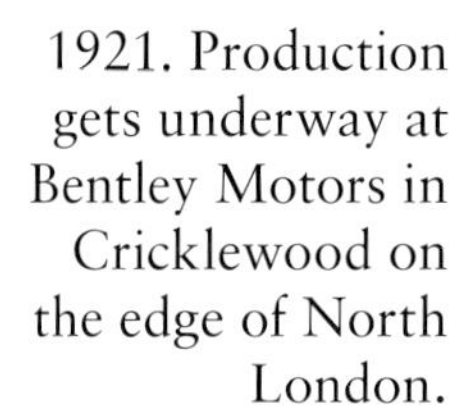

1921. Production gets underway at Bentley Motors in Cricklewood on the edge of North London.

Mechanic Leslie Pennal's dream comes true, seated next to W.O. for the 1922 Isle of Man TT. All three Bentleys finished, claiming the team prize.

1923. The very first Le Mans 24 hours gets underway, John Duff and Frank Clement's solitary Bentley No. 8 in fourth position.

Bentley No. 8 en route to the finish as the track deteriorates.

1924. The Bentley pits at Le Mans. Left to right, Frank Clement, W.O., A.F.C. Hillstead in background and John Duff. That year Duff and Clement gave W.O. his first victory.

Bacteriologist and racing driver Dr Dudley Benjafield used a 3 Litre Bentley on his rounds.

Woolf Barnato, who saved Bentley from bankruptcy, with his spectacular Gurney Nutting bodied Speed Six.

Artist, journalist, racing driver, the irrepressible S.C.H. 'Sammy' Davis.

Fabulously wealthy, spectacularly fast. Sir Henry 'Tim' Birkin with Woolf Barnato.

Le Mans 1927 Bentley Boys assemble. Front row, the drivers: Frank Clement, Leslie Callingham, Andre d'Erlanger, George Duller, S.C.H. Davis, Dudley Benjafield. Visible behind are Woolf Barnato, eslie Pennal and W.O.

Le Mans 1927, Bentleys nos. 1, 2 and 3 (Old No. 7) in the courtyard of the Hôtel Moderne on the rue du Borg Béle, the team's headquarters for the event.

Le Mans, 1927. Hood up shortly after the start, Old No. 7 rounds the hairpin bend at Pontlieue.

Sourced from the WOBMF

After the crash. Crowds gather to inspect the wrecked Bentleys on the corner at Maison Blanche.

Sourced from the WOBMF

Old No. 7, its headlamp crushed and mudguard mangled, receives attention in the pits.

Snatched from the jaws of defeat. Benjafield and Davis celebrate their historic 1927 victory.

A very special guest. Old No. 7 honoured at the Savoy Hotel.

The Hon. Mrs Victor Bruce. She set a world record, driving a 4.5 litre Bentley for 24 hours at Montlhéry in 1929.

1929 Le Mans. Bentley takes the first four places – the only works team ever to achieve that accolade at Le Mans. Left to right, Glen Kidston and Jack Dunfee No. 9 (2nd); Woolf Barnato and Tim Birkin No. 1 (1st); Frank Clement and Jean Chassagne No. 8 (4th); Dudley Benjafield and Andre d'Erlanger (3rd).

With his co-driver Glen Kidston (left), Bentley chairman Barnato celebrates his hat trick of Le Mans victories in 1930. A few months later Bentley Motors was up for sale.

Down but not out. His company sold from under him, W.O. would nevertheless find his way back to Le Mans, with Lagonda.

The highest bidder. Sir Henry Royce, W.O.'s nemesis.

on the track. Duff exploded. 'It's my car and I'll do what I damn well like with it!'

Armed with nothing but an innocuous-looking lemonade bottle – with a pint of fuel in it – Duff bicycled off up the track. When he reached the car it was surrounded by officials and gendarmes standing guard. He couldn't risk going near the petrol tank at the rear so lifted the bonnet, made a great play of fiddling with the engine and pipework long enough for them to lose interest, then without their noticing managed to dribble enough fuel from the lemonade bottle into the top of the fuel pump to get going again. Back at the pits, as more officials crowded round to oversee the taking on of petrol, oil and water, he made another show of appearing to work on a non-existent fuel pipe problem.

Both Sunbeams now began to suffer throttle trouble, and the French Chenard-Walcker took the lead with a Lorraine second. After struggling to complete another lap, Segrave retired his Sunbeam. Clement took over the surviving Bentley and set off in pursuit of Davis. For several laps the pair ran almost side by side before Clement left the Sunbeam behind as he strove to make up for the time lost on the fuel problem.

Out on the course and armed with the two stopwatches, Hillstead was relegated to an awkward location where he couldn't see the cars until they were right on him. As darkness fell he became tired, hungry and irritable, when, to his surprise, Benjafield turned up 'when by all rights he should have been resting'.

Hillstead begged him to get them to send someone to relieve him so he could get to the restaurant. Twenty minutes later Benjafield was back. '"They all seem pretty busy", he said, "but I've brought you something to be going on with." And produced half a cold chicken and a bottle of champagne. I blessed Benjafield from the bottom of my heart.'

At five on the Sunday morning, Clement was back at the wheel when he smelled fuel. He pulled over and opened the bonnet. The carburettor float chamber had broken loose and the engine was on fire. He managed to douse the flames, but the damage was done. Even if he *could* repair the car, with all the time lost on the previous problem, it would have been disqualified for failing to maintain the minimum average speed. So the second Bentley was now also out of the race.

By now a seasoned Le Mans timekeeper, Hillstead knew to stay at his post, as cars could disappear out of circulation for up to an hour or more while being worked on, only to suddenly reappear back in the race. But as the hours rolled on without a Bentley in sight, he felt his spirits sink to a new low as it began to dawn on him that both cars were out and in their gloom the team had forgotten to tell him.

Eventually H.M. appeared and delivered the bad news. Avoiding the pits where the mood was black, they walked back to the town, navigating their way through the gendarmes and officials with the help of a pair of accreditation armbands Hillstead had procured labelled *Presse* and *Ravitaillement* – refuelling. They settled up at the Hôtel Moderne and caught the next train to Paris.

Sullenly, the rest of the Bentley crew watched from their pit as Davis delivered a heroic performance with Chassagne as parts of the Sunbeam started to break. So bent was the back axle that the tops of the tyres were almost touching the bodywork. After he hit a ditch and several ever-growing potholes, the dashboard came adrift and he had to try to hold it up as he drove. At least three times he had to make use of the escape road at the end of the Mulsanne either because the throttle stuck on open or the brakes faded away. For a time, he and Chassagne looked as though they might win, but the car was disintegrating around them. A Lorraine finished first by 46 miles, with Davis and Chassagne's Sunbeam coming home a miraculous second. Of the forty-nine starters only twenty made it to the end.

W.O. said it was a 'black' Le Mans. Two cars lost, one of them through nothing but a miscalculation. For Benjafield, there was a hard but useful lesson. Moir, the man who had taught him how to be a racing driver, had himself committed the sin of driving too fast too soon.

'Playing to the gallery rarely paid dividends,' Benjafield observed later. 'It is rather similar to starting off at a 100-yards sprint speed in a marathon. It is the exception rather than the rule for the early leaders to be concerned in the finish.'

Privately, he was relieved to be out of the race. 'Bitterly disappointed as I was, I have often thought that it was the best possible thing that could have happened to me, for up to this time all my racing had been done on Brooklands track which could safely cater for more speed than any of the cars could attain, and thus it had all been foot hard down and steer. At Le Mans such tactics would not get one far and in spite of all the schooling from K.M. [Moir] I think it is more likely I should have put the Bentley into a ditch or sandbank on my first lap.'

The harsh lesson he learned that day was that 'the first lap or two of one's first drive are the most dangerous – take them gently – play yourself in as a good bat does in a big cricket match'.

Desperate for a fresh challenge to erase the bitter taste of failure, Duff took his car to Carrosserie Weymann in Paris who fitted a new lightweight, streamlined body. He borrowed Bentley mechanic Wally Hassan from the works and set off for the recently completed Montlhéry Autodrome, 16 miles from the capital.

Like Brooklands, it was the vision of one wealthy enthusiast. Alexandre Lamblin had built a 2.5km banked oval with 2,000 labourers and 8,000 cubic metres of concrete. An additional twistier road course inspired the *Automobile Club de France* to use it for the 1925 French Grand Prix, its inaugural race.

But it was not an auspicious launch. During the race, Italy's star driver Antonio Ascari was killed, and in any case, the circuit never attained the status of Monza or the Nürburgring as a Grand Prix venue. But the steeply banked oval track was ideal for Duff's purpose: to break more long-distance records.

His sights set on the twenty-four-hour record, he persuaded Benjafield to join him and share the driving. On the day, a combination of torrential rain and a series of mechanical problems forced them to give up. Duff would have to wait for the weather to improve. But Benjafield had to get back to his patients. Someone else had to be found with the time – and the appetite – to share the next attempt. So Duff put in a call to England and a relative newcomer to the Bentley club: Woolf Barnato.

29

A Diamond-Encrusted Spoon

In 1925 Woolf Barnato bought his first Bentley from Hillstead, a Speed model to which he had coachbuilders Jarvis of Wimbledon fit a smart, two-seater boat-tail body.

Already a paid-up member of the Brooklands 'set', and a source of fascination with his roguish reputation and his prodigious wealth, Barnato had dabbled in racing there since 1921, driving a variety of different cars from an 8-litre American Locomobile to a tiny Calthorpe.

Not long after he made the sale, Hillstead's eye was caught by an account in the papers of a courtroom battle over a disputed inheritance; the successful litigant – Woolf Barnato. He was about to become even richer – and Bentley was getting poorer.

Since the Le Mans debacle, Hillstead felt a certain gloom settle on the normally ebullient H.M. 'I was conscious of a growing feeling of unrest and began to analyse my period of service with Bentley Motors.' They had been in business for near enough five years, but it was still a hand-to-mouth existence as they scrabbled around for investors. And 1925 was looking as if they would make fewer cars in 1925 than the previous year. The prospect of Bentley going under started to look like a real possibility.

Armed with the news story about the inheritance, he put it to both H.M. and W.O. that Barnato should be sounded out. The brothers agreed and, as Hillstead had sold him his first Bentley, they decided he should make the initial approach. Given his fascination with country houses, he would at least get a glimpse inside Barnato's mansion. Hillstead was tasked with getting an appointment at Barnato's country estate, the 1,000-acre Ardenrun Place in Surrey, and motored out there one fine spring morning.

To say Woolf Barnato was born with a silver spoon in his mouth would be an understatement; diamond-encrusted gold would be more accurate. F. Scott Fitzgerald's *The Great Gatsby* was yet to be published in England, but had Hillstead got hold of an advance copy he would have instantly noticed a resemblance. Barnato's father, Barney, was born Barnet Isaacs, to an impoverished Jewish family in the 'rag trade' – selling second-hand clothes – in London's East End. He was also one half of a music-hall juggling act with his brother Harry. But Barney had ambitions to be a straight actor and improbably got the part of Othello. On the opening night the audience, thinking he was 'burlesquing', laughed uproariously. Barney was mortified and refused to join the curtain call, but the crowd chanted 'Barnet too! Barnet too!' until he took a bow. Ever after, he and Harry were known as the Barnet-Too Brothers – which evolved into Barnato.

Inspired by news of the recent diamond finds in South Africa, Harry emigrated and, in 1873, Barney followed him, armed with £50 and forty boxes of cigars to help pave the way. Knowing that claims were often abandoned too quickly by impatient prospectors, he sought the 'gleaning' rights and dug deeper. Ten years later, he was part of a new double act, with Cecil Rhodes and a half-share of the Kimberley Diamond Mines, a source of unimaginable wealth.

Expanding, he invited his nephews the Joel brothers to join him, married his long-term lover Fanny Bee and had three children. The youngest, Woolf – known as 'Babe' – was born in 1895.

By the time they all sailed for England on the SS *Christiana*, in 1897, Barney, now forty-four, was worth nearly £9 million, the equivalent of £1 billion today.

He never arrived home. Increasingly depressed and paranoid, he fell out with one of the Joel nephews, Solly, who was also on board. Whether Barney jumped overboard or was pushed was never resolved; the coroner's verdict was: 'Death by drowning while temporarily insane.' What was not in dispute was that Solly was also on deck at the time.

So Barnato grew up in the shadow of scandal, but also in the lap of luxury. A public-school education at Charterhouse and then Trinity College, Cambridge guaranteed an entrée into society.

At the outbreak of the Great War he enlisted as a private in the Royal Field Artillery, rising to captain and serving in France in the Ypres Salient in 1915, and later in Gaza. And after his elder brother Jack died in the Spanish flu pandemic, Babe became hell-bent on living life to the full.

By the time he bought his first Bentley, he had already divorced the first of his three wives and was attracting attention for his association with June Tripp, a star of stage and screen. A regular in the pages of *The Tatler* and *The Sphere*, he divided his time between his town house in Grosvenor Square and Ardenrun Place, where wild parties involved late-night races down the half-mile-long drive. In a twelve-car garage he kept a Hispano-Suiza for dashes to the South of France, a 3-litre Sunbeam, a runabout Model T Ford and a Rolls-Royce.

But Woolf was not just a fabulously wealthy playboy; he was a gifted all-round sportsman – a national-level amateur boxer, keen shot and powerful swimmer, who for two seasons in the late 1920s would keep wicket for Surrey. Celebrated cricketers Percy Fender and Jack Hobbs from Don Bradman's team practised in the nets below Ardenrun's five terraces.

Compared with other sources of finance that Hillstead and

H.M. had tried to tap, Barnato was in a league of his own. The court settlement that attracted Hillstead's attention arose from his decision to go after what he claimed were twenty years of the Barnato Brothers' profits illegally pocketed by his Joel relatives. A five-year investigation by the Barnato accountants helped deliver a verdict in his favour. But not content with the award of £900,000 – less £50,000 legal costs – he then sued for the twenty years of *interest*. When the dust finally settled, he had won about £1.4 million, then an unheard-of sum.

The pretext of Hillstead's visit to Ardenrun was to give him, a favoured Bentley customer, an exclusive demonstration of the new 6½ Litre. It was one of the last big country houses to be built in England, with electric light, central heating and even telephones – cutting-edge for 1909, though a bit recent for Hillstead's taste. Barnato had acquired it in 1921 and added his own little touches such as a golf course and, in the basement, a full-size mock-Tudor pub called the Ardenrun Arms, whose large oak-beamed fireplace was festooned with pewter tankards. It was the ultimate den in the ultimate playboy's playground.

On arrival, before he could show off the new car, Hillstead had to wait while Barnato was coaxed from his bed, by which time lunch was served. Once they had sat down Hillstead carefully manoeuvred the conversation round to the delicate matter of the Bentley finances, whereupon Barnato subjected him to a barrage of detailed questions about the business, which he struggled to answer.

Although it was not Hillstead's style to push for a commitment, he came away with the impression that 'something might be in the wind'. But he also had misgivings about the fate of Bentley Motors in such hands. 'He could take it up as a toy, have his fun and throw it to one side when the novelty had worn off.'

To Hillstead, Barnato was a sign of the times, about which he was becoming increasingly uncomfortable. While many of the landed classes he revered, hobbled by rising taxes and declining agricultural revenues, were cutting back and selling up, new people with new money seemed to be buying their way onto the top tables of high society with surprising ease.

This shift reverberated all the way up to the monarchy. The social circle of the Prince of Wales, the future Edward VIII, was much wider than that of his diffident, stamp-collecting father George V, more cosmopolitan and more likely to include industrialists and celebrities. This was also reflected in the Bentley clientele, which now included song-and-dance man Jack Buchanan, Hollywood film star Tallulah Bankhead and the actresses Gertrude Lawrence and Beatrice Lillie. For all Hillstead's misgivings, Barnato, the fabulously wealthy arriviste, rather looked like the man of the hour.

30

That Bloody Thump

In the 1920s, a generation ragged from combat was discovering the redemptive power to be derived from scaling heights and breaking records as a means of restoring faith in the human spirit, and reviving national pride.

In the summer of 1924, George Mallory disappeared on his third attempt at ascending Everest – many believed he had made it. And in May 1927, just weeks before Le Mans, Charles Lindbergh made his solo flight from New York to Paris. A nobody when he took off, by the time he landed he was world-famous. In the mid-1920s, Henry Segrave and Malcolm Campbell achieved celebrity status as they set their sights on breaking the 200 mph land speed record with specially commissioned aero-engined monsters.

Since Duff's efforts in 1922 with the Brooklands Double Twelve, when he achieved an average speed of 82.56 mph, interest in record breaking had increased dramatically for car makers and drivers, to the point where it was now a fashionable method of drumming up publicity for production cars.

Despite the trouble Bentley continued to have making a profit or securing finance, W.O. set his sights on the most headline-worthy record – driving at an average 100 mph for twenty-four hours on the Montlhéry circuit. Not only would this make the front pages, such an example of endurance would be a ringing endorsement of the Bentley's reliability at a time when the motor car was still regarded as a temperamental and unpredictable machine, prone to breaking down. And by backing a privateer like Duff rather than deploying a factory car, it was not a company expense. But to run for a full twenty-four hours with breaks only for fuel, oil and tyres, a second driver seemed essential. Benjafield was W.O.'s preference; it mattered very much to him who drove his cars, especially on such a high-profile stunt. Barnato had got himself noticed in a few races at Brooklands but his image was very much more of a playboy than a serious driver. But since this was Duff's project, W.O. was hardly in a position to protest, and Barnato relished the challenge.

The choice was a good one. Duff and Barnato pounded the banked French circuit for a trouble-free twenty-four hours. They averaged 95.03 mph, tantalisingly close to the magic 100 mph mark. The news didn't make the front pages, but it reverberated around the industry – even ringing alarm bells as far away as Derby.

What spooked Henry Royce's men about the Bentley's performance was not the record itself; there had been no change of heart about the 'serpent of speed'. It was because they knew all too well what it took for an engine to run for that many hours at continuous high speeds without any mechanical trouble. And it unsettled them.

Royce told his works manager Arthur Wormald to send someone down to examine W.O.'s machine at the forthcoming Olympia show when it was to make its debut. 'The recent extremely dramatic success of the Bentley on the track at Paris, apart from anything else, was an indication of the extremely effective system of lubrication throughout. It has frequently been brought to my notice by those who know the Bentley car, the extent to which they have reduced the amount of work necessary to be done by the owner-driver ... by making sundry pints of the lubrication automatic. It would appear that automaticity has not resulted in unreliability.'

Royce was also starting to recognise an unexpected development in his hitherto consistent world: the decline of the chauffeur as more owners took to the wheel. And his irritation with the upstart from Cricklewood was all the more pronounced, as W.O. prepared to launch a new model that took the fight right to Royce's own forecourt.

In Britain, Rolls hitherto had almost the entire top end of the market to itself. In the mid-1920s punitive import duty of 33.3 per cent on foreign cars penalised the American Stutz and the European contender, Hispano-Suiza, leaving the way clear. Commercial vehicle makers Leyland had tried and failed with their 'Eight', Napier had abandoned car making altogether and Daimler, though favoured by the royal family for official duties, lacked panache. But quite a lot had happened since *The Autocar*'s 1908 pronouncement that Rolls-Royce was 'the best car in the world'.

At Olympia, the 6½ Litre Bentley received a rapturous reception. Although W.O. never owned up to having Rolls in his sights, his choice of bodywork for the show car, a seven-seater limousine, left the visitors to his stand in no doubt: the 'best car in the world' had just been bettered.

There was even grudging praise from Royce's own men. Reported Percy Northey, a company lifer who twenty years before had driven an early Rolls to second place in the TT: 'This is the first time I have ever sat behind any engine which could be described as of a Rolls-Royce type.'

Worryingly, it produced 30bhp more than their own as-yet-unlaunched Phantom. However, in his own extensive report Ernest Hives, whom W.O. had dealt with at Derby during his Admiralty aero-engine period, chose his words more carefully, admitting that while it was 'the nearest competitive car we have tried – it is a good car but nothing exceptional about it'.

But this was a new market for Bentley. No longer were they aiming at daredevil types like van Raalte; this was a car for high society, bigger and more powerful, capable of sporting heavier, more elaborate coachwork. In a bid to persuade sales agents to commit to orders, W.O. and Moir embarked on a nationwide tour with the new model.

W.O. found himself frequently perplexed by sales agents' requests: 'nearly always unexpected things, and often very illogical and contradictory things – although to do them justice they were only reflecting that strange and perverse thing, public taste'.

Not everyone was wooed by the smooth, silky power of the new six-cylinder model. In Sandbach, Cheshire, they met Edwin Foden, a commercial vehicle maker whose firm was still producing steam road wagons. A 3 Litre devotee, after trying the 6½ he told W.O: 'It's a very nice car, W.O., very nice . . .' Then he hummed and hawed for a while. 'But you know,' he suddenly burst out, 'I do miss that bloody thump!' The six-cylinder engine was too smooth for the bluff northerner.

W.O.'s response, as soon as he got back to Cricklewood, was to plough on with yet another new model – an upgrade of the four-cylinder 3 Litre to 4½. It seemed the height of madness. Debts were mounting and the failure at Le Mans had added to their woes. H.M. could not help but share the board's exasperation and now even W.O., despite his loathing of the business side, could no longer ignore what was happening. He decided to take matters into his own hands with an appeal to Britain's most successful car maker, William Morris. Swallowing his pride, he drove out to Oxfordshire in the new 6½ in the hope of impressing the industry's leader into making an investment.

The works at Cowley, on the outskirts of Oxford, was on a scale W.O. had never seen before. Morris had transformed a former military college into a vast 40-acre assembly hall by roofing over what had been the parade ground.

The approach to car making of the two men was as different as their backgrounds. While the ex-public-school former railway apprentice W.O. obsessed over the engineering and performance of his cars, the self-made, self-taught Morris devoted himself to the art of maximising production and profit. Driving the hardest bargains with suppliers to keep costs to a minimum, he built his cars from as many off-the-shelf components as he could source.

And during the hard times at the beginning of the decade he gained notoriety for slashing his prices by a third. 'All our competitors called me a cut-throat and everything they could think of. But if I may say so it was the salvation of the motor trade. At that time all the manufacturers in this country were making very few cars at as high a price as they could possibly make. I had reversed that order to make as many cars possible at as low a price as possible.'

On the face of it, the two men had nothing in common. W.O. expected a tycoon, 'barking down a multitude of telephones, restlessly pacing the floor'. To his dismay, he found Morris's private office in a modest little house surrounded by the vast works which had grown up around it. The motor magnate was 'modestly phrased and with never a wasted word; and his appearance might be described as that say of a legal clerk dedicated to his calling'.

Morris inspected the new model and listened to Bentley's pitch. His response was polite but non-committal, noting that they were operating at opposite ends of the market, but he impressed W.O. with a homily on the virtues of avoiding bankers and insurance companies.

Morris was being economical with the truth. After the Armistice, to get back to peacetime production and then ride out the economic slump, he had had to raise almost £70,000 in loans and shares, a sizeable chunk of which came from a single aristocratic benefactor who had helped him back at the start. A few days later, W.O. received a polite note declining his proposal.

Bentley Motors was not the only car firm in trouble. In November 1925, Vauxhall Motors, makers of one of the few real competitors of the 3 Litre and drowning in debt, fell into the hands of General Motors of Detroit. Austin had only just avoided bankruptcy, and Wolseley – one of Britain's oldest and biggest car firms – was close to collapse. It was a volatile young industry; forty-six new car makers had come into existence between 1920 and 1925 – and thirty-five had gone bust.

With time running out, W.O. made an appointment to meet Barnato at his flat in Grosvenor Square. If the millionaire bon viveur could easily get through a rumoured £900 a week (more than £50,000 today) on parties and other revelry, surely he might find room in his portfolio for Bentley?

But when it came to negotiations the playboy diamond heir was no pushover. By his side were two men W.O. described as his 'cronies'; John Kennedy Carruth had been Barnato's business manager all through the inheritance battle, and Ramsay Manners, a Glaswegian whom Barnato had met in the army, managed his investment portfolio. While Barnato partied apparently without a care, they kept a close eye on the bottom line.

To their wary eyes, Bentley would be yet another of their boss's indulgences. And knowing that W.O. was in no position to negotiate, what they put on the table was not merely an investment – it was total control. The terms were staggering.

At an Extraordinary General Meeting at Hanover Court on 3 February 1926, the original Bentley Motors was effectively wound up.

The existing shareholders' £1 shares were to be cancelled and replaced with one-shilling ordinary shares, a paltry twentieth of the original value. The nominal capital of the reconstituted Bentley Motors Limited would be £175,000, with the bulk of the finance coming from Barnato, who now became chairman; Carruth and Manners would each be awarded 10,000 shares and join the board. While W.O.'s role would still be managing director, the job title in his new contract would be chief engineer, his salary halved from £2,000 per annum to a rather humiliating £1,000.

A press release issued to London's *Evening Standard* put a positive spin on the move, calling it 'merely a step in the steady growth and increasing prosperity of the company.' Not for publication was the evidence of how low the company had sunk; the sum required just to pay off all the old company's creditors came to £75,000 – about £4.5 million today.

It was a bitter pill to swallow, not least for Hillstead, the loyal and gifted salesman who had frequently gone out begging for orders, and even spent his own money keeping Bentley afloat. He wanted no part in the new regime and turned down a pay rise as an inducement to stay. With his disdain for what he called the 'sordid' business of finance, he was never going to approve of Barnato's crew. 'Right from the start we had operated as one large family ... the entire executive constituted of public school men. Somehow I did not relish the appearance of new faces in authority.'

One of Barnato's first moves was to find Bentley better premises to show off its wares. Hillstead disapproved of the 'large and elaborate' newly built showrooms at Pollen House in Cork Street, then home to the Royal Geographical Society and the Savile Club. To him it smacked of 'hard commerce as opposed to a friendly reception on reasonable terms'. He was not a man to embrace change and the world around him was moving on. The last straw for him came on a trip to Brooklands when he was horrified to find 'gramophone music' being played through the loudspeakers.

The bitterest pill for W.O. to swallow was the departure of his own brother, H.M., who kept on the old Hanover Court premises and became a car dealer in his own right. Ever amenable, he quietly took his leave. The unavoidable truth was that he and Hillstead had tried and failed to put Bentley Motors on a stable financial footing, and they were out of their depth. Enthusiasm and passion were not enough. Barnato had saved the company from imminent collapse. Now, at last, W.O. could focus full-time on his passion: the engineering.

31

The Brooklands Squad

Just before Hillstead left Bentley in the spring of 1926, a crisis broke which engulfed the whole country. Deteriorating pay and conditions for Britain's 1.2 million coal miners culminated in a nine-day strike, which, with the support of half a million transport, steel and dock workers, brought the country to a standstill. Not everyone 'came out' in sympathy, or even sympathised. An estimated 300,000 mainly middle-class volunteers stepped in to kept essential services going.

The strike did not spread to car factories. The motor industry was still relatively new and its workers had not yet been unionised. The pay was also better than in the older industries. William Morris, for one, was explicit about his reasons for paying better wages. 'A low wage is the most expensive method of producing. A moderately high wage gives a man an interest in life. Men are only going to work if they are going to earn more comforts, hobbies and amusements.' His brand of paternalism was not so different from W.O.'s feelings towards his own tiny workforce.

But many in the British establishment, with the Russian Revolution a recent memory, feared the worst. A *Daily Mail* editorial entitled 'For King and Country' was categorical: 'A general strike is not an industrial dispute. It is a revolutionary move which can only succeed by destroying the government and subverting the rights and liberties of the people.' But the printers refused to print it; they too were on strike.

Undaunted, the government decided to spread its message. Its house publisher HMSO – His Majesty's Stationery Office – would print its own paper, *The British Gazette*, to reassure the population that things were under control. The editor would be Chancellor of the Exchequer and former journalist Winston Churchill, and each edition would carry the additional headline: '*Please pass on this copy or display it*'. The first edition was ready on 5 May, the second day of the strike. But with the trains at a standstill, how would it be delivered?

A call went out to drivers willing to carry the papers to the provinces.

For wealthy Londoners with large, fast cars, the opportunity to drive flat out with the blessing of the authorities was too good to miss. Woolf Barnato, one of the first to line up, put himself at the head of what would be dubbed the Brooklands Squad, and many Bentley owners eagerly joined in. Neville Minchin in his Rolls-Royce also volunteered.

Hillstead, who was sharing a car, reported to Horse Guards Parade where he found Francis Curzon, the 5th Earl Howe – a Brooklands regular – in charge. His instructions: to collect his papers from a secret address and drive them to Bristol. 'There's no speed limit,' Howe assured him with a smile. 'And the police are out to help.'

As he passed Buckingham Palace, Hillstead touched 60 mph, and at Hyde Park Corner police held up the traffic to let him through. Noted Minchin: 'We moved off between 10 and 11pm amid cheers, the start being worthy of a Grand Prix race ... At about 45mph we got out of London, making detours to avoid troubled centres like Hammersmith. At places we were booed and shouted at by gangs of strikers. They realized we had newspapers on board but we were going too fast for this to trouble us.'

For the next eight nights, up to ten privately owned Bentleys along with Minchin's Rolls ferried newspapers to Cardiff and the other major cities. The first editions were no more than a single sheet, which soon grew to four. Minchin was delighted to find his own name in one, in a report of the Hurlingham Lawn Tennis Tournament in which he had just completed. Hillstead had a trouble-free run to Bristol, the only hindrance being the convoys of lorries distributing emergency food supplies.

Back in London, after a restorative lunch at the Berkeley Hotel, Hillstead was dropped off by the other driver and, in need of a ride home, happened on an ancient 'General' bus pulled up outside the Ritz. He looked up at the cab to see John Cobb – the holder of the land speed record – grinning down at him.

Cobb was not the only one. Another Bentley driver told Hillstead about his day of bus driving in Knightsbridge. 'It was lunchtime and as he happened to live in Eaton Square and so far as he could see there were no passengers aboard, he was tempted to leave the advertised route and partake of a little food under his own roof. Needless to say the conductor, also suffering from the pangs of hunger, readily agreed to a temporary retirement from duty. But at the very moment when the conspirators were entering the house they spotted a lone passenger sitting on the top and obviously puzzled by the unfamiliar surroundings. "As you're here you'd better come and have lunch with us", said the owner of the house. And that is precisely what the passenger did.'

Despite the establishment's fears of revolution, there was only sporadic violence. The army escorted food convoys without firing a single shot, and the Trades Union Congress called on its members to assist them. Thousands attended a football match in Plymouth between strikers and policemen and the biggest disruption to the diaries of London society was a one-week postponement of the Chelsea Flower Show.

32

The Slug

In spring 1926, with the ink barely dry on W.O.'s new terms of service, he and a squad of drivers and mechanics were back in France at Montlhéry.

Although his new finance men frowned on racing and record breaking, Barnato's personal enthusiasm for competition bought W.O. some valuable time. Having come so close to breaking the 100 mph twenty-four-hour record the previous year, he was determined to have another go. Reaching that milestone would be a huge publicity coup.

John Duff, Bentley's great trailblazer, had gone to America in search of new challenges, but Benjafield, who had partnered Duff's first attempt, was eager to try again. His own 'dirty little red car', the one that Moir had persuaded him to buy, was pressed into service, and, though it was an owner's car, received the full factory treatment. A new engine was fitted, as was an ultra-light, single-seat streamlined plywood and canvas body, supplied by coachbuilders Gordon England. However, its striking aerofoil profile did not appeal to everyone; with a fairing behind the driver's head that tapered downwards to a point at the rear, it was nicknamed 'the Slug'.

Since it was the car that would set the record, the number of drivers was not critical. Joining Benjafield this time was factory test driver and Duff's fellow Le Mans winner Frank Clement, champion jockey George Duller and Barnato, with Bertie Kensington-Moir along as reserve. There was also a whole team of mechanics, including Saunders, Pennal and Hassan.

On the first day at the track for practice, the drivers complained that the ride was so hard it was hurting their backs. In front of them, W.O. ordered Pennal to slacken the shock absorbers by letting them down by one turn of the spanner: 'I was just putting the spanner to the first one when W.O., who was standing by my shoulder, bent down, took his pipe out of his mouth and said quietly, "*Up* one turn, Pennal, *up*."

'So I tightened them each one complete turn. The drivers were all standing in front, still saying how awful it was and how sore their backs were. W.O. stood back with a completely expressionless face and asked who was going to try it now. I think it was Dr Benjafield who got in, and away he went. When he came round he was all smiles.

'"Different car, W.O.," he called, "different car – much better." It was really amusing, and W.O. looked across at me and with the faintest of smiles just nodded.'

To keep pit-stop times to the bare minimum, Pennal, Hassan, Saunders and the others practised their drill until they could change four wheels and eight spark plugs, fill the radiator and add twenty-five gallons of fuel all in under three and a half minutes. Saunders even managed to start work on the car before it stopped. 'I would be standing about thirty yards or more from the pits, and then I'd run along with the car. By the time it came to a standstill I'd got the petrol cap off, the rad cap off and the oil cap if necessary.'

Despite all their efforts, the first attempt was dogged with mechanical problems and had to be abandoned. But there was no question of giving up. Henry Segrave had broken the world land speed record in an aero-engined Sunbeam; now he was claiming he could easily snatch the 100 mph twenty-four-hour record as well.

At noon on 1 June they tried again, but despite the time of year the conditions were terrible; rain and gales blasted the track. They pressed on. With no lights on the car they navigated by trackside flares, but these were blown out by the gale.

By midnight all four drivers had taken their turn. Barnato, the last, was soaked and exhausted, so while Duller started the next stint, W.O. drove him back to the hotel where Moir and the others were resting. In the darkness, the crew listened to the constant drone of the engine as the Slug circled steadily at over 100 mph.

And then, around 1 a.m., silence.

The mechanics feared the worst. Leaving Hassan alone in the pits, Saunders and Pennal set off up the track in search of the car. Duller had lost control and spun the machine, bruising himself against the body, but had managed to keep the engine ticking over. Then he had somehow got it moving and headed on to the pits. Dazed and injured, he climbed out, expecting a teammate to take over. But none of them, not even Moir, the reserve driver, was there.

Seeing the whole attempt in jeopardy, Hassan grabbed Duller's goggles, jumped in and set off. Having found nothing, Pennal and Saunders returned to the pits, discovered what had happened and rushed to the hotel to fetch another driver, Clement. But when they reached the track again there was another shocking silence. Hassan and the car were nowhere to be seen – or heard.

In the darkness they slowly walked round the track until they came across a smashed barrier. 'It was a really substantial gate,' recalled Saunders, 'probably about sixteen feet high, made with real staunch wood and at the top a lot of wire to stop people climbing over.'

The Slug was upright, but had rolled at least twice. It was in a ditch, its tail and head fairing crushed and one of the wheels half off. 'And there was Wally, still in the car, with his head lying right back where the fairing had been – and absolutely lifeless.'

With a struggle, they extracted him from the cockpit, got him into the back of another car and, with Saunders half-cradling him in his arms, drove to the nearest village in search of a doctor. 'As we were going along, I looked at Wally and suddenly realised I couldn't see his face – it was all covered with mud – his eyes, ears, nose and everything. Then I see his mouth is all bunged up with muck and that. So I started putting my finger in and hunking it out . . . All of a sudden there was this great rushing, gurgling sound – just like unstopping a sink it was – and then he started moaning.'

Hassan was taken to the American Hospital in Paris. Since he was not part of the team, his drive would have disqualified them anyway. It was another crushing blow, but, as Hassan recovered, W.O. assured him it had been a plucky thing to do and they had managed to average over 100 mph for more than twelve hours. And besides, he had something more important to think about: it was just a few days to the next Le Mans.

33

Going All Out

After the failure of 1925 and the debacle at Montlhéry, W.O.'s reputation was at stake; he badly needed a success.

Bentley entered two cars in the 1926 Le Mans, both brand new 3 Litre Speed models, registered MK 5205 and MK 5206. At the wheel Clement was paired with George Duller, and joining Benjafield for the first time was Sammy Davis. A third 'privateer' machine, driven by George Gallop and Tom Thistlethwayte, was also being supported by the Bentley pit.

Davis was thrilled to be offered the Bentley drive at last. Even though he had competed at Le Mans before, this was different. He counted everyone in the Bentley team as a personal friend, and ever since his inaugural *Autocar* road test in 1920, felt he had a stake in the marque's success. And he and Benjafield were pleased to learn that their car had been given the number 7, which the French regarded as lucky.

As a newcomer to the Bentley team, Davis was in awe of the attention to detail being applied to their preparation. 'We had specially arranged spring clips holding the hood down, which could be released with a single pull, others that retained the hood with snap catches when raised, oil fillers outside the bonnet to save time, lamp glasses that could be wiped in a second – with bags to cover them for the first twenty laps – and separate switches for each lamp.'

Each of these features could shave a few precious seconds off the time the car was stationary in the pits. And there were other crucial tiny touches: all the bright parts of the instruments were painted over to block reflections from the lights of the cars behind. Even the ballast required by the regulations to match the weight of three passengers had been located in a lead-filled steel tube between the front wheels to balance the extra weight of the full tank of fuel out at the rear.

In the pits there were yet more innovations, some of them last-minute. A fuel tank on a giant tripod with a hose used gravity to speed the process of refuelling. Just days before the start, when they practised using the jacks, they discovered they were too high to get under the car if it had a flat tyre. And when the hood was up at speed, the wind tore its securing clips loose, so it flipped back over itself and trailed along the road. Davis also found practice fraught in general since the roads were not yet officially closed, allowing all manner of unexpected traffic, including on one occasion 'a colossal cumbrous machine, all hay and no cart, with a horse somewhere underneath'.

As the former jockey George Duller was a serial prankster, practical jokes crept into the repertoire of Bentley Boy behaviour. When one day the team encountered a passing horse and rider, he successfully lured the mount off its route, with a series of mysterious whickering sounds, to the obvious annoyance of its rider. He had also once swapped the cables on Segrave's Sunbeam so that when he pressed the accelerator it worked the choke, swathing him in a huge plume of blue smoke.

As the final minutes counted down to the 4 p.m. Saturday start, the cars, all polished and glinting in the sun, were manoeuvred into their positions. As Davis took his position on the track opposite Bentley No. 7, W.O. came over for a few final words. The look on his boss's pale and worried face expressed the weight of the responsibility on him, and left Davis in no doubt about what was at stake. He *must* make this race go their way. Expectations had been raised, not least by Bentley Motors' new owner. The pressure was greater than ever.

And that year the competition was top-notch. As well as the French Lorraine and Aries, the formidable Peugeot team had decided to enter for the first time. Alongside was a pair of OMs from Italy and two Willys–Overlands from America. Some of the road surface had been improved; the 5-mile near-straight stretch from Pontlieue to Mulsanne had been asphalted, but the rest was still traditional macadam crushed stone. The race would be faster but potentially even more hazardous.

Forty-one drivers lined up opposite their machines. As Charles Faroux dropped the yellow flag, they sprinted across the track and raised their hoods as the regulations demanded. Davis, glad of his practice and the final modifications, was thrilled to be driving for Bentley at Le Mans. He dived into the seat, stamped his foot on the clutch, hit the big brass starter and simultaneously pushed home the magnetos. The 3 Litre let out a furious bark as it burst into life. To save an extra second the car had been parked in first gear, so he let out the clutch and the car shot forwards, slewing into the scrum: 'the infernal hood, billowing out with air pressure seemed to trap every fume, to cut off light and air, to make it more difficult to see'.

Wheels almost touching, they descended on the Pontlieue hairpin, dropped right down to 15 mph and then off along the 2-mile-long straight towards Mulsanne. As the pack spread out, despite the hood acting almost like a parachute, his speed nudged towards 100 mph; Davis was going all out but being sure to keep the revs from going over the 4,000 mark. The pedals were specially designed so the drivers could 'heel and toe' – simultaneously scrub off speed and shift down from top to second while keeping the revs up – ready to be in the right gear for the fastest exit out of the next corner.

Then it was foot hard down, through the gears, and back into top, the next two corners flat out, alternating between second and third through to the last bend at Arnage. Away again, through the fast, twisty section to Maison Blanche, otherwise known as the White House Corner, a fast but blind bend before the climb up to the grandstands and the pits. This – if they were lucky – to be repeated for all of the next twenty-four hours.

After the obligatory first twenty laps, Davis pitted, but no rest quite yet. The next part he could almost do in his sleep. As the two *plombier* race officials cut the seals on the fuel oil and water caps, he collapsed the hood and snapped it fast into place. Staying at the rear he spun off the fuel cap, dropped the hose into the tank pipe then stepped forward to reach for the oil and water cans. Lubrication first, he poured until a bead of oil appeared in the level tap which indicated that sufficient had been taken, then he closed the level tap, snapped down the filler cap, unscrewed the radiator cap and added water. When the radiator was full, he spun the cap back on – but it jammed. All eyes from the pit were on him, but no one could help; those were the rules. Anyone else touching the car would disqualify it.

Davis took a deep breath, unscrewed the cap again, then re-screwed it back on, more delicately this time, making sure he meshed the threads. Back at the rear he shut the fuel cap ready for the official *plombiers* to step forward and seal the caps with fresh lead. Only then could he hand over to Benjafield. Davis had time only for a few words to warn him that the track was already getting cut up at the Mulsanne corner, before his co-driver was in the car, firing up and off.

After watching the car take off, Davis stepped out of the pits for a much-needed smoke before dropping in on the Aries pit where Chassagne, his fellow Sunbeam driver the previous year, was waiting to take his next stint. The camaraderie at Le Mans was strong even between rival teams, a far cry from the gladiatorial atmosphere in 1914 when competitors had eyed each other with mute contempt.

The giant board that recorded the race order told Davis what had been happening with the rest of the field. André Boillot, brother of Georges, was leading in his Peugeot, Rossignol and Bloch's Lorraine was second, with the lead Bentley of Duller and Clement third. Benjafield in their Bentley No. 7 was lying sixth.

But there was trouble ahead. Ignoring W.O.'s warning signals to watch his speed, Duller was shaving seconds off every lap as he chased down the Peugeot – until he failed to appear. As the cars screamed by, the Tannoy announced that he was digging frantically in the sandbank at the Mulsanne corner trying to free his car. After several agonising minutes, Davis saw him reappear. But it was not to last. A few humiliating laps later, Duller came to a halt with a broken rocker arm. One of the three Bentleys was now out of the race.

As the day faded, the casualties piled up; ten cars retired, seven with mechanical failure. Even in daylight and good weather, Le Mans was a brutal test of survival. As darkness fell the two surviving Bentleys came in, and the protective bags over their headlights were cut off. This apparently small detail paid off handsomely, as drivers in the adjoining pits had to scrub away at the glutinous cake of mud, squashed flies and tar that caked their lamps.

Back behind the wheel, Davis was in his element, finding it 'cold but thrilling. The run from Mulsanne through the woods to Arnage was fairy tale-like, as the lights threw sharp, goblinesque shadows from the trees, and here and there the warm glow of a fire showed a group of enthusiastic spectators.' Patches of white mist drifting across his path kept him extra-alert.

Then the windscreen of the lead Peugeot disintegrated, smashing over the driver as the wind took it. The previous year, Duff's had met a similar fate. Furious, Boillot pitted, threw the remains at his crew and roared off, only to be disqualified for not having a windscreen; the rules had been tightened up and cars had to finish with all their equipment intact. Evidently the French race officials made no allowances for their compatriots.

When Wagner's Peugeot's starter expired, its battery drained of acid, once again the rules prevailed. Cars could not be 'hand-cranked' back to life; electric starters were mandatory. The second Peugeot was out. This put the No. 8 'privateer' Bentley of Gallop and Thistlethwayte up to third.

By morning the pace of the survivors had increased. On instructions from the pit, Benjafield started to gain twenty seconds a lap on the Lorraines, now leading. But the other Bentley, No. 9, came to a stop, with the same rocker arm problem as Duller's car. This was devastating for W.O. The rockers, the levers that controlled the inlet and exhaust valves, were new, made out of the light alloy duralumin, but they had not been sufficiently tested – and now he was paying for it, dearly.

With only No. 7 still running, W.O. faced a stark choice: order Benjafield and Davis to drive defensively to stay in the race, or mount an attack on the Lorraines. Benjafield managed to overtake one which had slowed slightly, but W.O.'s calculations showed the lead Lorraine was running strongly.

His instructions were: hold position for now, *but* – if they saw him put up the all-out signal – drive like fury. Benjafield stormed into the pits, refilled and adjusted the shock absorbers, warning Davis that the brakes were 'none too good' as he handed over the car.

Davis jumped aboard, reached through the hole in the floor-boards, unlocked the right- and left-hand sleeves of the brake rods and took up as much 'play' as he could before roaring off back into the fray. He was now fully fired up, the higher stakes pumping even more adrenaline through him. 'Every driver is better for knowing that the situation is a bit desperate, that the team's hopes are concentrated on his car: there is a certain something which stirs in the blood to make a man capable of just that little bit more effort than he knows himself to possess, all trace of fatigue vanishes, and the driver becomes great and grim.'

Hillstead, a seasoned Le Mans observer from all his timekeeping, had noted Davis's precision the previous year. 'His corner work was set to a pattern which seldom varied. It was just as though he had a fixed mark for every operation, which – provided one makes allowances for the progressive wear of the brakes – is just as it should be.'

No. 7's engine showed no sign of faltering. As Davis reeled in the miles, he watched for the 'faster' signal, and a sighting of the Lorraine up ahead.

With the field now dramatically diminished and the cars spread out over the 10-mile circuit, the road ahead was deserted except for the long straight where there was a good chance of spotting a cloud of dust up ahead.

Gradually a 'squat blob' appeared in his path and grew in size and shape until it was recognisable as a back marker ready to be lapped. Davis overtook it and several more, effortlessly, then even his friend Chassagne's Aries and the third-placed Lorraine. He cheered silently as he passed the official minimum distance with still an hour to go. He was having the drive of his life.

But the brakes were near their limit. The mental markers he had made for himself – a tree, a gatepost or a kilometre post or farm building to tell him when to press the pedal – no longer applied. With the brakes starting to fade, points further from the corners had to be used. As he came past the pits, he slapped the external handbrake lever and gave a thumbs down.

With half an hour to go, as he came up the rise to the pits he leaned over to the oil pump lever and pushed it down to release more lubricant into the sump. Just as he did so he spotted the second Lorraine in trouble. This was it – and there was the signal from the Bentley pit: go all out!

Davis hunched lower in his seat and pressed on harder, only just making it round the next corner as he mashed the brake pedal into the floor. Charged with the excitement of the chase and trying not to get completely carried away, he bore down on the Lorraine.

Coming down the straight, it began to rain, a short sharp bout, but enough to mist up his goggles. At the same moment he came upon the Lorraine; the bigger car had superior acceleration to the Bentley. Either he had to pass it before the Mulsanne corner or wait until the next opportunity in front of the grandstand.

That wasn't an option.

He pulled alongside and they swept towards the corner wheel to wheel. With seemingly no room at all he just inched past. Again, the brake pedal hit the floor – now with almost no effect. He was committed to the corner but much too fast.

He grabbed the handbrake and heaved. On the wet road the back immediately slid. He checked it with the steering, but the car slid out again. They were at the corner and he was still going too fast – and sliding. He was the wrong angle for the escape road. He made one last attempt to stay on the track, but the car was now in a giant slide, on a course of its own. It just missed a tree but smashed through a fence and buried its nose in a sandbank, with one wheel in the air.

Unhurt, Davis leaped from the cockpit and dug frantically with his bare hands.

Then, from the other side of the fence, he heard a disembodied voice:

'*Attendez – une bêche.*'

And between the smashed posts appeared a spade.

It was against all regulations, but a marshal standing a few metres away merely smiled. Davis dug for his life, jacked up the rear, took out the floorboards and placed them under the wheels to use as a ramp. The wheels just spun; it was hopeless. Foresti in his Lorraine slowed and shouted to him, '*Quinze minutes!*' He had fifteen minutes left.

He was still digging at four o'clock when the race finished.

The victorious Lorraine team and the crowd all cheered. A course car brought him back to the pits where W.O. was waiting, stone-faced. Davis could not bring himself to meet his gaze. 'I have made a fool of myself,' he muttered, 'and broken up the car.'

It was an exaggeration. The car was driveable – but that just made his shame worse. There was nothing left to say or do. 'I went for a long walk and wished that I was dead.'

The Lorraines had not only won for the second year running, but claimed the top three places – an extraordinary achievement, which only served to rub salt in Bentley's deep and livid wounds.

After the winners' celebrations, Davis, Moir and some of the mechanics made the forlorn journey down to Mulsanne. 'No. 7 lay pathetically amid a huge crowd. We hauled the car out, dripping sand from every pore.'

Davis started her up and, to cheers from the remaining spectators and the competitors in the pits, 'with a lump in one's throat' completed No. 7's last lap.

34

The Desolation of W.O.

W.O. was desolate. In trying to obliterate the debacle of the year before, he had simply compounded it with another. Failing to finish twice in a row merely served to erase all memory of the earlier success. 'That none of our cars completed the course was nothing less than a disaster, and I returned to London in an awful state of mixed self-recrimination, anger and depression. We simply couldn't afford to go on like this, wasting time and money and energy which could be more profitably employed in the production of cars to sell.'

At the next board meeting he announced that the racing department would be scrapped forthwith and the team cars sold off.

There were two sides to W.O. One was the stubborn, driven perfectionist who refused to accept second best, who ignored doubters questioning the wisdom of launching bigger models; the other, perhaps compounded by the lack of a soul mate, could be crippled by self-doubt, as he was the night before the 1924 Le Mans when he suggested to Pennal that they should withdraw from the race.

No longer did he have H.M., his well-meaning brother, whom he could rely on to worry about how the next wages would be paid. Barnato's transfusion of cash had prolonged the life of the company, but at some cost to W.O.'s independence. Without first consulting him, Carruth, Barnato's 'crony' who was now on the board, invited the Spanish-Cuban aristocrat and amateur racing driver Pedro José Isidro Manuel Ricardo Monés, the Marquis of Casa Maury, to share the role of managing director. W.O., in no position to protest, accepted the imposition with his usual stoicism.

When he heard that there would be no more racing, Benjafield was furious; in the limited spare time he had in his very full life as a Harley Street specialist, he had worked hard to make himself a credible competitive racing driver. And having come so close to finishing Le Mans, he was not about to give up. 'After a week or two to recover from my disappointment at the culmination of the Le Mans race, I decided to buy the car that had stood up so nobly to the rough handling of Davis and myself for so long, and only failed us through our failing her.'

He telephoned Bentley only to be told that it had already gone to Henly's in Great Portland Street for disposal. Benjafield went straight round.

'She seemed jolly glad to see me and almost whinnied. I asked what sort of condition she was in and as usual the answer was "perfect". However the price shook me a bit, so I suggested that in view of the caning the car had received at Le Mans it was on the high side. I was assured that she had received no caning at all which resulted in my disclosing my identity. We had a quiet laugh and of course I came away with Old No. 7 together with a considerably lightened pocket.'

Late in August, Benjafield returned to France. The sixteen-lap Georges Boillot Cup race at Boulogne was like a miniature Le Mans; entrants ran in full road trim. And Chenard-Walcker and Aries were among the competitors. Benjafield persuaded Moir to co-drive Old No. 7 and look after the pit. Unusually, he also invited his wife, Vera, to come along.

By now he had grown in skill and confidence. The experience of Le Mans had put him at ease with racing on narrow, unpredictable public roads. Numbered 45 for this event, he decided not to press the car too hard, but drive consistently and see how far up the field he could get.

Early in the race he got ahead of Chassagne's long-time co-driver Laly and settled into what promised to be a long, unhampered run. 'There is something very pleasant in driving a thoroughbred car such as mine as hard as one can along roads kept clear of traffic by a continuous line of gendarmes and soldiers, with crowds of enthusiastic spectators to egg one on in perfect weather.'

But after six laps the brakes started to go 'doughy', and he had to press the pedal further and further to the floor to get any response. Valiantly, he nursed the Bentley along: 'by lifting a little earlier at the corners, using the gearbox more and the hand-brake a lot more, I managed to reach the pits before they failed entirely.'

When he pulled in to the pits, Moir gave him the good news: he was lying second and could catch the leading Chenard.

Feverishly, Benjafield adjusted the brakes and filled up with fuel and oil. Famously unmechanical, he had been drilled by Moir until he knew the procedure off by heart. But he lost four minutes in the process; he hoped he could finish without another stop. Back on the circuit he tried to restrain himself. He had been using maximum revs of 3,200, so the only way he could put on more speed was by taking more revs in the gears and braking later and harder into the corners, a gamble given how the brakes had performed before the stop. And with the circuit effectively a 21-mile-long triangle, its three tight corners ate away at them. He decided to take the risk and clipped twelve seconds off his next lap, but three laps later the brakes were fading again, an agonising turn of events as he was now on the leader's tail.

He was worried and it was getting hot. And though he had nominated Moir to be his co-driver, he decided to carry on himself, reeling off the eleventh and twelfth laps until he was in third place. As he passed the pits Moir held out the 'Faster' sign.

'We had very little in reserve and the brakes were once more getting woolly. And it was quite obvious they would not last more than the lap we were on. Just when I wanted them most, they were failing me.

'At the end of the long straight, slowing down for the right-angled turn we used up most of what was left, but we got round and were soon approaching a fast right-hand bend which could be negotiated at about 70 mph.'

He tore towards it at well over 80 mph, put his foot on the brake and got ... nothing. He arrived at the corner at least 15 mph too fast. 'I pulled her round and hoped for the best.'

The Bentley slid right across the road and smashed into a poplar. Benjafield's head and chest slammed against the steering wheel; he was badly winded. 'My first impression was that the whole of my chest had been stove in, my heart crushed, and that the bit of consciousness left to me was the last glimmering that would fade out as soon as the brain packed up for lack of blood supply. My dominant thought was – what would my poor wife say? She had come on the trip and was watching from the pits.'

Never comfortable with her husband's racing, Vera had made him promise not to take any chances – 'and now I'd gone and got myself killed. Finding myself still alive after a few seconds, I passed a hand down my chest and found with much relief the wall still there. I now became aware of the fact that my mouth felt different. On investigation I found that the four upper front teeth had been broken off flush with the gum and with the exception of a few bits embedded in my lower lip, which was pulp, they were stuck in the steering wheel.'

Soldiers and a gendarme extracted him from the car and, since he could just about stand, started to lead him towards a first-aid station. 'Suddenly it came back in a flash that the Chenard-Walker was just ahead, so in my best French, handicapped by the absence of teeth and crushed lower lip, I thanked them for their kindness and told them I must get on with the race.' He broke free and staggered back to the car, only to find 'her nose and tail almost meeting round the tree'. He found a phone and managed to get a message to the pits to say he was okay. It was just as well, as the death of one of the other drivers had just been announced.

For Benjafield, there were several lessons to be learned. He was glad, for a start, that W.O. had spurned his suggestion of a flexible spoked steering wheel. 'The rigidity meant that when I was thrown forward my weight was distributed equally over the whole wheel which had it been the flexible variety would have been concentrated in a much smaller area, viz., the steering column and the result must have been much more serious.'

But he regretted not handing over to Moir. 'The elementary mistake of running into a fast bend with too much speed in a car without any brakes was undoubtedly the outcome of fatigue. And finally it was better to finish second or third in a big race than not finish at all.'

For the second time, Old No. 7 had left the track in a race, this time with serious damage. But having come this far with what was, after all, his own car, Benjafield was not going to give up. If anything, the crash strengthened his resolve. He took his precious Old No. 7 to the service department for a comprehensive rebuild. He was going back to Le Mans for one last try.

But Bentley had left the field; Barnato's people regarded racing as not only pointless but actually damaging to the marque. Going it alone without the meticulous attention to detail W.O.'s pit crew could provide would be a gamble, possibly suicidal. He consulted Moir, who suggested a direct appeal to W.O. At this stage of the game, what had he to lose?

Benjafield proposed to W.O. that he use Old No. 7 as the nucleus of a team of cars, possibly with other privateers if that helped. Even though W.O.'s influence within Bentley Motors might now be diminished, Benjafield knew there was one aspect of the man that nothing could extinguish: his competitive spirit.

Sammy Davis had observed this as well, right back in their motorcycling days, before the war, when he was still an apprentice in the railway sheds. Racing had driven W.O.'s designs, from the transformation of the humble D.F.P. into a Brooklands record breaker – to the creation of the extraordinary 3 Litre: an apparently everyday touring car that won major international races.

W.O. had been shaken by Barnato's terms, and still felt contempt for his financial advisers. But he had come to realise one thing that gave him cause for optimism: what actually drove Barnato was not money at all, and certainly not partying: it was competition. This was what made both their hearts beat faster. And for all his monosyllabic diffidence, W.O. was an astute reader of men. When the moment called for it, he could be very persuasive.

Now he outdid himself, and convinced Barnato of 'the absolute necessity of wiping off those two humiliating defeats. You can't, having won a race and then failed twice in succession, just lie low and hope that everyone will forget. They don't.'

All talk of wasted energy and money was now banished, and by November they were hard at work preparing cars for the following June. As a delighted Benjafield put it, reason – or perhaps madness – had prevailed.

35

A Bit Like an Animal

With Barnato's blessing now secured, the preparations for Le Mans moved into a higher gear. Throwing himself into the project like a man possessed, W.O. convened a meeting at Cricklewood to study the race regulations as soon as they were published. Previous experiences were systematically evaluated and all technical initiatives discussed: engine modifications, axle ratios and fuel tank specifications.

And for 1927 new features were added to the cars. Oil fillers were fitted with quick-release caps so valuable seconds could be saved by just having to slam them shut rather than screw them down. And drivers now reached them through a hole cut into the bonnet so it wouldn't have to be unstrapped and lifted. Lastly, refuelling was simplified and speeded up with a giant funnel into which thirty gallons could be poured at a time, freeing the driver to attend to other duties as the tank filled up.

However, the question of who would drive was an emotive one. As the only Bentley driver who had raced in all the previous Le Mans, Clement was a given, as, of course, was Benjafield, since he was supplying his own car. The others were less certain. After the humiliation of the year before, Davis was desperate for the chance to make amends, but he knew there were other contenders.

Unbeknown to Davis, W.O. had decided to go for broke and enter the first of his brand new 4½ Litre four-cylinder cars. It would be a high-profile launch for the new model, and W.O. thought that if he put Davis behind the wheel, he could write it up for *The Autocar*. Davis was delighted – and relieved. But there was a hitch. Benjafield was furious.

Since he had been the driving force behind Bentley's return to Le Mans by offering up what was now his own car, he should have first pick of co-driver. With Davis offered his own drive in the new 4½, he couldn't be co-driver of Old No. 7.

As far as Benjafield was concerned a bond had been forged – not just between him and Davis, but with the car itself. To his surprise, Davis, although mindful of being accused of ingratitude, concurred. He asked to be relieved from the 4½ Litre. 'I was very grateful to Sammy for backing me up in this crisis since there was no doubt at all that the new 4½ had a far better chance of winning than a car which is smaller and slower. I could hardly have blamed him had he asked to be released and strictly speaking in the interests of the team I should have given way. But this time both Sammy and I owed a great deal to No. 7 and furthermore she had behaved irreproachably in her two major races. In this third effort profiting by our respective mistakes in the previous year we hoped to make atonement. Therefore to give her a strange driver after all this did not seem fair.'

It was a brave move; seeing the impact on W.O. of the previous year's debacle had driven home to Davis how much 'racing is a business for the firm concerned, if a sport for its drivers'.

W.O., that astute reader of people, knew the value of great teamwork and gave way. The final line-up was Frank Clement and Leslie Callingham in the new 4½, Davis and Benjafield in Old No. 7 and George Duller and Andre d'Erlanger in the new 3 Litre.

Even before they arrived in Le Mans, they'd begun. Moir, who managed the pit, made the drivers practise every part of the pit-stop routine, and even filmed them on a cine camera so they could watch themselves and hone their skills.

For Benjafield – who was not at all mechanically minded – this was particularly helpful; the drill instilled the discipline demanded by W.O. and served as a reminder that they were part of one big machine that must not fail. In the courtyard of the Hôtel Moderne, where Old No. 7 was parked each evening, Davis noticed a lone magpie would come and sit under the car. Ever the optimist, he decided this was an auspicious sign. They christened him Marco. Superstition was taken very seriously among the drivers, who all wore St Christopher medals. Most importantly, 'it was extremely bad luck to wish any French or German driver good luck'.

At the track there were more changes. W.O. moved his pit signaller, the man with the job of sending his instructions to the drivers, down the track away from all the distractions of the flood-lit pit area, and linked him up with a dedicated field telephone. He also installed a timekeeper for each car armed with not one but several stopwatches; they could burn through the life of a stopwatch in less than twenty-four hours.

The pit itself was tightly organised. W.O. was installed on a high stool on the left with a couple of stopwatches round his neck to keep tabs on the times of the competition. Three timekeepers at a table, their stopwatches hooked on a clipboard, filled in forms to record the performance of each car. There was even space for one or two strictly vetted guests. 'We had a very firm rule about that which had to be applied with particular severity to the hordes of young women who followed the exploits of their favourite drivers.'

At the opposite end of the pit, Nobby Clarke, who had built the first 3 Litre engine, supervised up to eight pit mechanics, with fuel, oil and fresh tyres ready to be handed to the drivers, the fuel in large metal churns lined up on the counter in readiness along with the oil cans and water. Seasoned competitors, they had – or thought they had – every eventuality covered.

The days in the run-up to the race were long and intense, with 7 a.m. starts for yet more drills. They practised refuelling using milk churns, during which Benjafield managed to overturn at least one, got drenched and had to strip to the waist, provoking much mirth. As his son Patrick observed, 'He couldn't do up a nut without crossing the thread.' It made him an easy target for the dark joker George Duller, who during practice recruited Benjafield supposedly to help lift a damaged cylinder block out of a car. Duller directed him to climb a ladder, sling a rope over a beam and make a noose out of one end. 'Then George, with an expression a graven image would have envied, said to Benjy: "Now put the loop round your neck and jump off." For a moment it looked as though Benjafield was going to go through with it before the penny dropped and we had much ado to preserve George's existence.'

Amid the larking around, Davis was worried. 'To my mind a car is a bit like an animal and if it likes you then the combination is successful but if it doesn't then you won't succeed.'

And Old No. 7 was not behaving. The engine was taken apart and rebuilt – to no avail. 'The problem was it wouldn't give any power and was extremely slow . . . it just seemed to lack the will to succeed.'

36

Carnage at Maison Blanche

As four o'clock approached on Saturday 18 June, the anniversary of the Battle of Waterloo, entrants in the fifth *Vingt-Quatre Heures du Mans* readied themselves for the start. As Le Mans custom dictated, the cars lined up diagonally down one side of the road, the drivers facing them on the opposite side. When the yellow flag dropped, each man dashed to his car and put up the hood before starting up and tearing off towards the Pontlieue hairpin.

The Motor recorded the excitement: 'With a sharp hard bark, the engine of the new 4½ Litre Bentley sprang to life, and Clement, amid enthusiastic applause, got away first. "*Un Anglais, comme toujours*" exclaimed the crowd. Barely a second later Benjafield too let in his clutch and sped off close on Clement's heels.'

D'Erlanger, in only his first race, was slower off the mark in 3 Litre No. 2, three down the pack from his teammates, but by the end of the first lap he was up in third behind Benjafield. 'One heard the drone of the engines over across the pines, where with open throttle, the cars raced from Pontlieue to the Mulsanne corner, then, cutting in and out, round the Arnage bends before a speck in the distance grew swiftly into the form of the first car round. It was No. 1, the 4½ Litre Bentley, holding the road perfectly and being driven beautifully by Clement, having covered the 10.7 miles in 9 min. 35 secs. from a standing start.'

On his second lap Clement broke the lap record at 71.9 mph. The new car had enormous reserves of power. Laly in the Aries along with the team of Salmsons, the only serious competition, were soon miles behind.

At the end of the first hour the Bentleys were first, second and third, Clement leading Benjafield and d'Erlanger with Laly in fourth and three other French makes close behind: Salmson, Fasto and Th. Schneider. Such was the superiority of the 4½ Litre Bentley that by the eighth lap Clement had lapped Laly's Aries. It had all the makings of a Bentley walkover, but there were twenty-three more hours to go. Just after 7 p.m., Clement pitted to take on fuel and water and collapse the hood.

In what was now a seriously slick operation, Clement had the Bentley tanked up with twenty-seven gallons of fuel and ready for Callingham to go in 3 minutes and 23 seconds. Ten minutes later Old No. 7 came in.

The Bentley rule was that the arriving driver, who was already caked in road grime, would attend to the car, so his co-driver would not be covered in oil and grease before he got behind the wheel. Benjafield folded the hood, uncovered the lights, refuelled and handed over to Davis in 3 minutes 17 seconds. He was pleased to find he wasn't the slowest. D'Erlanger, the new boy, took 4 minutes 43 seconds before Duller could get away. And in the Aries pit, Laly struggled for a good six minutes before Chassagne could start his run.

As dusk crept over the pines, the air began to chill and a clammy mist settled on parts of the track. Headlamps went on and W.O., to put a bit of safe distance between them, signalled to the drivers to spread out. Davis, lying third, left enough of a gap behind Duller so Old No. 7's headlights would not dazzle him in the rear-view mirror.

Neville Minchin, the ever-present enthusiast and spectator, had motored down to Le Mans in his Rolls-Royce with an old school friend. As darkness fell, he persuaded his companion to follow him away from the noise and lights of the grandstand in search of a better vantage point. 'We scrambled through fields of potatoes and crops, over ditches and streams, steadily making our way.'

Eventually they reached Maison Banche, the long, whitewashed farmhouse right on the road that blocked the view round the bend named after it. They started walking away from it, alongside the track.

'When we were about fifty yards further on we heard a noise back by the house and we stopped for a moment to listen. A car came past us, then a moment later a loud crash was heard. We turned to go back just as the first Bentley passed us.'

Callingham, whose 4½ Litre had twice broken the lap record, had already lapped several slower machines. He thundered down the road out of the village of Arnage building up speed, ready to blast through the turn at Maison Blanche. The white farmhouse sat hard against the road. Davis, like all of them, knew the drill. 'It was a tricky blind corner which you approached downhill, but you had to go as fast as possible because after the bend it was all uphill to the pits and a good speed made all the difference between holding top all the way and having to change into third.' That meant going as fast as humanly possible into the blind bend.

Callingham rounded the corner at what must have been 70 mph, to find a car, broadside in the road, his path completely blocked. Pierre Tabourin had lost control of his Schneider, smashed through a split chestnut fence into a farmhouse wall and bounced back into the middle of the road, where the crippled car stalled.

There was no time to brake. Callingham made a desperate attempt to skirt around the wreck, but the 4½ hit the bank that bordered a ditch on the edge of the road, catapulting him out of the cockpit, over the bonnet and onto the road.

Coming up equally fast in the No. 2 Bentley, Duller, with only his mud-caked headlights to show him the way, saw the silhouette of the Schneider and attempted the same manoeuvre, realising too late that Callingham's stricken Bentley was right in his path.

As a former steeplechaser, Duller did what came naturally and jumped from his steed. The impact of his Bentley smashing into the 4½ pushed it out of the ditch and *back* onto the road. The front end of the 3 Litre flew upwards and crashed down onto the two wrecks, creating a single mound of mangled metal. Seconds later, a fourth machine, Thelusson's Schneider, joined the pile.

Old No. 7 hurtled towards Maison Blanche at over 80 mph, Davis at the wheel. Something on the road caught in his lights – he didn't know exactly what – maybe fragments of chestnut fence or other debris scattered by the impact. He couldn't decipher what he had seen, but it was enough to make him brake fractionally harder than usual just before he rounded the blind corner.

The spectacle that faced him was nothing like anything he had ever seen before. Barely distinguishable in the failing light was a tower of twisted metal, partly lit by a lone headlamp still beaming forlornly up into the darkening sky.

In the split seconds left, there was little he could do, but something was better than nothing. There was no way round the pile-up, so to avoid slamming into it head-on he gripped the wheel tight in his left hand, heaved on the handbrake with his right and deftly threw the Bentley into a broadside skid in the vain hope of deflecting the impact away from the radiator and engine.

Stunned by the succession of searing crashes, Minchin and his companion peered round the blind corner. 'A horrible sight met our eyes. The road was blocked solid with cars. Cars on their sides, cars upside down and just as we reached them, yet another crashed into the wreckage.'

Minchin turned and ran back up the track in the dark towards the oncoming cars to warn them. 'I stood in the middle of the road, as long as I dared, making what signs I could and frantically waving my handkerchief. At this point the cars would be doing nearly 90mph.'

In the field where he landed, some distance from his stricken machine, behind a hedge that bordered the track, Duller, blood pouring from his mouth and badly winded, struggled to his feet. Discovering he could stand, he too set off in the direction of the approaching drivers.

Briefly stunned by the shock that had thrown him hard against the wheel, Davis half climbed, half fell out of Old No. 7 onto the road. It was suddenly quiet, but for the hissing of broken radiators and the sporadic crackle of oil dripping onto hot exhausts. The heap of mangled wreckage that loomed over him focused his mind immediately. Where were the others? He imagined the worst as he began a frantic search for survivors. The cockpits were all empty. Turning round when he found no one, he caught sight of the silhouette of Duller, struggling up the track. Together they started looking for Callingham and the others. Tabourin, the first to crash, appeared out of the darkness with a broken arm, clutching his chest, and dropped to his knees.

Minchin returned to the crash site where he found Davis, but in the murk, severely shaken, both tried to communicate in French until they recognised each other. Minchin borrowed a mattress from the dazed occupants of the farmhouse and persuaded Tabourin, who couldn't walk, to lie down on it so that they could carry him inside.

Davis inspected Old No. 7. The front axle was pushed back out of alignment, the offside wing chewed up and the head and side lamp completely squashed. Not visible to him and only discovered later was that the dumb irons, the curved chassis extremities that protrude beyond the front wheels, were bent – and the neck of one of the steering ball joints cracked. Again he examined the crash site. There was a narrow gap between the wreckage strewn across the track and the farmhouse wall, perhaps just enough of a gap to squeeze through – if the car would drive. He climbed back in and pressed the starter.

Old No. 7 shuddered back to life. He put it in gear and braced himself for the wrenching screech of metal against metal as he reversed out from the rest of the pile.

After another quick look round with a flash lamp Davis got back behind the wheel, selected first and inched his Bentley round the wreckage. As he drove slowly away by the light of his one remaining headlamp, he heard the screeching crunch of yet another car joining the pile-up. All told, seven cars would be involved: the three Bentleys, two Schneiders, the Aries and a SARA.

The distance from the White House back to the pits was short – only 200 metres – but he took his time. The surviving lamp was dim and one front wheel shimmied drunkenly on its hub. He peered at the instruments: was there any oil pressure? Was the radiator okay? Gingerly, he reached the pits and came to a stop in front of W.O.

With a horrible sense of déjà vu, Davis tried to avoid his stare. Under the arc lights the car looked a wreck. There was a brief, stunned silence before a torrent of questions. No one else could touch the car; it was still all down to him to see what he could do. He grabbed the jack and set about changing the bent front wheel as the race officials crowded round, demanding to know what had happened. Still too stunned to say much, he set about doing what he knew mattered most – attempting to repair the damage.

Regulations decreed that the mudguard had to be over the wheel and cover a third of the tyre, so he heaved the chewed remains into a rough approximation of its original shape. Two lamps pointing forward was another stipulation. He coaxed the one good headlight back into action with 'energetic and somewhat violent efforts', and, as a substitute for the other, lashed a Smiths Wootton police lantern to the scuttle.

Then he strapped the battery box back onto its place on the running board. Leaning over the counter, desperate for a closer look, W.O. kept repeating: 'The axle, look at the axle!' Davis did not want to look; he preferred just to hope that it was intact. When he did finally bend down and shine a torch on it, he made sure he blocked W.O.'s view so that he could make the assessment for himself. It did not look promising. 'The axle was well back on the right-hand spring and a little bent, the frame was bent, the front cross tube that was carrying the ballast was bowed.'

It wasn't yet time to hand over to Benjafield, and, besides, he wasn't going to let anyone near it until he was satisfied it wasn't about to fall apart. Straightening up, he turned to W.O. 'I'm going on.' Deaf to W.O.'s entreaties and before he could attempt to stop him, Davis climbed back in and pushed the starter.

Escorting Duller on foot back to the pits, Minchin was astonished to see Old No. 7 disappear up the track and into the night.

The steering had no return action, the brakes refused to bite simultaneously and the absence of a proper offside lamp made cornering in the dark an even greater challenge.

Davis pressed on, anger boiling up as the realisation set in that even though the car was still running, any idea of a win was hopeless. After a few miles he began to accustom himself to the quirks of the damaged steering and brakes, adding a little more speed with each lap, and slowing to a crawl at Maison Blanche to pass the crew struggling to clear a wider path between the wrecks as midnight approached.

When he finished his allotted 214 miles, exhausted but relieved, Davis pulled into the pits where Benjafield was waiting. As he went through the routine, he quietly gave his co-driver a rundown on the quirks to expect and how to compensate for them. 'At least I knew the extent of the damage, Benjy knew only by hearsay, yet without a moment's hesitation he took on, determined as I was to get No. 7 to the finish.'

Benjafield had to grapple with the Bentley's erratic handling. In the darkness, every bend, gradient and corner over the 17km circuit felt different from his last stint. And as the hours wore on, the car's narrow tyres on the looser surfaces had begun to dig deep ruts into the racing line. But he tried to settle into a steady rhythm. The experience at Boulogne had taught him the value of consistent, measured driving. Then, deep into the night, the weather took a turn for the worse.

Rain poured down, engulfing the cars in a fog of spray, mud and grit. Jean Chassagne's Aries now held a commanding lead, the hugely experienced driver well up to the task of keeping his position through the night, despite the conditions.

At midnight Benjy came into the pits, a sidelight dangling by its wires from the chewed mudguard. Davis took over again, the weather now even more of a challenge than the damaged Bentley. His goggles leaked and steamed up, cutting his visibility even further until he switched to a visor.

By the time dawn broke the wind had changed, shepherding the clouds away and bathing the damp track in pale morning sun. Davis pressed on, buoyed by finding he was gradually passing several other competitors until he was up into second behind the Aries, though Chassagne was still several laps ahead. With each lap he got a little nearer. Gradually Davis came up close; there was a chance to overtake.

But seared into his memory was last year's disaster when he had buried the car in a sandbank after overtaking too fast. The stretch of road between the pits and the Pontlieue hairpin was narrow, too narrow to pass, yet Chassagne let him through. He soon realised why.

Chassagne leaped on his tail and used the Bentley's slipstream to tow him along the faster stretches before snatching the lead each time before the corners. The Frenchman was conserving his car while trying to wear the Bentley out. With four laps still in hand, Chassagne brought the Aries in for the changeover.

But, once refuelled, the Aries wouldn't start. The starter motor was sticking. It *had* to be made to work. A push start would mean instant disqualification; those were the rules. Finally, after frantic attention, the engine burst back into life and Laly roared off, the Aries' lead over Old No. 7 now cut to four minutes.

Davis pitted for more repairs, tying down a wayward rear wing that had come loose on the crash side, but the engine was holding up and the brakes were still just about doing their job. Despite its injuries, Old No. 7 was getting back into its stride, but the overwhelming urge to speed up had to be resisted. By 11 a.m., the Aries had come back with a vengeance; it was now 43 miles ahead. For Benjafield, back behind the wheel again, survival to the finish was the best he could hope for now.

As midday approached, the pit crew watched their only surviving car circle the track. The mood was tense and few words were exchanged; they all knew the entire reputation of the Bentley name hung by a thread, as precarious as the barely tethered remains of the smashed mudguard. Even to finish with a badly bent car now seemed naively optimistic.

Despite a sleepless night, W.O. focused hawk-like on the rest of the field, timing the opposition with the stopwatch round his neck. As the Aries came past, he listened even more intently; had he detected a slight change in its engine note? He turned to Davis. 'Can the car go any faster?'

Davis swallowed and told him it could. Crazy as it sounded, with the car still working, what was left to lose? Once again, the gambler in W.O. edged ahead of prudence. The next time Benjafield came round, the wayward mudguard still flailing in the wind, W.O. ordered the pit signaller to hang out the sign:

FASTER.

Surely not? But Benjafield knew there could only be one reason: something was up with the Aries. He pressed harder, shaving the gap between him and the leader down to just one mile. Faster on the straights, Old No. 7 was more of a handful round corners, yet still good accelerating out of the slow Pontlieue hairpin. But it wasn't enough – not yet.

The big blue Aries cruised on at the same speed. W.O. wanted him to feel threatened enough to respond – in the hope that the French car would break. Laly came in to the pits to hand over.

A veteran at forty-five, whose experience went all the way back to the very first race at Le Mans in 1906, whose calm and focus was legendary, Chassagne had taught Davis most of what he knew about endurance racing. Immediately the Aries' speed increased as he found reserves in the Bentley that had been beyond the reach of his teammate. 'He's gained fifteen seconds,' reported the timekeeper.

Each lap his speed went up, but as he went by W.O. cocked his ear as if listening for the footstep of a deer in a forest. His optimism had cost him dear in the past, but he was becoming more certain: yes, he could hear something not quite right with the Aries' camshaft drive.

Benjafield was fast using up his resources. He had screwed the brake adjustment down as far as it would go, the front shock absorbers were badly in need of adjustment and the battery box on the running board was working itself loose again.

Coming over the rise before Mulsanne, his mind already on maintaining momentum through the next two difficult corners, he saw in the dip beyond – he didn't dare believe it – the Aries, with Laly out of the cockpit, head down, peering under the bonnet.

The four laps between them were now down to three. His heart in his mouth, Benjafield completed the next lap and there was Laly again, still stationary.

The next lap, the Aries was gone – back at the pits. When he came round again, there was no sign of it. Such was the mystery of Le Mans that, at 10.726 miles, the circuit was so big that two machines could be forty or fifty seconds apart yet never catch any sight of each other.

Now the loose battery forced Benjafield to make an emergency stop at Pontlieue. Working furiously, he strapped it back into position, hoping against hope that the Aries would not reappear.

All he could think about now was the survival of Old No. 7, the car he had rescued from sale by buying it himself, crashing it and getting it fixed, then throwing down the gauntlet that he was taking it back to Le Mans. It was the reason they were back there at all, and the whole future of Bentley Motors now seemed to weigh on its tired, bent chassis. Nothing else mattered.

He had just about decided to slow down and nurse the Bentley home when he caught sight of the Aries one more time, up ahead at the roadside, its bonnet up. On its 129th lap it had finally expired. W.O. had diagnosed it perfectly: the camshaft drive had failed.

With less than an hour to go Benjafield was now, impossibly, in the lead, but with a car that was still trying to shed its loose parts. Yet the engine was still pulling well and, with no pressure to find and pass another rival, he could go a little easier on the brakes. All he had to do now was keep going to the flag.

Then, to the shock of W.O., Davis and the pit crew, Benjafield pulled Old No. 7 in and stopped. For a second there was silence. Then he beckoned Davis over and told him to get in and drive the last laps. There was no time to argue. Benjafield manhandled his co-driver, the man who had saved their car from oblivion, into the driving seat.

It was an extraordinarily chivalrous act. All the more, given what had happened almost to the minute the year before. So the last glorious laps were Davis's to savour on their beloved battered machine as he cruised towards the yellow flag, what he called 'the greatest sight in motor racing'. At an average of 61.36 mph, they had covered 90 miles more than the regulation minimum: 1,472.5 miles.

Among the first to congratulate Davis and Benjafield was

Chassagne, their greatest rival, followed by the Lorraine team, all of whom had also retired. A collective admiration could be felt all around the pits. This was not a time for umbrage; all the entrants knew what skill and courage it had taken the Bentley drivers to nurse a damaged car through night and day, wondering with each lap whether it would be the last.

Each of them also knew exactly how Davis was feeling after the humiliation of the year before, and what had to be going on behind W.O.'s ever inscrutable expression. No one doubted for a moment that they deserved their win and that, despite the pile-up at Maison Blanche, the biggest racing accident since the 1903 Paris–Madrid, and the loss of both their other cars, this would be forever Bentley's race and W.O.'s day. For his part, Davis insisted the glory was Benjafield's. The only thing the doctor knew about cars was how to drive them, which he did with great panache.

Jubilation spread around the city. From the moment the race ended, everyone knew this was a story that would be told for generations to come. That 1927 was the race that would put Le Mans on the map. There was a triumphal procession round the streets of the city, drinks on the house from M. David at the Hôtel Moderne, and more drinks from M. et Mme Eriau at the Hôtel de Paris. Even Marco the magpie paid his respects by visiting the space beneath Old No. 7's battered front end. Only later did Benjafield and Davis get to see for themselves the state of the ball joint on the steering, which was millimetres away from shearing off and finishing them for good.

As usual, W.O. merely murmured his satisfaction. He had gambled everything – his reputation, the Bentley name, the future of the marque – on this one race. And in those dark hours through the night and rain, as it looked almost certain that for the third time running no Bentley would finish, he had had time to reflect on the folly of returning to Le Mans for the race that had caused him so much grief, which, when he first heard about it, he had dismissed as madness.

Several reports recalled the last time racing crashes made news. 'Even the Paris–Madrid – the race which is a classic so far as the number of crashes is concerned – never produced such an amazing sequence of events as last Saturday's and Sunday's 24 hour race at Le Mans,' exclaimed *The Motor*. And a sequence of events in which no one was killed made it surely racing's greatest ever miracle.

The victory not only made Bentley's name, it also put Le Mans on the map. Faroux and Durand's twenty-four-hour endurance event was no longer a French curiosity but a major sporting property that would, from here on, grab attention far beyond the automotive press.

The Tatler wrote: 'That second win at Le Mans, coupled with the amazing circumstances in which it was accomplished, created a sensation in motor racing circles', and was 'easily the biggest thing in European motor sport'.

Even the *Daily Mail* paid tribute with an editorial, calling it 'a wonderful triumph for British engineering skill'.

Back in London, *The Autocar*'s publishers hosted a white-tie dinner at the Savoy to honour Benjafield and Davis, one of their own correspondents. During the meal, Sir Edward Iliffe called for silence and announced that 'a lady who was entitled to be there' was waiting outside. The doors were folded back, her engine roared and with her one headlamp blazing Old No. 7 took her bow.

Davis and Benjafield were honoured by Bentley on 29 June and by the Royal Automobile Club on 1 July, when, in his speech, Bentley chairman Woolf Barnato, alluding to Duller's now famous journey over the windscreen, announced that henceforth all drivers would be issued with a gyroscope and a parachute.

Later, when he asked Benjafield what he could do to show his appreciation for the win, he jokingly replied: 'Oh well, a million. But as you probably haven't got it, then something for my hospitals.' Some months later, over lunch, Barnato passed him an envelope containing two 'very large' cheques.

The Bentley win was received at home as a great national triumph in a sport where Britain had until then at best been an also-ran. But it was more than that; it was a vindication of the best human virtues, relentless pursuit of the prize but also co-operation and teamwork, a far cry from the fiercely nationalistic combat of the 1914 Grand Prix, when Mercedes slayed Peugeot just days before the start of the Great War.

For these Bentley men who had come through that apocalypse, who had seen things and experienced losses that would take a lifetime to process, if ever they would be – this was their finest hour.

Winning was glorious, but feats of endurance restored faith in human endeavour, and survival against insuperable odds. Staying the course, coming back to the race after all seemed lost, was the most compelling expression of what it meant to be human. W.O., who had sacrificed so much in the pursuit of engineering excellence, who gambled his family name and his reputation again and again, deaf to the warnings of the naysayers, had finally got his reward.

Typically, he took a passive role in the celebrations. He absolutely loathed being the centre of attention; it was also his preference to acknowledge the contribution of others rather than draw attention to his own. Davis, Benjafield and all those around him knew full well what that victory meant for him – and what the consequences of a third failure would have been.

His business had been rescued, perhaps not in the way he would have preferred, and his reputation had been restored by the outcome of a race which no one could possibly have imagined. Had there been no White House crash, the likelihood is that the Bentley team might have cruised to the finish and everyone would have breathed a sigh of relief. There would have been approving notices in the motoring press. That Benjafield and Davis snatched victory – from not so much the jaws of defeat as somewhere deep down in its digestive system – was historic.

37

The Schoolboy and the Playboy

No one was more thrilled about the triumph at the 1927 Le Mans than fifteen-year-old Rivers Fletcher. Already a confirmed Bentley enthusiast, he had written to Hanover Court four years earlier politely requesting a brochure. His filed letter carried a scribbled note from H.M: 'Schoolboy, send catalogue but do not follow up.' Since he talked of little else, his chums at school even nicknamed him 'Bentley'.

Sadly, it was not the sort of hobby of which his religious parents approved. 'My mother wanted me to go into the church but instead of reading divinity I would only have continued to read *The Autocar*.'

His father, a reluctant stockbroker whose passion for sacred music far outstripped any enthusiasm for money, disapproved not only of the cars themselves but also of the new Bentley chairman Woolf Barnato, because of his unseemly associations with women of the stage and screen. But it so happened that through the network of men in the City they were very loosely acquainted, and an introduction was arranged.

When Barnato asked young Fletcher what he knew about

Bentleys, Rivers responded with a torrent of specifications, performance figures and racing successes. Barnato, highly amused, said of course he should join the company. He would speak to the works manager at Cricklewood and start him as a general apprentice straight away. Rivers could not believe his luck. 'I felt that life was going to be perfect.'

It almost was. On his first day, he was dismayed when at 5.30 a loud whistle blew and everyone made for the door. 'What was wrong? Was there a fire?' His wage was 9/6d a week, but he would gladly have paid them.

When he moved to Pollen House, the Bentley showroom in Cork Street, he got his first glimpse of the exotic world of Chairman Barnato, through his head chauffeur Cyril du Heaume. 'He knew his way round the Continent and was very discreet. He needed to be as Barnato's life was full to overflowing.'

Among the stable of Barnato's private cars was a specially made limousine bodied by coachbuilders Thrupp and Maberly. 'The front compartment was a single-seater only . . . the rest of the body making a large L shaped boudoir. This "room" had windows with blinds so that the boudoir could be totally enclosed.' One must presume he did not share the details of this specification with his parents.

Fletcher's duties included driving the boss's cars down to his country seat – another source of parental disapproval. 'I thought Ardenrun was lovely but my father hated it, saying that it was pseudo Georgian . . . There was a magnificent ballroom with a balcony and a stage big enough for a large orchestra.'

Despite his lavish parties, Barnato had a reputation for what W.O. called his 'extraordinary parsimony'; he was famous for never sharing his cigarettes; Moir claimed to have once managed to extract one, though carried the scars from the lid of the gold case across his knuckles ever after.

But Fletcher the protégé soon discovered a different side to their chairman. Although too young and too menial to be invited as a guest, if he dropped a car during one of the many parties, Barnato would let him come in, 'just for a time, to meet some of the drivers and famous people from the theatre. In this way I was rather spoiled by Barnato and he obviously took pleasure in this sort of generosity.'

Fletcher would come to severely test this generosity. One wet morning he was told to drive one of Barnato's cars round to his flat. 'To reach Grosvenor Square from Cork Street, I usually drove down Bruton Street, hanging the tail out and feeling like Le Mans, when I lost it completely. The Bentley swung right round and hit a taxi head on. Nobody was hurt but both cars were an awful mess ... The Chairman's 4½ looked a sorry sight, with the front axle pushed back and the radiator gushing water all over the block.'

He ran back to the showroom and told the manager, Mr Longman, who looked aghast. It was – of course – one of the chairman's favourites. He told Fletcher to go straight round to his flat and explain himself. 'So off I went, feeling like death. At Grosvenor Square the butler kept me waiting in the hall, every minute making me feel even worse. Eventually I was ushered upstairs to where Barnato was having his breakfast. Sitting beside him was a gorgeous blonde whom I recognised immediately.'

Fletcher shakily mumbled his explanation. 'Every time I looked up, the Chairman was scowling at me over the top of his egg. Then when I reached the part of my story when I told him how I had shunted his 4½ into that taxi, that beautiful blonde put her hand on the chairman's shoulder and smiled at him. Barnato turned and grinned back at her – he had to smile, she looked so ravishing. He turned to me, still with a grin on his face and said: "Now Rivers, you will never do that again. Run along." Off I went, mumbling my apologies, and I never heard any more about the incident. In fact some weeks later, when the 4½ had been repaired, there was a message asking me to deliver the car to Ardenrun.'

Another insight into Barnato's true character comes from someone much closer, his daughter, Diana. He and Diana's mother divorced not long after her birth in 1918, triggered partly by his widely publicised affair with the singer and actress June Tripp (later to star with Ivor Novello in the seminal Hitchcock film *The Lodger*). Diana's parents remained on good terms, but she had been instructed by her mother never to kiss her father's girlfriend. After being allowed to stay up during a party she was saying goodnight to the grown-ups when: 'June got up from her chair in all her beauty, crouched down beside me with her arms outstretched ... "Kiss me goodnight too?"

'I could feel a surge of heat suffusing my body. This was a very difficult situation; someone was going to be very angry with me but I had to tell the truth. "Mama said I wasn't to kiss you," I blurted out. June only laughed, as I added, "Because you are a very wicked woman!" and fled out of the room in tears.'

As she waited for her father to come up, she expected a severe scolding, but he merely remarked: 'You are very small but you were quite right; and I like it that you are so honest.' Words every child would hope to hear from their parent.

Barnato was the closest 1920s Britain ever came to a real-life Jay Gatsby. He seemed to have it all. A powerfully built, devilishly handsome, permanently tanned six-footer, with a swept-back mop of tight, curly hair and deep-set eyes under a broad brow, he exuded excitement and action, a man in a hurry for the next adventure. Not self-made like Gatsby, he nonetheless seemed to have catapulted himself into high society with a haste that some found indecent.

His unlimited wealth and brash behaviour were too much for the likes of Hillstead, who feared he would debase the Bentley pedigree. Without Barnato's investment, Bentley would have gone under. Yet W.O. never quite lost his ambivalence towards their saviour with 'his numerous and mysterious and intricately involved interests in the City'.

W.O. observed that Barnato 'never liked lending money and anyone in debt to him was never allowed to forget the fact . . . what he wanted next to success was value for money. It was almost a mania to him, as it is with so many rich men.'

While this may be accurate, the description unwittingly betrays W.O.'s own inbuilt disdain for the grubby matter of finance. This attitude extended to Barnato's financial advisers who 'heartily disapproved of their master's rash venture into the motor car business, which they viewed with the gravest suspicion and of which they were totally ignorant'.

For men like Hillstead, H.M. and W.O., born into comfortable affluence, who came of age in the Edwardian era, Barnato's hedonistic lifestyle was a reminder that the tectonic plates on which British society was built had shifted. After the Great War, the aristocracy faced a triple whammy: the decline in land values, rising wages and a shrinking pool of domestic and agricultural labour; many servants went away to fight and were either killed or simply didn't return. On top of this, death duties doubled in 1919 to 40 per cent on estates of £2 million or more – a seismic shock to a landed gentry for whom little had changed in hundreds of years, now that so many of their boys had perished in the mud of Flanders.

All this made it harder for the old guard to keep up appearances; many were reduced to cooking and even answering their own front doors, which somewhat rubbed their faces in it, while *nouveaux riches* like Barnato were living it up with their town and country residences, weekend parties, live jazz bands and lavish quantities of cocktails. The open promiscuity also provoked an only partly authentic moral outrage among them, a fair few of whom had their share of blonde breakfast companions in their Mayfair flats, but would never have received a guest – or a delivery boy – at the same time.

Barnato, the son of a Jewish East Ender who had gained

respectability via Charterhouse, Cambridge and a distinguished war record, was simply demonstrating an often overlooked feature of the British establishment: that, with a handful of the right attributes – and enough money – doors could be opened with surprising ease.

One of Barnato's more noble qualities was his genuine and serious belief in sportsmanship. This above all was what won over W.O., who was pleasantly surprised to find that on all matters to do with racing his chairman deferred unfailingly to him and, when driving, followed his orders to the letter.

It also helped that, with Barnato's backing, W.O. could at last have a separate dedicated racing shop. The premises, leased from coachbuilders Vanden Plas in Kingsbury, north-west of London, wasn't much to look at – a long shed with a hard-packed earth floor and room for several cars to be made ready for racing – but its presence signalled a very serious intent. In 1928, there was no question: they were going back to Le Mans.

38

Full Throttle

The story of the 1927 Le Mans did as much for the event itself as for Bentley's own reputation. One measure of that was *The Motor* chartered a plane to rush its race reports complete with photographs and sketches back to Fleet Street to be first on the news stands with their full six-page write-up.

Other British firms Alvis, Lagonda and Aston Martin all signed up to race and there was a long queue of drivers wanting to try their hand. First in line for a Bentley drive was Barnato, but he was not W.O.'s first choice. 'Maybe he was company chairman and a very experienced driver at that but he didn't know the Sarthe circuit or have any but second-hand knowledge of the subtleties of driving a 24 hour race.'

But W.O. was in no position to resist. And when it came to the choice of co-driver, it's hard to imagine another person cut from similar cloth to Barnato, but Bernard Rubin was.

The son of a Lithuanian who made a fortune trading pearls in Australia, he almost died serving in the Royal Garrison Artillery in the war and endured three years of treatment before he was able to walk again. The death of his father in 1922 made him extremely rich and extremely determined to make the most of it. Barnato helped Rubin get back on his feet, literally, as he emerged from a long convalescence, giving him the use of his flat in Grosvenor Square where they partied long and hard.

W.O., who prided himself on his ability to choose the right man for the job, must have made a tactical decision and let his chairman have his way. Their car, however, was not a newcomer to Le Mans but the repaired 4½ Litre from the previous year, the first Bentley casualty of the Maison Blanche crash.

In the second Bentley was another newcomer to the team.

~

Sir Henry 'Tim' Birkin was the scion of a wealthy Nottingham lace-making dynasty. Motor racing was not a boyhood passion but a substitute. The war had given him an inexhaustible passion for speed and danger. Having served with the Royal Flying Corps in Palestine, Birkin, twenty-two at the time of the Armistice, had made every effort to settle down. He married and joined the family business, but neither stuck.

By 1928, he had left his wife, bought a Bentley and with his brother Archie – to their parents' horror – entered a race at Brooklands. Having lost one son in the war, they were implacably opposed to such wilfully dangerous pursuits. A few weeks later their worst fears were realised when Archie was killed on the Isle of Man, practising for the motorcycle TT.

Instead of giving up racing, the loss of his brother merely stiffened Birkin's resolve. From then on, he would devote himself to racing with an intensity that bordered on the obsessive. In his memoir *Full Throttle*, which he dedicated 'to all schoolboys', he claimed to have got 'more excitement out of a few minutes in a car, than most people out of a lifetime, and I know they could do the same if they chose; motor racing holds such a variety of thrills and such a multitude of difficulties beset it that any other sport pales utterly by comparison'.

Despite his small physique and a raging stammer, he cut a flamboyant figure, always with a blue and white spotted silk flying scarf around his neck whenever he raced. For W.O., Birkin was another mixed blessing. 'Tim's weaknesses were his love of playing to the gallery and his complete ruthlessness with his cars; I know of nobody before or since who could tear up a piece of machinery so swiftly and completely as Tim.'

These were hardly the qualities required for a twenty-four-hour endurance race. Wisely, W.O. partnered him with the steadiest, most mature Le Mans veteran available.

Jean Chassagne, their chief adversary in 1927, knew the *routes* of the Sarthe region intimately when *Les Vingt-Quatre Heures du Mans* was just a gleam in the eye of Durand and Faroux. Now forty-seven years old, he had been in the very first French Grand Prix in 1906 and put up a furious battle with Jimmy Murphy's Duesenberg in the 1921 French Grand Prix, on the precursor of the current Le Mans circuit. He had mentored newcomer Sammy Davis in 1925; perhaps he could work the same magic on Birkin.

W.O.'s own nominees were Clement and Benjafield. As last year's winner it was appropriate that Benjafield should feature in the team. What appealed to W.O. about him was his steadiness and experience. 'Tough, thick set, totally bald and wonderful fun at all times except perhaps during the hours immediately before a race. Benjafield worried, a useful asset in a racing driver, and if his pit work sometimes bordered on the ludicrous (I don't think Benjafield ever finally discovered which way the hub caps should be rotated on a Bentley!) he was a grand driver who forgot all his worries about his car and how he would perform once he got going.'

With Clement, who had competed for Bentley in every Le Mans – and had won with Duff in 1924 – the pair more than made up for any inexperience or impetuousness among the newcomers.

A measure of how far Le Mans had come in the five years since it started, with a row of rain-drenched, half-timbered tents beside a muddy track, was captured by Birkin, awed by the preparations for the big event. 'Special trains, special boats and special aeroplanes are run at special fares; journalists have every possible machine put at their disposal, to get them back with their reports and photographs for the evening editions.'

He found English tea being served by French waiters and 'crowds pushing their way towards the cars hiding them completely from view, of the tents pitched for the night, of the picnics and the programme sellers'. The narrow streets of medieval Le Mans were full of traffic, 'battalions of gendarmes blow their whistles and regiments of foreigners pester them for information . . . Such was the scene upon which I came, thrilled and rather frightened at the prospect of so great an event.'

This year, the entertaining ritual of erecting hoods at the start was abandoned, as the ever higher average speeds had begun to make the shaky fabric structures even more of a liability. The rules now also permitted folding windscreens, and, although they were non-standard, the 1928 Bentleys were each fitted with an enormous third headlamp centrally mounted in front of the radiator, to help with visibility through the night on the long, dark straight to Mulsanne.

Bentley would have its work cut out, not only against the French but a contingent of powerful new cars from America: four Chryslers and a 4.9-litre straight eight Stutz, the latter entered by the Parisian coachwork pioneer Charles Weymann. His French drivers Robert Bloch and Eduard Brisson were also seasoned Le Mans campaigners.

At the circuit, the Bentley entourage was swollen with wealthy young men purporting to be potential customers and the whole atmosphere of the event moved up a level. For mechanic Wally Saunders it was a glimpse into a different way of life. In the 'Hartford Hotel', a refreshment pit laid on by the manufacturers of Hartford shock absorbers, 'they'd have all the wine, champagne, chickens, and everything that went with it. They'd have the head chauffeurs, butlers, secretaries, and heaven knows what, hangers on too.'

As he learned the circuit under Chassagne's watchful eye, Birkin, too, thrilled at the spectacle: 'The tents of eager spectators dotted among the trees, the heather – invisible for the crowds. The pits and grandstands face each other for three hundred yards. Diplomatic Frenchmen hang them lavishly with the flags of all nations, until with their fronts like shop windows and the counters with mechanics behind them, they give a good imitation of a high street in Shopping Week. In front and on top of them and of the grandstand, whenever there is any room not required for spectators, you are confronted by titanic hoardings in the brightest colours, advertising cars, petrols, oils, spare parts and insurance policies. To an advertisement agent there can be nowhere more like Paradise.'

The thirty-three competitors started in bright sunshine. Brisson in the Stutz got away first, but by the end of the first lap the three Bentleys were in front, led by Birkin. His average of 72.7 mph was broken on the next lap by Barnato at 74 mph. Brisson replied with 75.5 mph and on the fourth lap Clement topped it with 76.2. W.O., usually so mindful of the twenty-four hours to be survived, threw caution to the wind. 'I let the team have their head as I knew the morale effect of these opening laps was important, particularly to the rather more temperamental Continental drivers ... Everyone was having enormous fun and the crowds were loving it.'

On the twentieth lap, Birkin blew a tyre near Pontlieue, and the shredded remains wrapped themselves around the brake drum, jamming the operating rods. To save weight, the team had opted not to carry jacks. In the event of a puncture, they would drive back to the pits on the rim – *slowly*. Furious Birkin spent an hour and a half, armed with only a pocket knife, hacking away the remains of the rubber to free the wheel. But on the way back, driving with the bare metal rim, and a complete lack of discipline, he touched 70 mph.

The wheel couldn't take it and collapsed at Arnage, sending the car into a ditch. Birkin abandoned it and dashed back to the pits, arriving half dead with fatigue. The rules were that the car could only be worked on with whatever tools it carried. Chassagne, his co-driver and a veteran former mechanic, sprang into action. '*Maintenant, c'est à moi,*' he informed W.O., and, before he could protest, helped himself to a pair of jacks and, with one under each arm, slipped through the back of the pits, out of sight of the patrolling officials, ran the 3 miles back to the car and changed the wheel. They were back in the race, but Birkin's impetuousness had cost them the best part of three hours. And the drama was only just beginning.

Clement and Benjafield were in the lead, with Barnato and Rubin second. The competition was beginning to scatter; two Lagondas collided and an Aston Martin broke an axle. But on lap twenty-six Benjafield pulled in, the engine running rough, with a spray of oil over his legs. It was a fractured oil pipe. They were prepared for that; the cars were fitted with double pipes – it was just a matter of switching over the supply.

More worrying was *why* it had happened. While they worked on the car the driver's door kept coming open; the chassis was flexing more than it should. Clement identified the problem; this year a sharp diagonal ridge ran right across the road at Maison Blanche. Taken at high speed to aid the long climb up to the grandstands, the double jolt of the ridge sent shock waves through the chassis, causing rapid fatigue.

All through the night, the Bentleys and the Stutz exchanged the lead. But by dawn Benjafield and Clement's car was done for; the flexing had caused the top radiator hose to come adrift. Starved of water, it came to a stop out on the circuit miles from the pit. There was nothing to be done. Regulations decreed that water could only be added during specified stops. Benjafield and Clement were out of the race.

W.O. could only hope the same fate did not befall his other two cars. All his attention was now on the least experienced pair, Barnato and Rubin, as they sought to keep the tail lights of Brisson and Bloch's eight-cylinder Stutz in their sights.

But no more than that – for now. Despite having only half the number of cylinders, W.O. was privately convinced his car was faster, but it made sense to conserve its resources rather than go for a full-on battle for the lead. And Barnato, despite his exalted position and his natural sportsman's will to win, was, contrary to expectations, obeying W.O.'s orders to the letter. At one point, sensing how close Barnato had got behind him, Brisson deliberately wagged the Stutz's tail, throwing up a hail of loose gravel. Barnato couldn't resist pulling up alongside and giving him a V sign, but he kept to team orders and returned to his position as instructed.

At 2 a.m., W.O. gave the signal – *faster.*

Barnato took the lead. His driving style was another surprise. To W.O.'s experienced eyes, he appeared to be slower than the others, yet on the stopwatch he was actually producing faster times than more flamboyant drivers and opened up a commanding lead. In a few hours he had mastered the counter-intuitive art of endurance driving – the conservation of energy and resources.

At dawn, a thick mist rolled over Maison Blanche, obliterating the blind corner. The drivers had to navigate it by the tops of the trees. Miraculously, there was no repeat of the previous year's crash. By noon on Sunday, Barnato and Rubin were leading by 20 miles.

Victory now depended on wearing down the Stutz as it struggled to catch up. But the next time Barnato pulled into the pits the mechanics were horrified to see that, as he stepped out of the car, the door gaps flexed. It was the same chassis fatigue that had caused Benjafield and Clement to retire. There was nothing to do but press on.

An hour before the end, Barnato had extended his lead to 70 miles, but as he came past the pits he gave a thumbs-down signal; the chassis was now visibly sagging in the middle, so much so that the bonnet had been forced back and now overlapped the dash. The Stutz was also struggling; it had stripped the teeth off its top gear. Both cars were now fatally wounded. As they entered the twenty-fourth hour it was touch and go if either of them would make it to the finish.

As four o'clock approached, Barnato was still ahead by 7 miles, but the flexing was getting worse, his door kept coming open and the accelerator had begun to stick. If he timed it right he could crawl to the flag and avoid having to do another lap – if . . .

But as he approached at what he thought was the right time – there was no flag. He was too early. The clock on his dashboard must have gained a couple of minutes. He had to complete another 10-mile lap.

As he passed the pits he felt water on his face. He thought it was rain, but the sky was blue. He looked at his instruments just as the temperature gauge shot up to 100 degrees Celsius. The radiator hose had gone; the engine would be red-hot. Painfully aware of letting down the team, not to mention the shame of the Bentley chairman failing to finish his first Le Mans, he nursed the car along as slowly as he dared. 'I switched off down every possible hill and tried to cool the engine off and I was listening for the slightest little sign of tightening up, at which I was determined I was going to stop and let it cool off and start again . . . Never in my life have I been more thankful to get to a finishing line.'

Showing exemplary nerve and discipline, Barnato managed to bring the car over the line just after 4 p.m. Bentley had won for the second year running.

The Stutz had narrowed the gap to 8 miles, quite an achievement for a car with no top gear. Not to be completely overshadowed, Birkin, who had fought his way up to fifth, managed – in an extraordinary final flourish – to break the lap record on the very last lap – at a staggering 79.73 mph. Incredibly, the chassis survived – until halfway back to Dieppe on the drive home.

In its own way it had been just as nail-biting a race as that of 1927. W.O. was amused by the sight of Barnato, bedecked in flowers grinning in between swigs of champagne, 'looking like a prep school boy who's just scored the winning try'.

Barnato, being the polar opposite of W.O., drank up the attention. 'He loved having his photo taken and all the rest of it,' Wally Saunders recalled. The surprise was that, for all his barnstorming showmanship, Barnato made an unexpectedly responsible team player. Wally Hassan was impressed. 'He'd do exactly as he was told . . . Barnato loved his racing, there's no doubt of that. He was very, very skilled, driving to orders. He was an excellent driver, had to be to do it. He could really steel himself to do exactly what was wanted.' He soon earned the respect of mechanics, who recognised his commitment and grit.

It was another example of how expectations – and prejudices – ran ahead of reality where Barnato was concerned. His inherited wealth and extravagant lifestyle fostered the assumption that he was merely a brash playboy living for the moment, but his capacity to manage his wealth so astutely, along with the discipline he applied to his sportsmanship, belied this. It also spoke volumes for W.O.'s management skills that, on the track and in the pits, Barnato, his chairman, would do just what he was told.

But W.O. knew that once again they had also been lucky. If Brisson's Stutz had not lost a gear, the more powerful car would have won. It was one thing to achieve success, another thing to maintain it.

Thirsty for more action, Birkin took his car to the German

Grand Prix at the newly opened Nürburgring, a race open to sports cars. To his chagrin he was 'hopelessly outclassed' by bigger supercharged Mercedes and came eighth. Yet the Daimler-Benz chairman found reasons to be impressed with the Bentley's performance: 'Its running was so accurate and its lapping so regular that people could almost set their watches by it.'

But the subtext was clear – even though Birkin had driven flat out, his Bentley was no match for the Germans. Britain's only competitive machine was about to be left behind. It was down to him to see that didn't happen.

39

Bentley v. Bentley

Famously impatient, Birkin was in no mood to wait for Bentley to answer his call for more power. He took matters into his own hands, a move which did not go down at all well with W.O: 'Tim ... had the constant urge to do the dramatic thing, a characteristic which I suppose had originally brought him into racing. His gaily vivid, restless personality seemed always to be driving him on to something new and spectacular, and unfortunately our 4½ Litre was one of his targets.'

A supercharger can boost an engine's power by more than a third. Instead of relying on natural atmospheric pressure to supply air to the fuel mixture, it blows or forces it in. W.O. disliked the whole concept. 'To supercharge a Bentley was to pervert its design and corrupt its performance ... Of course we were after speed and acceleration but not by any falsely induced means; and I always held that the supercharger applied to the Bentley engine was a false inducer ... I disliked the easy short cut provided by the supercharger which was against all my engineering principles.' Birkin did not have any principles when it came to the pursuit of speed. If W.O. refused to countenance supercharging he would go elsewhere.

Amherst Villiers was a freelance engineer who had supercharged racing Vauxhalls and even a Rolls-Royce. Birkin approached him to fit one on his Bentley. The effect was dramatic, pushing the power of the 4½ Litre from 110 to 175 bhp. Thrilled by this improvement, this was the car he wanted to race; but knowing W.O.'s opposition he would have to find another backer, and brought into the Bentley world one of its most surprising and unlikely champions.

Dorothy Wyndham Paget stepped fully formed from the pages of an Evelyn Waugh novel. Her fame would come from her horses, which won the Cheltenham Gold Cup seven times, and her notoriety from a prodigious gambling habit, her girth and her hundred-a-day consumption of Balkan Sobranie cigarettes. She led a chiefly nocturnal existence, attended by a retinue of female staff whom she addressed not by name but by a colour she chose for each of them.

Born in 1905 to a British industrialist and an American heiress, Paget was a problem child. Expelled from five schools by the age of fifteen, she was sent as a last resort to a finishing school in Paris run by a Russian émigré whose niece would become her lifelong companion. On her twenty-first birthday she received a cheque from her American grandfather for one million pounds (more than £61 million today), and from her father a Rolls-Royce.

By the time she met Tim Birkin, in her mid-twenties, she had already left a trail of disappointed suitors who belatedly got the message that she was emphatically not interested in men. But she *was* interested in speed. Birkin saw an opportunity and invited her to take a drive with him. Trussed up in a beret and favourite tweed overcoat she called 'speckled hen', she cut an unlikely figure among the glamorous ladies of the Brooklands set, not that she gave a damn. Birkin took her up to 130 mph on the banking and she was hooked – enough to bankroll his venture: a stable of racing supercharged 4½ Litre Bentleys. He set up his own workshop in the new town of Welwyn Garden City and persuaded other Bentley regulars to join him: Clive Gallop, who had worked on W.O.'s first engine, and Bertie Kensington-Moir, to help him field his own team.

W.O. vehemently disapproved of the 'spurious glamour' of the Birkin–Paget endeavour. 'They would lack in their preparation all the experience we had built up in the racing department under Clarke over ten years. I feared the worst and looked forward to their appearance with anxiety.'

In its first races in 1929, the 'blower' Bentley's brutish charisma excited crowds, but failed to finish. Undaunted, Birkin decided he would take his cars to Le Mans. But to qualify, it had to be a proper production car, with a minimum of fifty built for sale to the public.

He went straight to the chairman. Barnato agreed to build fifty. It was a measure of how much W.O.'s authority had slipped within his own company that such a major decision could be taken over his head. But W.O. had also been quietly tackling the power issue; his solution was already proving itself on the road.

The big six-cylinder 6½ Litre had been developed as a challenge to Rolls-Royce, a smooth, silent machine that could power a limousine. The compelling logic was to turn it into an endurance racing car and the job was actually quite simple: two carburettors instead of one and revised camshaft profiles put the power up from 140 to 160bhp.

Early in 1929, Nobby Clarke, the man who had put the very first Bentley engine together in the hayloft, was preparing the ultimate racing machine in W.O.'s brand new machine shop. It would be called the Speed Six and by April it was on sale. *The Motor* was impressed. 'To produce a car with the velvety silence and flexibility of the Six and combine it with the fierce acceleration and fiery impetuosity of the old three litre and the four and a half litre was no easy task but Mr W.O. Bentley and his engineering staff have been more than successful.'

Maynard Greville of the *Morning Post* heartily agreed. 'I consider this car to be one of the most remarkable engineering achievements of the century, the balance of speed, silence and flexibility having been maintained in a unique manner. Regardless of price, this car is the nearest to the ideal road vehicle that I have ever seen.'

Sammy Davis's first time at the wheel took him by surprise; it would test the limits of his skill – and his hyperbole. Arriving at Brooklands to report on the 500-mile race, he was taken aside by W.O. '"Will you drive the Six?" Naturally I answered, "Yes, if the stewards will allow it."' W.O. had already got their permission.

'I climbed into the seat, made feverish efforts to discover what all the levers did – I had never tried the six cylinder before – the engine was started up and away we went ... The wind howled like the hosts of demons, the big car simply throbbing with animal life, simply flew, the rev counter needle went up, 120, 124, 126, 128 miles an hour ... I didn't know what our signals were, I did not know when to come in, and I had to identify the important instruments as and when I could; the rev counter was obvious but for a long time I thought the thermometer was the oil gauge ... If one gripped the wheel hard the car was all over the place, and it nearly pulled one's arms from their sockets, but if the wheel rim was allowed to play through one's fingers the big car did, in fact, steer itself, save for a little guidance here and there ... Verily the car was alive, time after time it seemed to gather itself together, and jump from the banking at a pace that really thrilled, as wild a ride as ever Valkyrie dreamed, to the musical roar of exhaust behind and the howl of the wind past the small oil-stained screen.'

But it wasn't all plain sailing. 'There was a sudden loud report from the back of the car, followed by a whole series of further reports, and before I could do anything my right elbow which was outside the car, was hit by a terrific blow. For a moment I was afraid the arm was broken; it was quite numb and my hand wouldn't close round the steering wheel, but sufficient strength, accompanied by fearful pins and needles soon returned to show it was not badly damaged. Looking cautiously round after I had slowed, I saw the tread had come off the right rear tyre.'

The track was littered with casualties. A Thomas Special caught fire, an OM blew up, a Sunbeam's springs collapsed, an Amilcar broke a valve, a Delage and another Sunbeam both blew their engines and Birkin's supercharged Bentley went up in flames.

To his astonishment, Davis came second at an average of 109.4 mph. 'That anybody could step straight into a car without knowing anything about it and without preparation, yet be second at that speed, seemed to me a real miracle of luck which by all the rules could not happen.'

The new car appeared to put the faithful 4½ litre into the shade somewhat, but not before a woman on a mission came to W.O. with a proposal he couldn't refuse.

40

The Other Bentley Girl

The Honourable Mrs Victor Bruce was the polar opposite of Dorothy Paget. She was petite and pretty with pale green eyes and freckled cheeks and five foot two out of heels. Among the Brooklands smart set she easily blended in with the other wives and girlfriends. But the fact that she adopted her husband's name is one of her many contradictions, not least because, even after she dumped him for someone else, she preferred to be addressed as Mrs Victor Bruce. *Mister* Victor Bruce would remain forever in her shadow.

Born Mildred Mary Petre in 1895, from an early age she liked to score 'firsts'. She was the first woman in Britain to be given a speeding ticket – aged fifteen – riding an 8hp Matchless motorcycle belonging to one of her five brothers, and was fined six shillings. By 1920 she had given birth to a son, Tony, from an affair with Stephen Easter, a married man nearly twice her age. But bringing up a small boy did not slow her down. The same year, she acquired her first car. 'I decided I wanted a car – a fast car with a leather strap round the bonnet like those used on race tracks.'

Naturally, she gravitated towards Brooklands and met Victor Bruce, who was just about to become the first Englishman to win the Monte Carlo Rally, in a 2-litre AC. In February 1925, a week after his victory and on the proceeds of his 25,000-franc prize, they were married at the British Consulate along the coast in Menton. Her son became Tony Easter-Bruce. The following year, in another AC, with Victor as passenger, the new Mrs Bruce won the first Monte Carlo rally Coupe des Dames, setting off from John O'Groats and driving the whole way herself – for extra publicity.

Selwyn Edge, the pioneer racing driver and now boss of AC, had been the first to establish a twenty-four-hour speed record, in 1907. He sent the Bruces off to Montlhéry where together they achieved 1,000 miles at an average of 60 mph. Their next trick the following year was a shattering 15,000 miles in under ten days. Piqued that Mildred was getting rather more publicity than the AC car he had provided, Edge's enthusiasm for the Bruces began to ebb. In any case, Mildred was ready to up her game. The single-handed twenty-four-hour record was held by AC driver Thomas Gillett. She decided she wanted to break it, but it would need a much more powerful car. In May 1929 she made an appointment to see W.O. at Cricklewood.

Perhaps W.O. was forewarned, because he asked Barnato to join them. She got straight to the point. 'Briskly I told them that I wanted to borrow one of their cars, why I wanted it, and where I was going to take it.'

Her request was to borrow a 4½ Litre Bentley for a twenty-four-hour run at Montlhéry. 'W.O. said, "Who's your co-driver?"

'I told him, "I've no co-driver, I'm going alone."'

There was silence as the two men exchanged a look. Barnato's brow furrowed. He too had attempted twenty-four hours at Montlhéry – but with Duff and others, not on his own. Bruce thought she had blown it but then W.O. piped up.

'I believe she might do it . . .'

The only car available at that short notice was the 4½ allocated to Birkin and Howe for the upcoming Le Mans. 'Before they could change their minds I said, "Do you think your engineers can squeeze a hundred and seven miles an hour out of her?"'

Bruce knew that Thomas Gillett had had six months to prepare for his solo effort, training for it 'like a boxer'. Bruce had one week. So she went straight to Bond Street 'and bought myself a pale blue leather jacket for the occasion. It had no special padding but I thought it looked very smart.' She was hoping for sponsorship from Dunlop, which was refused when they heard she was going it alone.

In Paris the night before, she wrote her mother a last-minute letter from the Hôtel Astra.

'Dear Mama, I'm over in Paris just about to make an attempt on the twenty-four-hour record. I hope to drive the whole time myself and cover the about two thousand miles in twenty-four hours. If you buy Friday and Saturday's *Daily Sketch*, you'll be able to read all about it. Expect to be back in England on Sunday.'

Until it arrived at Montlhéry the next day, Bruce had never driven a Bentley. 'It was so vast that my feet barely touched the pedals and my head barely topped the dash board.'

She borrowed three cushions from the official timekeeper's hut, sat on one to help her see over the bonnet and put the other two behind her back so she could reach the pedals. To reach the handbrake outside the body she virtually had to stand up.

With the car were Hassan, Wally Saunders and Jack Sopp. Hassan, having crashed the Slug there three years before, knew all about the challenges of Montlhéry. The weather was dull and hurricane lamps had been placed at intervals round the track. Rain started to fall and the track became greasy. He suggested postponing a day, but she knew the track and suggested a practice lap. The Bentley was a world of difference from the AC. Straight away she touched 105 mph, faster than she had ever driven before. 'The extra speed meant I was much higher than I'd ever been on the banking . . . Constantly it seemed poised to leap over the top.'

She pulled in and had a cup of tea. As noon approached it was raining harder, but the officials from the *Automobile Club de France* had arrived, ready to monitor the run. She had driven through a lot worse; she decided to start.

She settled to a steady 107 mph, keeping the revs at a constant 3,000rpm, applying slightly more pressure when she turned into the wind, easing fractionally when it was behind her. She felt dizzy on this giant wall of death but concluded that it was 'simply a matter of sticking it out until I got used to it'. Every fifty-seven seconds she flashed past the pits – fifteen hundred times if she was to last the full twenty-four hours.

The plan was to stop every three hours for a maximum of three minutes for both her and the car to refuel.

The bumps in the track battered her furiously. The mechanics had tightened the shock absorbers to stop her bouncing right out of her seat. On her first stop she insisted they loosen them. Hassan said he wouldn't dare: 'You'll go over the top.'

As dusk settled on the track, 'my world shrank to the confines of the Bentley. The red storm lanterns were stars to guide me. I was averaging 105 mph and going like a dream.

'I became like an automaton, sitting rigidly, scarcely moving, with only two main thoughts in my mind: the rev counter and staying awake.'

Deep in the night, still averaging over a hundred, she nodded off.

'It was the change of the engine sound that woke me. I heard the rushing sound of the hoardings at the top of the banking.'

She pulled the Bentley clear of the edge and plunged down towards the pits, climbed out and went into the pit to get something to drink. On the bench was a mineral water bottle. She grabbed it and took a swig. 'I felt as if I'd been struck by lightning. It was BP petrol, set aside for a spirit lamp. I choked and fought for breath.'

The combination of the vapour in her lungs and the fluid

in her stomach could have killed her. She lost fifteen minutes coughing it up.

Furious, but now wide awake, she climbed back in. Wally Saunders rode with her for one stint at 3 a.m. to help her stay awake.

'My God what a good driver that woman was – she really handled that car ... The banking was terrifically steep, much steeper than Brooklands – you couldn't run up it – and it gave the sensation of sort of bearing down on you. Well, I just couldn't keep my eyes open, what with the warmth and the rhythm of the engine and the red lights round the perimeter ... it felt like we were going up one continuous hill ... Mrs Bruce, she was really plucky, sitting there, drenched in oil, driving like hell.'

To make up time she cut out one stop and drove for a continuous six hours. As the sun rose, so did her hopes. As noon approached Hassan held out a pit board with a big number 10 on it: 'a beautiful sight.' They were counting her down, her elation rising as they diminished. After the final '1' she pulled to a stop.

The crew had to lift her out of her seat, but as soon as she could stand she made straight for the timekeeper's hut to get the official word. The single-handed twenty-four-hour record was hers, at an average of 89.57 mph, comfortably breaking Gillett's AC time, plus the fastest for 2,000 miles. Saunders was in awe.

'That's no light task, handling a 4½ litre single-handed for twenty-four hours. It'd be damn tough for a man. My God what a woman she was!'

Earl Howe, president of the British Racing Drivers' Club, en route to Le Mans, had made the detour to see how she had got on. 'Would you be too tired to drive me to Paris for some lunch?' he said.

She thought it a delightful idea. When coffee came Howe made a proposal – honorary life membership of the BRDC: another 'first'. 'Unfortunately I never heard him. I'd dozed off for a moment.'

At Le Mans a week later she was feted. Barnato, as victor the previous year, was allowed a pre-race lap of honour and invited her to accompany him. She was the only Bentley driver of either sex ever to achieve a solo twenty-four-hour record.

41

THE REAL BENTLEY BOYS

The swollen ranks of the Bentley entourage descended on the 1929 Le Mans like a troupe of entertainers – which in a way they were. The pit was split into two, one under Nobby Clarke, the other – which would have been the blower team – managed by Moir. The supercharged cars were plagued with teething trouble, so the Paget-backed team fielded ordinary 4½ Litre cars. The next challenge was completely unforeseen and nothing to do with racing or cars. A smallpox scare in France led to a ban on anyone unvaccinated entering the country. Dr Benjafield enthusiastically came to the rescue, with 'a special vaccine calculated to raise large blisters on nitralloy steel, and to prostrate any ordinary human. Practically everyone therefore had a dud left arm and was feeling anything but chirpy on landing, while at Le Mans Benjy had to hold sick bay parades daily, inspecting craters of the Messines variety in people's arms with equanimity and a bedside manner unrivalled in all of Harley Street.' (The Battle of Messines in 1917 was remarkable for the Allied deployment of underground mines which caused particularly large craters.)

Then, the regulation was suddenly withdrawn – great news – but the team found out that Benjafield had failed to inoculate himself. As penance he was sentenced to 'wheel changing practice in the sun of the Hôtel Moderne backyard whenever a Bentley could be spared.'

The mechanics had not lost their sense of humour during the scare. A frequent target were the gendarmerie, whose officiousness irritated them as much as their habit of begging free refreshment. Leslie Pennal recalled a cocktail they prepared for them in a champagne bottle: 'vin blanc, bisquet and Castrol R . . . and a sandwich of Belmolene – engine grease.'

They could afford to relax a little; after six Le Mans, they knew their stuff. 'We became the best prepared team over there. It was all the lessons we'd learned over the years, from the early days . . . other teams they were taking their blocks off, fitting new valves and that. We used to see other racing stables working all night and we'd say, "They're still learning – they haven't got down to it like we have".'

Nobby Clarke and his mechanics had come a long way with W.O. Now that Bentley's name made the front pages they looked askance as the growing band of illustrious titled drivers were featuring in the press as 'The Bentley Boys'. 'We were always called the Bentley Boys . . . It didn't dawn on us for ages that the drivers were being called the Bentley Boys as well. We had called ourselves that for so long, right from the beginning, that we just thought of ourselves as the Bentley Boys – and we were proud of it.'

As Wally Saunders recalled, 'the town was ours, it really was – they'd got little time for their own people – it was always "Vive la Bentley". And when us Bentley boys went out, when we did get the time to go out and have a bit of fun, I mean they really thought something of us. We could have had the town.' Event organiser Charles Faroux, however pleased he was to see the success and fame his race had achieved, nevertheless railed at the absence of competitive French cars. 'It's a disgrace – I am ashamed of my country. Perhaps next year.'

Benjafield was down to partner Barnato, who was looking to repeat his win of the previous year, but when it became apparent that the supercharged cars were not going to be ready, he gave up his seat to Birkin, another measure of the doctor's gentlemanly character and respect for team spirit. Vacating his seat in the team's fastest car, Benjafield was certain to lessen his chances of a win.

W.O., for his part, put aside whatever feelings he had about Birkin and his cars and agreed that he could join Barnato – though this time he was to keep strictly to team orders. 'As to the drivers we were always fortunate in having a mile-long waiting list which included the best amateurs of the day. The final choice was always mine and I was looking for drivers who were fast and steady and untemperamental who would do as they were told.'

The outcome was never in dispute. The Speed Six led from the start. The biggest excitement was during the night when Brisson came into the pits: his exhaust pipe was glowing red. 'No sooner had the driver begun to refill than the whole back of the machine went up in flames, the glare showing in the sky for miles around.' Brisson was badly burned but Chiron managed to get the car back into the race – until the petrol tank split.

Then the 4½ Litres were plagued by mysteriously malfunctioning lights. Travelling at around 100 mph they were plunged into complete darkness with no warning, only to come back to life, jolted by the next pothole. The problem was an intermittent power supply, 'which resulted in the comic spectacle of Benjy coming in with no lamps and no starter motor working, then banging the battery box with a huge spanner, a process that excited that unfortunate component into action, whereupon the headlamps lit and the starter motor functioned.'

But the main drama of the race came just minutes from the end as Faroux prepared to drop his yellow flag at 4 p.m. The leading Bentleys were overdue – all of them. Everyone who could remember the events of 1927 or had heard the story had their hearts in their mouths – all except the Bentley team.

The four cars had been ordered to pause at the roadside on the Mulsanne Straight to form up, 'then the whole lot quietly, impudently, but impressively, came slowly over the finish line ahead, tails up, in battle order'.

The Speed Six cruised to victory. The Stutz briefly held third, but in the end positions 1–4 all went to the Bentleys. Birkin boosted the lap record again to a superb 82.984 mph.

Nobby Clarke was not only thrilled but relieved. Before the start, M. David of the Hôtel Moderne told him he had bet all his savings on a Bentley win. 'After the race he took me into his back parlour, opened up a special private cupboard and produced a bottle of 1898 Absinthe. He kept telling me it was forbidden in France, which I thought was just his French "baloney" but my hat! I soon found out why. When I went to get up I couldn't move a muscle from the neck downwards.'

The celebrations went on well into the night. Drivers and mechanics tended to party separately, but not always. Francis Richard Henry Penn Curzon, the 5th Earl Howe and at forty-five the oldest of the new drivers, joined the mechanics when they hit the town. By now well out of control, they accosted a band playing in the market square, stole some of their instruments and led them back to the Moderne, where they all climbed in through a window and continued to jam, musicians and Bentley Boys together.

In the 'upstairs downstairs' world of the 1920s, Bentley mechanics enjoyed a privileged position. Leslie Pennal increasingly found himself crossing Europe on Bentley business as a roving trouble-shooter. After Le Mans, W.O. sent him on to Paris to look at the car of a Mr Waterhouse. Arriving in the evening, he was given dinner by Waterhouse who plied him with brandy while he pumped him for details about the race. 'All I remember in the end was him taking me to my room and into the bathroom where he worked the geyser for me – he didn't say so but I'm sure I was incapable of doing it myself.'

The next day Pennal fixed the car and they test-drove it down to Chartres, where he was treated to lunch – a once unimaginably exalted life for the East End boy who had started out sweeping the showroom floor.

On another occasion he went to Cannes with Rubin and Barnato on 'a real fast run'. On arrival Barnato threw a dinner for all the vacationing Bentley owners and announced that there was a mechanic in attendance at their garage if they wanted any adjustments, free of charge. 'I used to sit on the shore enjoying the sunshine. If anyone needed me at the garage the boy there had only to run a little way and call me. All I'd got to do was slip in at the back, put my overalls over my shorts and walk through to the front to attend to the owner.'

One morning a couple came in straight from an all-night pyjama party. 'Oh my goodness were they tight – as tight as owls – and kept trying to tell me there was something wrong with the starter.'

Sometime later when Pennal was back in London the man came into the works. 'When he saw me he gave me such a look as if to say, "You know nothing". But he needn't have worried. That was part of the job – not knowing anything. Or rather, knowing what you were to see and what you were not to see.'

42

The Smile of the Tiger

In 1929, Bentley Motors celebrated its tenth year, and – at last – its first profit. The first 3 Litre now looked like a relatively modest cruiser beside the awesome battleships now in production. The works and the service department had expanded and W.O. finally had his own machine shop. He was already well on the way to building his next car – a formidable 8 Litre.

The impact of the Wall Street Crash took its time to reach Cricklewood. At the start of 1930 the works were humming and at Kingsbury, in the racing shop, a pair of Speed Sixes were taking shape for that year's season. Old No. 1 as it was now affectionately known, the car in which Barnato had won the previous year's Le Mans, was rebuilt, while, up in Welwyn Garden City, Tim Birkin's blowers were being readied for their belated assault on Le Mans, bankrolled by Dorothy Paget.

Put in charge of the Birkin operation, Clive Gallop struggled to make the supercharged engine reliable; he would later admit to W.O. that the whole idea had been a 'major error'. But Birkin made headlines by repeatedly breaking the Brooklands lap record, culminating in a spectacular 135.33-mile run.

Barnato, seldom out of the papers, was also proving to be a worthy ambassador for the brand. In 1929, those without a

Bentley – or the inclination to drive the length of France – travelled to and from the Riviera on *Le Train Bleu*. A couple of British cars had made headlines by beating the train on its dash back to Calais. In March, Barnato, on one of his many trips to the Carlton Hotel on the Croisette at Cannes, accepted a bet to go one better: that he could reach his club in Pall Mall before the train even made it to Calais.

It sounded crazy, but in reality, like everything Barnato did, there was method behind the madness. 'We waited in the Carlton bar till we got word from the station that the train had left (5.45 p.m.), we finished our drinks and left . . . I had already arranged for a garage pump I knew at Lyons to remain open after midnight and for a petrol lorry to be at Auxerre at 4 a.m.'

They braved rain and fog for the first 500 miles and soon after Paris burst a tyre, but made up time and pulled onto the quay at 10.30 a.m., ready for 'an excellent breakfast' in the station buffet, while the car was loaded aboard the ferry.

After crossing the Channel, they reached the West End of London at 3.20, four minutes before the train arrived in Calais: 'News of the run had already preceded us, for the hall porter was waiting with the time clock message stamping machine.'

The society papers lapped it up. It was an informal wager but, because Barnato was chairman of Bentley, the French Motor Manufacturers Association took umbrage. They pointed to an agreement signed by Bentley in 1929 as part of their application to exhibit at the next Paris Salon d'Auto, not to enter any competition in France that was not officially approved by the Association.

Refusing to accept that Barnato was acting as a private individual, they imposed a fine of £160, and threatened them with expulsion. Bentley replied that they would neither pay nor exhibit, and even threatened in return to withdraw from Le Mans.

Few expected them to miss the race, but it was a measure of their stature at Le Mans that such an idea could send shivers through the French authorities. As it was, the entry list was down – particularly the number of French cars, only three in a depleted field of seventeen. And to really rub salt in the wound, ten of those were from Britain. When French designer Gabriel Voisin complained about the British 'domination' of what was now France's premier motor race, it was no exaggeration.

In June, Bentley rolled into Le Mans in style. The works and Paget–Birkin teams had separate pits and separate mechanics. They even had their own ties, designed by Davis: red and grey for the blower drivers, green on dark blue for Bentley. Benjafield, Davis noted, was entitled to wear both, and 'always came to the right party in the wrong tie'.

But now Bentley was faced with a truly formidable competitor. The 7-litre Mercedes-Benz SSK was an awesome machine, with an engine bigger than the Speed Six *and* a supercharger. The design had been a leaving present to Mercedes from their recently departed chief engineer, a little-known professor from Bohemia: Ferdinand Porsche. Mercedes also had years of experience with superchargers, going back to their aircraft and submarine engines in the Great War.

Their driver, Rudolf Caracciola, was from a much humbler background than Barnato and Birkin. The son of hoteliers, he had started out as an apprentice mechanic but was ambitious. He made his name at the first German Grand Prix in 1926 in a three-year-old borrowed Mercedes. Having stalled on the grid, he was a minute behind the leaders when it started to rain and then fog descended. With no idea where he was in the field, he just kept driving and passing slower or retired cars. Only after the finish did he discover he had won. The ecstatic German press dubbed him *Regenmeister* – the Rain Master. His co-driver, the hugely experienced Christian Werner, had been a test driver for Mercedes since 1911. The pair had already made their intentions clear by beating Bentley in the 1929 RAC Tourist Trophy.

Sammy Davis was delighted to be reunited with his old team, but he noted the party atmosphere among his fellow drivers was dampened by W.O.'s warning that they had 'got' to win. Anything less against the lone German car would be an embarrassment.

'The very fact that to win was essential meant a greatly increased mental stress on all concerned' – all the more given the lingering doubts about the reliability of Birkin's blowers, despite his impressive show of speed at Brooklands. With the Mercedes' superior engine size and power – and proven reliability – the fear was that Caracciola could follow the Bentleys around the track for as long as he chose, then in the closing laps use the supercharger to surge ahead.

Although business was taking him out of the country for longer intervals, Barnato returned for the event. Having won twice in a row, to do anything other than to go for the hat-trick would be against all his competitive instincts. As co-driver, W.O. chose Glen Kidston, who had come second in 1929 and was the only Bentley driver whose life story could put Barnato's in the shade.

Aviator, big-game hunter, motorcyclist, motor boat and motor car racer, Kidston was the son of an industrialist and a neighbour of Barnato's in Grosvenor Square. In the Great War, as a naval lieutenant aged just fifteen, he was torpedoed, rescued and then torpedoed again – in the same morning. In the 1920s as a submarine commander, he survived when his experimental craft got stuck on the seabed, surfacing long after all hope had been given up. In 1927 he crash-landed an aeroplane in an East African swamp and in 1929 he was on board a Junkers airliner en route to Amsterdam when it crashed in Surrey. His clothes on fire, he punched and kicked his way out of the fuselage before re-entering to try to save fellow passengers. After he'd hacked his way through a mile of woodland, his clothes were still smouldering when a passing motorist picked him up. For Kidston, motor racing – even at Le Mans – was hardly a challenge.

A few days before the race, Charles Faroux and the *Automobile Club de l'Ouest* gave a lunch for the Bentley and Mercedes teams at a charming riverside hotel. 'At first things were difficult; Caracciola and his wife appeared ill at ease; none of us could talk German; only a few of us knew French.'

Then a dachshund called Moritz fell into the river. The successful international effort to rescue the animal broke the ice and bonhomie prevailed. Benjafield discovered Frau Caracciola could speak English and French and 'even W.O. came out of his shell ... and we all ended up with toasts in the English, French and German manners.'

As the race approached, the Bentley team talked tactics. According to Benjafield, one idea was for one of the Bentleys to pass the Mercedes at high speed down the straight and then disappear up the escape road to tempt Caracciola into taking the corner too fast.

It made sense for the two Bentley teams to work together, but, having tasted victory with Barnato the previous year, all Birkin wanted was to win again – in his own car. In practice, Birkin was very fast, but W.O. was convinced that his machine, for all its speed, did not have the stamina to go the full twenty-four hours. He also knew Tim well enough to know that he would be unable to resist going flat out all the way.

The day before the race, a problem emerged which none of them had foreseen. The French-supplied petrol disagreed with the supercharged Bentleys, causing them to overheat, so it was decided to run Birkin's cars on pure benzole. But that required a last-minute modification to the engines, to raise the compression ratio, which meant removing the compression plate between the crankcase and the engine block – no simple task on one car, let alone three.

Despite W.O.'s misgivings, he ordered his own mechanics to help Birkin's team. 'The mere fact of seeing the cars with their cylinder blocks off convinced me that there would be trouble; things like that cannot be done just before a race even if necessity compels.'

There was another problem. In pre-race practice, one of the Birkin cars had run its bearings and then thrown off its flywheel. Even with all the mechanics on the job, working round the clock, they could only prepare two of the three.

But W.O. had learned of a key difference between the superchargers on Birkin's Bentleys and that on the SSK. Where the blowers on the British cars were engaged all the time, those on the Mercedes version were operated by the driver when the throttle was wide open and he needed an extra burst of power, and only sporadically, for no more than fifteen seconds.

Davis also reported what he had gleaned from Mercedes at that riverside party; to formulate their own race strategy, they had pored over Bentley's lap times from last year's race. But had they accounted for the fact that in the absence of a credible competitor W.O. had ordered the team to slow down and conserve their engines?

Armed with Davis's intelligence, W.O. now came up with a simple but cunning plan. It would require Birkin's help, without necessarily asking him to do anything other than what came naturally. But it would in effect mean persuading him to give up his dream of a second victory.

As 4 p.m. approached, and as the cars formed up in front of the grandstand, the weather was baking hot, tempered by a slight breeze. Emile Coquille, the man from Rudge Whitworth who had originally proposed the race through the night, prepared to drop the yellow flag. The Mercedes got away first, pursued by Kidston and Davis in their Bentleys, a Stutz, then Clement's Speed Six, another Stutz and Birkin in fifth place.

At the end of the first lap, Caracciola screamed past the pits, supercharger engaged, which to W.O. made it sound like a 'stuck pig', but was also music to his ears. Already, Birkin was up to second with Davis close behind, making sure that Caracciola's mirrors were full of Bentley. 'I kept the Big Six going for all it was worth to harry the Mercedes if possible in the hope that the driver would be forced to keep the blower in gear. On the curly section from Arnage, the German car gained, on the straight I took back a little of that gain; round after round the machines roared, and when Caracciola looked back after Mulsanne the green Bentley was always in sight, a little too near for comfort.'

The German had taken the bait; he was racing for all he was worth, the Bentleys pushing him, close enough to worry him but not to overtake – yet – and 'rousing the spectators to tumultuous applause, applause one heard above the roar of the exhaust and, hearing, appreciated. No more wonderful run than that opening two hundred miles, itself once upon a time enough for a whole race, could be imagined; the very fierceness of it thrilled.'

On the fourth lap, Birkin set a new lap record of 88 mph. 'I could see the car more clearly now through the dust . . . I decided to wait for the straight before Mulsanne and there pass him; we roared down the hill towards it and took the bend and came into the three kilometres of clear road. I heard the supercharger wailing as I approached.'

Birkin then heard a different sound, much closer, a loud, metallic crack. He glanced round and saw a crumpled mudguard. Unbeknown to him, a tyre had thrown its tread. But he was closing in on the Mercedes, which was right in the middle of the road doing 125 mph, the barest margin either side. Mulsanne was coming up.

Birkin pounced, forcing his way past the completely unsuspecting Caracciola, with two wheels on the verge. There was just time to change down and take the corner. Caracciola was flabbergasted. With his supercharger wailing he hadn't heard Birkin approach. Just as dismaying, he could see the tell-tale white line of canvas on the Bentley's stricken tyre, and yet it was charging ahead.

Having taken the Mercedes, Birkin could not afford to slacken. Passing the pits, he noticed agitated gestures from the crew. Coming out of the Arnage corner on the next lap, the Bentley lurched wildly and skidded. 'I knew only then that a tyre had gone; it was torn to shreds and as I hobbled to the pits at under forty, the Mercedes passed.'

Davis rounded Maison Blanche to see Birkin, 'limping slowly with one rear tyre torn to pieces, a fuzzy ball of tangled cords'. It was his turn to take up pursuit, piling on power and hyperbole as his machine thrilled him, 'like some great feline under one as it took the curves'.

Coming up to pass an Alfa Romeo, he hugged the kerb; a stone flew up and ricocheted off the right lens of his goggles. It didn't smash, but turned the glass into a mass of cracks. Tiny splinters fell into his eye. He tore off the goggles and fumbled for the spare pair; this time nothing had been left to chance.

After a stint of twenty laps, he came in and handed over to Clive Dunfee, Davis's protégé on his first Le Mans, and went to *The Autocar*'s own pit for some tea and to get the glass extracted from his eye. 'Sitting there, thrilled by the recent run, I was at peace with all the world, save when the eye gave a nasty prick.'

Then he noticed Palmer, the *Autocar* man who was keeping track of the British entrants on a large scoreboard, frowning at him. His car was missing. Davis dashed back to the Bentley pits to discover why. It was an eerie replay of his own misfortune in 1926. 'Coming down to the first turn, always very dangerous in one's first race, Clive had gone far too fast; the car had skidded right across the road and into a heap of sand.'

His eye pulsing with pain under a 'most theatrical' bandage, Davis ran down to Pontlieue and dug for an hour, using a spare headlamp glass as a spade, which *The Motor* commented was 'about as hopeless as trying to drain the North Sea with a teaspoon'.

As dusk fell he discovered that it was to no avail. 'The steering was gone and two wheels bent, the car undriveable . . . I felt as miserable as could be. But that was nothing compared with Clive's feelings, as I knew only too well – no one on earth could comfort him.'

As dusk turned to darkness, it was now Barnato's turn to hunt down the Mercedes, to keep close in his mirrors until W.O. gave the order to pass, then slow just enough to tempt the German to repass. Barnato was issuing a warning; it wasn't only the blower Bentleys which had extra power reserves.

Birkin was now lying seventh, frustrated but nevertheless exhilarated by the drama and spectacle of the race going into the night. 'In the pits the shaded lamps glared inwards, and coloured lanterns hung around the dancing places. The air was cool to those not racing, and few attempted to sleep; in the car parks crowds of private cars lay huddled together like shadows, until one would swing out and join the river of lights back to the town. But, whatever the weather, there would have been many to watch the great struggle between Mercedes and Bentley.'

W.O.'s strategy was working. Mercedes increased their pace. Caracciola and Werner had no choice but to keep using the supercharger through the night, its banshee wail audible all round the track. Following W.O.'s instructions to the letter, on lap forty Barnato passed the Mercedes again, and then again two laps later, allowed him to repass. On the forty-third lap, Barnato filled up with thirty-seven gallons of petrol and handed over to Kidston. The Mercedes led until its pit stop on lap forty-six. It was off the road for seven minutes. Even though the rules had changed, allowing both drivers to work on the car together, the Mercedes team were nothing like as well-drilled.

Birkin in seventh place battled on. During refuelling, a Stutz burst into flames: 'the glare was blinding as we passed it and the margin of road so small that we drove through almost a wall of flames. The fading glow lit up the tall trees, throwing the figures of the crowd around into silhouette, and for hours the dark smoke drifted like a ghost across the road.'

Into the night, W.O.'s cat and mouse strategy played out. Barnato's co-driver Kidston was well in the lead after the Germans' pit stop, as Werner, having taken over from Caracciola, tore after him. After thirteen more laps Kidston let Mercedes reclaim the lead. Barnato took over again and on lap sixty-five was back in the lead.

Then, almost as if on cue, at 2.23 a.m. on the eighty-third lap, the Mercedes pulled into the pits for the last time, water spewing from a blown gasket. For Caracciola, the race was over. W.O. went over to offer his commiserations; he must have smiled inside when they told him that according to their calculations they had expected to be leading by a full lap at that point in the race. Officially the explanation was battery failure; it was customary for teams to try to blame mechanical failure on a proprietary component, but W.O. was in no doubt. Forced into continuous use, the supercharger had cooked their engine.

Birkin, still hammering on in the darkness, had extracted from W.O. an understanding: if one of the supercharged cars found itself in the lead, the works Bentleys would not try to beat it. With Stutz the only serious remaining threat, he still had a hope, if a faint one. But it was never to be.

Birkin's car expired after twenty hours with a broken con rod that smashed its way through the crankcase. Benjafield in the other supercharged car drove a Herculean ten hours after his co-driver fell ill – and even Dr Benjy couldn't cure him – only to retire with a collapsed piston.

It was a triumphant moment for Bentley of truly historic proportions. Not only had Barnato won, he had got his hat-trick, an achievement which would not be matched at Le Mans for another forty years.

Frank Clement came second in what was his eighth consecutive Le Mans for Bentley. The supercharged cars for all their sound and fury still had a way to go to match the other Bentleys' endurance. And W.O.'s five wins set a bar so high for future competitors that more than a quarter of a century would pass before it was equalled by Jaguar.

After the finish, Benjafield looked across at W.O. 'Never before have I seen such a smile on the face of the tiger.'

43

Les Camions Rapides

Just as Bentley's triumph was front-page news, so too was speculation about its future in racing. To the outside world, their cars could not be matched for speed or endurance. Nor could any other make of car of the day match such stellar competition success. And *Les Vingt-Quatre Heures du Mans* – trimmed to the snappier 'Le Mans' – was now as firmly fixed in the public consciousness as *Le Prix de l'Arc de Triomphe* or the Grand National.

Faroux, Durand and Coquille had achieved their dream of racing through the night, but not with quite the outcome they envisaged. Wearying of the monotony of yet another Bentley triumph, Faroux wrote: 'The moment has arrived when the French automobile industry must decide whether to reassert itself or allow the decline to continue.'

Bentley Motors solved the problem for him by formally withdrawing from competition. Even without the financial crisis engulfing the world, it was the moment to retire on a high note, and the notes wouldn't get much higher than this.

But Bentley was not quite done with France. Before the end of 1930, and before Dorothy Paget cut off her life support for the blower venture, Tim Birkin risked making a complete fool of himself – and his car – by entering the French Grand Prix.

While Le Mans had prospered, the Grand Prix was struggling. The 1930 season had been a fiasco. Four out of seven races in the Grand Prix calendar had to be cancelled due to lack of interest. So in a rare break with form *L'Automobile Club de France* threw away the rule book and opened their race at Pau, near the border with Spain, to all-comers.

Looming over a field dominated by sixteen petite Bugattis, Birkin's 2-ton supercharged Bentley, shorn of mudguards and headlamps to reduce wind resistance, looked positively elephantine, provoking mirth among the French spectators. Ettore Bugatti called it '*le camion le plus rapide du monde*' – the fastest lorry in the world. But Faroux wasn't laughing. 'I have seen the Bentleys at Le Mans, and I know. I am Faroux, I am not a bloody fool.'

As it happened, the circuit, in the foothills of the Pyrenees – with its long straights and tight hairpins – suited the British machine's raw power. Birkin scythed his way through the field until on lap ten he came upon a crashed Bugatti, the driver Louis 'Sabipa' Charavel sprawled across the road, unconscious, right in the Bentley's path.

With no time to slow, Birkin aimed for the narrow gap between the driver's head and a stone wall and squeezed through, so close that blood was found on his front tyre. He finished a remarkable second. Mme Charavel personally thanked Birkin for sparing her husband's life.

It was indeed a good note to go out on. Dorothy Paget's enthusiasm for bankrolling the blower venture had waned. A few weeks later, the four remaining Bentley blower team cars were put up for sale in the classified pages of *Motor Sport*.

44

The Maharajah's Displeasure

After a board meeting early in 1930, Woolf Barnato asked his finance man Jack Carruth to inspect the books and give him a report. He delivered his findings on 24 June, in a 'Confidential Memorandum to Captain Barnato from Mr Carruth'.

Carruth was only doing his fiduciary duty. Even so, W.O.'s distaste for him was undiminished. But there was no point shooting the messenger. This was the first time in Bentley's existence that an in-depth audit had ever been conducted, and it did not make for happy reading.

The profits for the year to 30 March 1929 had been £28,467, their best year. For the year 1929–30, they were put down as £1,023. In fact, 1929–30 was a loss maker but Carruth elected to show a token profit 'so we may not have further embarrassment from the creditors'. He noted the 'general unfinished stock' at the end of the fiscal year came to a value of £74,000. But even if all that stock could be sold it would still mean a loss of approximately £12,000.

By massaging the figures to show a nominal profit, Carruth was buying Barnato some time to consider his options. His decision, when it came, would be shocking. His response was to remove W.O. from his position as managing director, along with his own friend the Marquis of Casa Maury, and replace them both – with Carruth. For some time W.O. had felt his own influence in the company slipping. Now he faced the humiliation of demotion to chief engineer. Not only that, the board commissioned a new 4 4-litre engine from an outside designer, Harry Riccardo.

Thanks to the financial crash, the euphoria of the 1930 Le Mans triumph was very short-lived. Throughout W.O.'s career, circumstance conspired to rob him of satisfaction – in 1914, his Tourist Trophy D.F.P. halted by the war, the reward for his aircraft engine work disputed and downgraded, the hostile shareholders who balked at the expense of racing, the oppressive presence of Barnato's people who caused the departure of his faithful brother, and now the knowledge that even as he clinched his fifth Le Mans, his business was going under. All these years he had doggedly soldiered on, absorbing blow after blow, from the death of his first wife Leonie in the Spanish flu pandemic, to the failure of his childless, loveless second marriage to Audrey. Seven years younger than him, she had different priorities. She was never going to sit on an oil drum in the pits, nor wait patiently at home while he worked late into the night at Cricklewood. Still under the same roof, she had carved out her own busy social life and was seldom around to comfort him.

In the face of all these setbacks, W.O. remained resolutely Sphinx-like and dignified. Bentley Motors had always struggled. His focus was always on building the cars, rather than building the business. Delegating that task to his brother H.M. and Hillstead had been a mistake. Barnato had come to his rescue and provided the cash with which to keep racing and, finally, equip a proper machine shop – but it was all too late.

What W.O. relied on was his capacity to brazen things out. He hated to ask for help or admit defeat. His last mentor had been

Wilfrid Briggs, his superior at the Admiralty; there were no wise counsellors to help him navigate the adverse currents of markets and finance. His thick skin made him seem cold and aloof. His discomfort in moments of jubilation was dismaying. But his focus and determination as well as his decency inspired a loyalty among those around him that bordered on devotion. Unlike William Morris or Henry Royce he was not an autocrat, yet he could motivate a team to deliver 100 per cent. Never was that more evident than in October 1930 when, with the economic storm swirling around them, W.O. and his team prepared to present his masterpiece.

The star of the London Motor Show at Olympia was without doubt the 100 mph 8 Litre Bentley. No fewer than six versions were exhibited, each graced with bodywork from the country's foremost coachbuilders: Thrupp and Maberly, H.J. Mulliner, Gurney Nutting, Park Ward and Freestone & Webb. In the teeth of what would become a devastating economic depression, it is hard to imagine a more inappropriate car.

Always eager for a headline, the press were ecstatic. *The Autocar*, which had once dubbed Rolls 'the best car in the world', pronounced W.O.'s 8 Litre 'Motoring in its very highest form'.

For a full-scale seven-seater limousine to be able to travel at 100 mph was unheard of. This was W.O.'s Sistine Chapel, the culmination of all his hours of deliberation, and thousands of miles pounding the *routes nationales*, chasing down every imperfection until it was right. It was also a direct threat to Rolls-Royce's Phantom II. Superior insulation and close attention to vibration combined to make the 8 Litre a more refined ride than the Rolls – and faster by nearly 10 mph.

Also on show at Olympia was the supercharged 4½ Litre, of which Birkin had persuaded Barnato to build fifty, in order to qualify for Le Mans. Most still had yet to find buyers. Some were even shorn of their superchargers to make them more docile – and saleable.

At Bentley's official motor show luncheon, Hubert Pike, W.O.'s long-time service manager and friend since prep school, announced a road show tour of Britain with a convoy of cars. There would also be a new service depot in Paris, headed by Jean Chassagne no less, and declared that a similar initiative was underway across the Atlantic. 'That is why our Chairman Captain Woolf Barnato has gone to the United States,' he told the assembled party.

This was at best wishful thinking. Barnato – as far as W.O. was aware – was busy pursuing his future second wife. Perhaps there was a hint of truth in Arthur Hillstead's warning that he might take Bentley up as a toy, 'have his fun and then throw it aside when the novelty had worn off'.

But the world was changing. Even the most benevolent benefactor would be shirking their duty if they did not take a cold, hard look at the prevailing economic conditions, and their impact on the prospects of a luxury brand.

Although it had the cushion of its aero-engine business, Rolls-Royce was also feeling the effects of the Wall Street Crash. An attempt to assemble cars in America had been an expensive flop; now, with its home market shrinking, having to contend with Bentley's new model posed a serious problem.

In January 1931, Rolls' managing director Arthur Sidgreaves wrote to Henry Royce at his winter retreat at La Canadel on the Côte d'Azur: 'I am sorry to say that this car appears to be becoming a formidable competitor of the Phantom II.'

He attached a memo from the Maharajah of Rewa, an otherwise faithful Rolls customer, who had sampled the new Bentley. Sidgreaves reported that the Maharajah was *only* taking his Phantom II back to India with him because he couldn't get a good enough price for it in part-exchange for a Bentley and 'unless we had a very good answer to the 8 Litre Bentley we should find ourselves not in the premier position, as he (the Maharajah) felt sure that a number of the Indian Princes, once they had experienced the Bentley car, would buy it in preference to anything else'.

But would there be enough Indian princes to keep Bentley afloat? By the end of 1930, an air of desperation had entered the boardroom. Since the first loan of £40,000 in 1923, the company had been meeting the interest payments but had not made any inroads into the capital. Two further mortgages with the London Life Association, in 1927 and 1929, stipulated payment within fifteen days of the due date, otherwise they would call in the capital sum. And such payments as they did manage were being made not from income but from other loans guaranteed by Barnato.

On 9 June 1931, without so much as a word to W.O., Jack Carruth made a call to Arthur Sidgreaves. He wanted to know if Rolls-Royce would be interested in a partnership. A day later, he followed it up with a lengthy letter marked 'Strictly Private and Confidential'. It is an extraordinary document, not least because it contains a barely veiled threat.

First, Carruth disclosed a devastating trade secret – an unsold stock of a hundred finished chassis. Then, having indicated he was acting with the authority of his chairman, he did not mince his words: 'Captain Barnato is a very determined man on any matter which affects his personal prestige ... He may say that the large quantity of material purchased but not yet completed has to be completed and put on the market at reduced prices.' In other words Bentley might dump unsold chassis onto the already shrinking market, causing Rolls a major headache.

Carruth went on to point out that a receiver liquidating the business could do the same and that 'either contingency must have a very great effect on Rolls-Royce'. He then laid out the merits of his proposal for a partnership, highlighting the assets – including W.O. himself – whom he described as 'a designer of the first rank. He is a young man who originally became eminent as a designer of aeroplane engines, and I have no doubt that Rolls Royce would find his cooperation extremely useful.'

It's no wonder that Carruth was held in such contempt by W.O., who would never have dreamed of addressing a fellow car maker like this. It also betrayed his ignorance of the industry, to think that the managing director of Rolls-Royce would need to be briefed on W.O. of all people: the man who had brought the aluminium piston to Derby in the Great War and delivered the secrets of the overhead cam Grand Prix Mercedes when Henry Royce came to design his first aero-engine.

But Carruth did make the more astute, if somewhat presumptuous, observation that Rolls-Royce merged with Bentley would 'cease to compete and cater for different aspects of the luxury market'.

In his closing words, the newly appointed Bentley managing director made no secret of how he saw his primary role: as that of the chairman's *consigliere*. 'The advantage to Captain Barnato, with whose interests I am primarily concerned, is that the Company on these lines should go on to success and any question of his own personal prestige would be obviated.'

On 15 June the payment Bentley owed to London Life became due – to be paid within fifteen days. The clock was ticking.

A few days later, Sidgreaves replied to Carruth asking for more details about Bentley's finances. But when Rolls' chief accountant ran his eye over them, he decided it would at best be a drain on their own already strained finances. Sidgreaves informed Carruth that by their calculations, the suggestion that they put up thirty to forty thousand pounds to gain control would 'only be a temporary palliative since there was no other cash available for current expenses'.

On 23 June the Rolls-Royce board rejected the proposal. Barnato and Carruth now faced a stark choice: pump yet more money in to keep Bentley afloat or call in the receivers. Given the dire economic climate – and Bentley's finances – only one of these options made business sense. They informed London Life that Bentley Motors was unable to meet their payments.

Barnato's explanation to *The Star* on 10 July was short and to the point. He neatly summed up the state of the car market as it headed into the void. 'People can no longer afford to buy expensive motor cars. Motoring is either a necessity or a luxury – there is now a limited public who can afford luxuries. It is a matter of getting from one place to another, and third class gets you there as well as first class.' As a gesture of goodwill, he paid all Bentley employees a month's wages.

Leslie Pennal was in Hereford, preparing a car for its owner, when he got the letter from the Official Receiver. 'It was a terrible shock; I hated to think that Bentleys were going to be no more. In fact I just couldn't believe it, and I could imagine the awful feeling at the Works.' He was instructed to do no more work and return immediately. 'I was very unhappy about that, and I'm afraid I disobeyed.' He finished the car he was servicing and went on to another job. 'It seemed the proper thing to do: Bentleys may have gone broke but that was no reason, I felt, for leaving an owner not quite satisfied.' Wally Saunders was in Ireland when he heard. 'It wasn't just the job we were losing – Bentleys were special to us. Sort of stunned we were.' Rivers Fletcher was holding the fort at Cork Street with Bertie Kensington-Moir when they were given the order to stop trading, which prompted Moir to remark sardonically: 'Stop trading? They never started, Rivers, they never started.'

With Bentley's predicament no longer a secret, the Receiver's task was to keep the business ticking over until he was able to dispose of it either in one piece, or, failing that, its constituent parts. By a cruel irony, Patrick Frere, who was appointed on behalf of London Life, was an old friend of W.O.'s brothers Hardy and H.M. Ruefully, W.O. realised, belatedly, that Frere was just the sort of man he should have had on board from the start to manage his company. For the few months he was in charge, he actually created an atmosphere of comparative calm, recharged the service department and managed to retain W.O.'s design staff.

By a happy chance, the news of Bentley's predicament caught the attention of yet another friend of H.M. Bentley's: H.T. Vane, chairman and managing director of Napier & Son, in Acton, west London. Dating all the way back to 1808, Napier had been among the first precision engineering firms in Britain, with a steam-powered printing press among other innovations before going on to cars. A Napier had won the 1902 Gordon Bennett race and Charles Stuart Rolls had been an enthusiast before he discovered Royce.

But soon after the Great War they abandoned car making to concentrate on aero-engines, though their V12 Lion did find its way into Malcolm Campbell's record-breaking Bluebird cars and boats. With the country in the grip of recession, the Napier board decided they should look for another revenue stream.

What attracted them to Bentley was W.O. himself. As well as his Rolls-Royce-beating cars, his reputation as the designer of Britain's most successful rotary aero-engine was a further advantage. For W.O. – and for Frere, who seemed to care more about Bentley's future than Carruth did – this came as extremely promising news. Buyers of a luxury car business in the current climate were likely to be hard, if not impossible, to find.

Napier was just the sort of engineering-led business that W.O. respected. They all met at Hanover Court, the old Bentley & Bentley headquarters that H.M. had kept on, and the broad outlines for the specification for a future Napier–Bentley car were agreed.

With Frere's blessing, W.O. threw himself into what he did best, designing a new car. It would be inspired by the 8 Litre, but smaller, lighter and lower – and potentially even faster. The motoring press soon got wind of this possible tie-up and began enthusing at the prospect of another thrilling new W.O. design, with the added excitement of Napier's impending automotive renaissance.

Wally Saunders, whose father had worked as a racing mechanic on the original Napiers, was beyond relieved. 'We began to feel things weren't going to be too bad after all, especially after we knew that W.O. and the design staff, who'd been kept on, had actually started on the new car.'

Napier tabled an offer of £84,000 for the whole of Bentley Motors Ltd which received court approval on 20 October. A contract of sale was drafted and approved by Napier, Frere and London Life. But the Bentley board had commissioned their own independent valuation which came up with a figure more attractive to Carruth and his master – of over £140,000. Napier agreed to look at improving their offer.

But when news of the proposed tie-up reached Derby, it presented Rolls MD Sidgreaves with a new problem: a competitor on the road joining forces with a rival in the air was potentially a greater threat than Bentley being dissolved and dumping unsold chassis on the open market.

The stage was set for a battle as nerve-jangling as any Bentley had faced on the racetrack. In keeping with his duty to get the best deal, Frere persuaded Napier to up their offer to £103,675, and on 17 November the court met to sign the agreement. It should have been a mere formality. Plans for the new Napier-Bentley were already taking shape. W.O., H.M., Frere and Vane, the Napier MD, set off together from Hanover Court, looking forward to settling Bentley Motors' fate.

But as the proceedings got going, a lawyer stood up and asked to address the court. He introduced himself as a representative of an entity called the British Equitable Central Trust; he was there to offer a figure higher than Napier's. For a moment no one spoke, then Napier's counsel asked for a brief adjournment. When they returned he made a higher bid. But the judge reminded them that his court was not an auction house and instructed both parties to return at 4.30 p.m. with sealed bids.

When they were opened, the mysterious rival's bid was £125,275, £25,500 more than Napier's. There was a stunned silence. Just at the moment of salvation, W.O. was cast back into the unknown. No one had ever heard of British Central Equitable Trust, and no one knew of its intentions – or even if it had any connection to other automotive interests. Ever the master of understatement, W.O. found it 'an odd and unpleasant sort of situation not to know who now controlled my future, and the firm which bore my name'.

The answer to the mystery came from the unlikeliest source. For several years, W.O. and his wife Audrey had been living separate lives, albeit under the same roof. Later that night after W.O.'s day in court, Audrey arrived home from a cocktail party. She told W.O. she thought she had overheard a man claiming he had just taken over Bentley Motors. Curious, she sought to find out the man's name.

'"It was Arthur Sidgreaves," my wife told me. "Who is he?" "He's the managing director of Rolls-Royce", I told her.'

45

Return of the Sphinx

With no warning whatsoever, Bentley Motors had been sold to Rolls-Royce. What would they want with it – and with W.O.? His fate lay in their hands; he was contractually bound to his company and its successors *'in perpetuity'*.

On 20 November 1931, W.O. made an appointment to see Sidgreaves. The meeting was inconclusive. He was then sent for an audience with Henry Royce at his base in Sussex. It was the first time the two had met. Royce was a semi-invalid with only two more years to live, but from his summer and winter bases in West Wittering and the Côte d'Azur he kept an iron grip on the company's designs. His opening question to W.O. was wilfully disingenuous. 'I believe you are a commercial man, Mr Bentley?'

W.O. chose his words carefully; he did not want to appear vain. If he took umbrage, he hid it well. He suggested that he was more of a technical man, and noted that like Royce he had started out in the running sheds of the Great Northern Railway. Perhaps, he hoped, this connection would prise Royce open, but the old man merely accepted it with a nod.

Afterwards, Royce sent a memo to Sidgreaves: 'If we were to let him have the run of the Derby designs, experiments and reputation, Rolls-Royce would teach him infinitely more than he would help us.'

The words serve as a testimony to the kind of tunnel vision that the elderly Royce excelled at, just at a time when the company would soon be in dire need of design leadership. The job Rolls offered W.O. was a very public humiliation, as *understudy* to the technical adviser to Sidgreaves, based not at the works in Derby but in their Mayfair Conduit Street office with the sales team, just opposite the building where, ten years before, he and his team had designed the first Bentley 3 Litre. But he wasn't in any position to refuse. Handcuffed by his contract, he was at Rolls' mercy to do with him whatever they chose. Worse, he was still in debt to his company to the tune of £2,480 plus interest.

W.O. asked Sidgreaves to release him from the contractual handcuffs and the debt in exchange for giving up all claims to royalties, so he might go and work for Napier's. When Sidgreaves refused, W.O. tried to start legal proceedings, arguing that the agreement had been nullified by the liquidation. But Napier, perhaps stung by so publicly losing out on Bentley, were also losing interest in W.O.'s services. He had run out of options.

What Sidgreaves did need was to secure ownership of the Bentley trade mark. In exchange, he offered to clear W.O.'s debt. It was another bitter pill to swallow, but W.O. was seriously out of pocket – and another expense was on the horizon – his impending divorce from Audrey. There was one other concession; if W.O. accepted, Sidgreaves would release him from those handcuffs – after five years.

If W.O. thought Carruth was a hard-hearted operator, Sidgreaves ran him a close second. The Rolls MD was also a lot wilier than Barnato's man. Carruth had approached Rolls-Royce with a very poor hand to play, and played it badly. Inviting Sidgreaves to take a stake in a company having hinted it might be liquidated made little sense; once the company had gone into receivership, only then would its true liabilities be disclosed. All Rolls had to do was watch and wait for their closest competitor to self-destruct.

In fact, Henry Royce was under no illusions about the threat W.O.'s company had posed. As far back as 1925, he wrote to his team, 'Regarding the Bentley, the makers are evidently out to capture our trade.' It was clear to everyone in Derby that the Phantom II was inferior to the 8 Litre, but Royce did not see any merit in buying one to study it. 'We can see in which way it can be better than we are ... for high-speed performance, because it has four valves per cylinder. It would appear more costly than ours to produce for equal silence.'

Arthur Robotham, who had been taken on by Rolls-Royce as a premium apprentice after the Great War, had also been well aware of Bentley for a long time. In 1924, Neville Minchin, whose firm supplied Rolls' batteries, had driven up to Derby in his then new 3 Litre to show to him. And Robotham had been impressed by both the quality of craftsmanship and its performance.

And despite the managerial utterances to the contrary, the 'serpent of speed' had indeed tempted Royce, who, a few months before his death, wrote from La Canadel that he *would* like to design 'a high-speed sports car, not expecting much in the way of sales but for the good of ordinary sales'.

It would be two more years before the public found out what Rolls had in mind for Bentley.

For those without intimate knowledge of the company's finances, the dissolution of Bentley Motors was an outrage. Dudley Benjafield was flabbergasted: 'Of course we had weathered several financial crises in the past, but never in our blackest moods had we considered the possibility of the complete eclipse of the company that produced his wonderful cars for the sake of a few thousand pounds.'

To Wally Hassan, taken on as a boy of fifteen, W.O. had created a unique workplace. 'He had the priceless facility for gathering good types – the right types – together and building them into a team ... there were lots of good men who were glad to come and work at the bench, and some of them had quite lowly jobs ... Everybody had a real interest in the work – even the blokes who bolted the chassis together had some degree of keenness. You don't come across that very often.'

~

As a full-time employee of Bentley Motors, Frank Clement had kept a low profile compared to the other Bentley drivers. But he had been there from the start, the first to drive a Bentley in a race, had driven in all eight Le Mans and was still on the payroll when the axe fell. He did not own the trophies he had won; they were the property of the company, proudly exhibited in the Pollen House showroom.

When Clement enquired after them he discovered they had all been shipped up to the Rolls factory in Derby, so he asked if he could buy one. 'After a terrific palaver I was allowed to choose one ... Later when he ran into a Derby man and asked about the rest of them he was told they were gone, "sold for old silver".'

Leslie Pennal was kept on right to the bitter end at Cricklewood. 'The worst I saw with my own eyes was the breaking up of the 8 Litre crankcases ... I walked in there one day and found two labourers with sledge hammers trying to break up those beautiful things ... I was so shocked that I just stood still, and while I was standing there our storekeeper, Mr Conway, came in. He looked grim, and I just turned away. It was dreadful.'

There was no room for sentiment. The men from Derby had seen the threat and contained it. Rolls-Royce quickly established Bentley Motors (1931) Limited and would eventually produce a line of Bentley-badged cars promoted as 'the silent sports car'. But at no stage was W.O. let anywhere near the development of the cars which would carry on his name, nor was he invited to join the new company's board. One person who was asked was Woolf Barnato.

Just before the liquidation, he bought a number of Rolls-Royce shares and served on the new Bentley board for the rest of his life, a willing and enthusiastic ambassador for the marque.

W.O., the architect of Britain's motor-racing glory, had every reason to be bitter about the cloak-and-dagger circumstances of the takeover. It is a measure of the man that he threw himself into the lowly job Rolls had found him without a hint of complaint. An engineer by heart and soul, although kept at arm's length in London, he was welcomed by the Rolls design team on his visits to Derby and as if by osmosis was drawn into their development work, but, as he noted, 'Of course it was all rather tame after the exciting and adventurous days of Bentley Motors, and I could never quite throw off the feeling that I was nothing more than a hostage – a dangerous ex-enemy confined (with all reasonable comforts) to my Elba.'

In January 1934, his loss of status was partially alleviated by a third and very happy marriage to Margaret Roberts Hutton. Like the first Mrs Bentley – if not the second – Margaret enjoyed a demanding drive, which was just as well since their honeymoon turned out to be a long-distance winter road test over the Stelvio Pass to Lake Como.

A year later, the end of Rolls' contract with W.O. was in sight. On Friday 12 June 1935, Sidgreaves took W.O. out to lunch. The two men had evidently put aside any animosity as the occasion was quite convivial. Sidgreaves made W.O. an offer: five more years, no change of status but a significantly better salary. W.O. reacted with his customary poker face. He was forty-seven, happily remarried, in the prime of his life. He said he would give the offer his consideration and allowed the conversation to move on. Sidgreaves then let slip that Rolls was about to make a bid for Lagonda, which, like Bentley Motors five years before, was about to go into liquidation. And in another eerie coincidence, that very Friday was final practice for the 1935 Le Mans, and, despite its problems, Lagonda was competing.

W.O. had more than a passing interest in the outcome of the

race because, unlike Sidgreaves, he knew that Rolls was not the only bidder for Lagonda's assets. And in his pocket was an offer from the other party – the position of chief engineer. That Sunday afternoon, Lagonda won Le Mans; a few days later, Rolls failed to win Lagonda. W.O. politely declined Sidgreaves' offer. He had found his escape road. And soon he would be back at Le Mans, once more, racing in the dark.

Epilogue

This is not the end of the story of Bentley, nor even the beginning of the end. For many of the Bentley Boys and Girls, all still in their prime, their time with W.O. was merely the launch pad for further exploits, worthy of a whole shelf of books, though most of them if pressed would have agreed that this was their finest hour.

In August 1944, Sammy Davis, fifty-seven years old and back in uniform as a REME major, made a poignant visit to Le Mans just days after the Germans had departed. Relieved to find the city relatively unscathed, he was compelled to check on the roads that made up the circuit. 'Down the straight to the Café de l'Hippodrome all was well . . . Mulsanne Corner good, the run to les Esses too and a good broad road as before to the White House turn. Coming round White House – fast on principle – we got a shock: the road was gone. In its place was a mass of bomb craters, unexploded bombs, the wreckage of a hundred Boche aeroplanes . . . With difficulty we got to the grandstand, a mere skeleton, those wonderful pits were gone where we had worked so hard and slept so fitfully as the 24-hour race went on.'

The race was revived in 1949 and Davis continued to be a regular attendee, right into the late 1960s, driving his 'Frogeye' Austin Healey Sprite all the way there and pitching his tent in the spectators' campsite, passing unnoticed in his beret, puffing on his pipe. The city did remember, though. In 1965 Rue SCH Davis was named in his honour and he, along with General Patton, whose

Third Army liberated Le Mans, was made an honorary citizen. He also acquired his own *Tue Belle-mère*, the motor tricycle made by the Bollées of Le Mans, and was a perennial participant on it in the London–Brighton run with his amenable second wife, Susie, up front. His first marriage to Rosamond before the Armistice, when by his own admission he was still struggling to come to terms with the war, ended in divorce. Davis's judgement was that 'In wartime one is a different person in almost every way in contrast with one's peacetime personality ... I could not live the life expected.' But they did have one son, Colin, to whom Davis was devoted. Colin followed his father into motor racing and won the gruelling Sicilian road race, the Targa Florio, in 1964. Sammy Davis continued to draw, paint and write to the end of his life, telling Benjafield's grandson, Robert, that he had painted the Maison Blanche crash scene more than ten times. He died on his ninety-fourth birthday when a paraffin heater in his flat toppled over during the celebrations.

After its 1927 triumph, Benjafield sold Old No. 7. It came to an ignominious end, repainted yellow and wrapped around a lamp post. Only the log book survives, in the Bentley Drivers Club archive, the automotive equivalent of the Dead Sea Scrolls. In October 1930, Davis and Benjafield had one more never-to-be-forgotten race at Brooklands – against each other. The BRDC 500 mile was open to all-comers, Benjafield in a mighty blower Bentley locked in a titanic David and Goliath battle with Davis, who was in a tiny blood-orange Austin 7. Davis won – on handicap. Ever after, they remained friends and shared a passion for building model boats and aeroplanes out of balsa wood.

Through the 1930s Benjafield continued to divide his time between his patients and the racetrack. At the age of fifty-three he was back in the Royal Army Medical Corps for the Second World War and back in Egypt where he improvised yet another boat – from a tin bath this time. On the long voyage home, while tending a colleague with a carbuncle, he wrote an account of the Bentleys at Le Mans which he read each day to his patient.

He gave up racing, but remained an enthusiastic member of the British Racing Drivers' Club, which he had founded in his dining room at Wimpole Street. He never retired from medicine. Though he was far more interested in his patients than his professional reputation, and received no credit for his pioneering work treating Spanish flu victims, it is striking that as recently as 2003 his 1919 paper for the *British Medical Journal* was still being cited in articles on vaccines.

After the war, he became a doting grandfather to his son Patrick's children, Robert and Helen. Aged ten, Robert was sent off to boarding school with a supply of stink bombs Benjafield prepared for him in his laboratory and the school matron was sent vials of experimental vaccine for her to inject into Robert and report the findings. As soon as Robert could reach the pedals he was taught to drive the doctor's black Citroën Traction Avant Big Six.

Although an attentive grandparent, like many servicemen whose children were born during the Great War, he was a distant and ungiving father. Despite their shared interest in motor sport, Dudley Benjafield showed little affection towards his son, Patrick, until the weeks before his death in 1957, age sixty-nine. By that time, Patrick had become a notable photographer for *Autosport* magazine. Though most of them are without a byline, several of the best images of Stirling Moss, Mike Hawthorn and many others in action on the track are his.

~

All the original Bentley Boys, those who had joined the company in their teens, continued on to a lifetime of distinguished service in motor engineering. Leslie Pennal continued as a travelling trouble-shooter for Rolls-Royce until the Second World War swept him into the Bristol Aeroplane Company's experimental department. But he continued to care for early Bentley cars whose inner workings he knew like the back of his hand. At his funeral in 1974, a Bentley owner was heard to say that his car was doing very well since Pennal last serviced it – in 1947.

Wally Hassan, a mere fifteen years old when he started at Cricklewood, was retained for a time by Barnato. Their Bentley special eventually achieved a shattering 143 mph average at Brooklands. Then, after a stint at ERA in the late 1930s, he was spotted by William Lyons and helped develop the original Le Mans-conquering XK Jaguar engine. He moved on to Coventry Climax where he created a power unit, ostensibly for a fire pump, that would take Cooper and Lotus to the top of Formula One. Back with Lyons in the 1960s, he was part of the team that designed an awesome V12 which would power Jaguar to more Le Mans victories, in 1988 and 1990. Hassan's *eight* decades of motor sport achievement must be an unrivalled record.

Woolf Barnato reckoned that, in all, Bentley set him back around £120,000 – more than £7 million today. As a business decision, on the eve of the Great Depression, pulling the plug on Bentley made sense. In 1933, as if to signal that the Gatsby era was over, his beloved Ardenrun Place burned down. Ever the master of understatement, W.O. noted 'a trace of reserve' in their subsequent meetings. As a Rolls-Royce shareholder and member of the subsidiary Bentley board, Barnato was an enthusiastic promoter of the marque on his frequent trips to America. He married again, twice, and in the Second World War served as a squadron leader in the RAF responsible for airfield defences. When he died in 1948, his funeral procession was led by Old No. 1. Not until 1962 would his Le Mans hat-trick be equalled.

Arguably, Barnato's greatest achievement was his feisty daughter Diana, who refused to kiss his girlfriend goodnight. Diana

Barnato-Walker inherited her father's spirit. A keen flyer, she delivered aircraft to their bases in the war and in 1963 broke the sound barrier and the women's air speed record. She always regarded her father as her chief inspiration. After his death she wrote, 'not only did I lose a father but a good friend'.

For Mrs Victor Bruce, her twenty-four hours at Montlhéry were a mere appetiser. In 1929, in a powerboat christened *Snotty*, she broke the record for crossing the English Channel. The following year she bought a small biplane from Selfridges and, just after getting her pilot's licence, set off on what would be the first solo flight from Britain to Japan. Flying became her passion from then on. She launched her own air service, pioneered mid-air refuelling, and in the Second World War ran a business repairing airframes for the RAF which made her a millionaire. Later in life she rekindled her love of fast driving, improving on her Bentley time with a 118-mph lap of Thruxton Circuit, at the age of seventy-eight. Asked why she preferred to be known as Mrs Victor Bruce, she retorted: 'I'm not a women's libber!'

After his Montlhéry attempt, John Duff, who had delivered Bentley its first Le Mans win, set off for America. Having come a respectable ninth in the 1926 Indianapolis 500, he decided to take his chances on the wooden board tracks that had sprung up across the nation. Board tracks were known for their particularly high banking and high fatality rate. In all, the Altoona Raceway in Pennsylvania claimed the lives of three Indianapolis winners and, after a serious crash there later that year, Duff gave up racing. He moved to Santa Monica and put his other skills to work; his fencing and horsemanship made him an ideal Hollywood stunt double for Gary Cooper in *Beau Geste*. He returned to England, became a show jumper and died in 1958 in Epping Forest, when he was thrown from his horse.

Abandoned by Dorothy Paget, Tim Birkin was determined to carry on, even if it meant parking his patriotism. With Earl Howe he won the 1931 Le Mans in an Alfa Romeo, and it was a bitter moment when, during the post-race celebrations, he was handed a telegram. It was from Benito Mussolini congratulating them on their victory – 'for Italy'.

In the 1933 Tripoli Grand Prix Birkin finished third but burned his arm on a hot exhaust pipe. Back home, Benjafield asked him what the bandage was for. Birkin said it was nothing. Benjafield insisted on taking a look and found that not only was the burn in a bad state, Birkin had serious blood poisoning. But he wouldn't go to hospital because he was due in Germany for a race at the Nürburgring. 'If you don't go in there is every possibility you will not get to Nürburg or any other race,' warned Benjafield. Birkin did go to hospital but it was too late. He died aged thirty-six. In his racing memoir *Full Throttle*, published the year before his death, he wrote, 'If I blamed anything for my devotion to cars . . . it would be something blamed already for so many troubles, that one more can make no odds – the war.'

After sharing Bentley's last Le Mans victory with Barnato in 1930, Glen Kidston followed Mrs Bruce aloft, with a record-breaking flight to Cape Town. Bentley attracted those born into fabulous wealth, but the Great War alerted them to the responsibilities that came with it. In August 1930, relaxing on the Côte d'Azur after his Le Mans win, Kidston sat down and wrote a long letter on notepaper from the Majestic Hotel in Cannes to his younger brother. 'If you want a good time and nothing else my few words of advice are worthless. Life is not merely a procession of amusements – it is a serious business, and we, those better placed and better educated than our compatriots, have a duty firstly to our country and secondly to the world, showing some return for our mortal span on mother earth.' His life ended in an air crash in South Africa at thirty-two.

W.O. Bentley returned to Le Mans in 1939 with his awesome V12 Lagonda. It didn't win but as a road car it was more than a match for Rolls-Royce's Phantom III. Once again W.O. was getting up the noses of his erstwhile colleagues in Derby. *Motor Sport* pronounced it 'one of the greatest automobiles that has ever happened'. After the war he created a more modest six-cylinder twin-cam engine for Lagonda, but by that time the company was about to go bust. Having bought Aston Martin, David Brown was urged to take a look at what was left of Lagonda and bought the company on the strength of W.O.'s new engine. This, transplanted into the first of the DBs, went on to spectacular success, powering Aston Martin to post-war competition fame which culminated in victory at the 1959 Le Mans.

Materially, W.O. did not have a lot to show for his vast contribution to Britain's automotive heritage. He and his wife Margaret settled in a small cottage near Guildford and drove a Morris Minor. Robert Benjafield, who used to drive his grandmother over for tea, was struck by the quiet modesty of this shy elderly gentleman.

W.O. was always quick to acknowledge the contribution of others to the realisation of his dreams, but perhaps his true genius was his judgement of character, and ability to recognise potential in those who had no idea of what they were capable. Sammy Davis must have been thinking of him when he wrote, 'Though the machines themselves are interesting beyond belief, it is knowledge of men that counts.'

~

No one sums up the unique experience they shared better than Leslie Pennal, who was there at the birth of the very first Bentley: 'We were working for W.O. and for the car. The car was W.O. and W.O. was the car – to us they were one.'

Acknowledgements

My thanks go first and foremost to two people with direct connections to the Bentley generation. Robert Benjafield has been a huge resource and support, providing me with previously unpublished writing by his grandfather and giving me his own insightful impressions of several key players in this tale. He has also acted as an invaluable sounding board and a wise advisor on the pitfalls of excessive nostalgia. Barney Walker, grandson of Woolf Barnato has been an equally enthusiastic supporter and directed me to his mother Diana's own wonderful memoir. Barney also led me to some recently discovered film footage of the family's magnificent house, Ardenrun Place, featuring some amusing horseplay between Barnato, Benjafield and friends.

While checking sources for my previous book, *High Performance*, in the Royal Automobile Club library, I found myself competing for the bound 1947 volume of *The Autocar*. Vivian Bush was combing the classified ads in the hope of tracing a previous owner of the 3 Litre Bentley he now owns – and races. Not only do I have Vivian to thank for my first ride in a 'W.O.' Bentley – around Silverstone – but also for agreeing to read my first draft and giving me his very detailed and unvarnished notes.

Michael Barton eased my induction into the W.O. Bentley Memorial Foundation and its remarkable archive at Wroxton. My thanks to the team at the W.O.B.M.F. for their enthusiasm and advice before Covid intruded. Through Michael I also met the Society of Automotive Historians. My thanks to Anders Ditlev Clausager, Malcolm Bobbitt *et al.* for their warm welcome and their enthusiasm.

Andrew Nahum, former curator of technology and engineering at the London Science Museum, navigated me through the mysteries of the rotary aero-engine and the virtues of the aluminium piston. He also kindly read sections of the manuscript for technical accuracy.

University College London medical research scholar Talia Pittman guided me superbly through the treatment of Spanish Flu and helped me to properly appreciate Dudley Benjafield's pioneering contribution.

James Castle and Patrick Uden were, as always, great sounding boards. Automotive author Russell Hayes helped me with some invaluable fine detail about the more elusive Bentley characters. And eminent racing driver and journalist Tony Dron provided his own memorable take on the Bentley Boy phenomenon, as well as the unique challenges of racing at Le Mans.

As my erstwhile executive coach, Polly McDonald helped steer me towards writing. But, having as a child travelled to Montlhéry in 1959 with her father Gordon in his own beloved 41/2 Litre Bentley on a record-breaking mission, gave me her own unique insights into the Bentley obsession.

My thanks also to Steve Cropley, Richard Bremner, Giles Chapman and my fellow Simon & Schuster author Alan Judd for numerous suggestions and general cheerleading. The same to my lifelong fellow enthusiasts and great friends, Jason Hartcup, Martin Rudland and Philip Skinner.

Confirmed non-car enthusiasts author Manda Scott and editor Bill Massey were the first to convince me that the tale of Old No. 7 was worthy of a wider audience. And Jonathan Taylor and Simon Berthon both assured me that the story had an appeal beyond the automotive cognoscenti, as did my very special agent Mark

Lucas of The Soho Agency, who eased it towards publication and provided his customarily sharp and insightful observations on the manuscript.

At Simon & Schuster, publisher and author Iain MacGregor was instrumental in making *Racing in the Dark* happen before he absconded to Headline, delivering me into the immensely capable hands of Ian Marshall and Frances Jessop, who have been extraordinarily attentive and inspired in their shepherding of the manuscript to publication. Thanks also to Craig Fraser for his brilliant attention to the design and to Victoria Godden for proofreading.

Everyone in the Calman–Grimsdale household had a hand in this project. My thanks to my daughter Lydia for choosing the title, my son Lawrence for creating the map of the Le Mans circuit as it was in the 1920s, and Stephanie, my wife and in-house editor, who has read and re-read *Racing in the Dark* until she could drive Le Mans blindfolded.

Endnotes

Chapter 1: Dangerous Men

'cracked up entirely . . .' in S.C.H. Davis, *Motor Racing* (Iliffe & Sons, 1932), p. 54.

'spiralling down in flames . . .' and 'grief, courage and fear . . .' in W.O. Bentley, *My Life and My Cars* (Hutchinson, 1967), p. 69.

'Motor racing provided . . .' in Tim Birkin, *Full Throttle* (G.T. Foulis, 1933), p. 16.

Chapter 2: Seven Tons of Coal

'a slow, inefficient, draughty . . .' and 'They filled my dreams and ambitions' in W.O. Bentley, *My Life and My Cars* (Hutchinson, 1967), p. 11.

'I didn't like doing things . . .' Ibid., p. 15.

'I had to know . . .' Ibid.

'slashing and stroking . . .' Ibid., p. 16.

'gave me more . . .' Ibid.

'the barrier dissolved . . .' Ibid., p. 21.

'The sensation of being . . .' Ibid., p. 28.

'a rough, narrow and second-rate highway . . .' Ibid., p. 32.

'For a brief time . . .' Ibid., p. 31.

Chapter 3: The Outlaws

'such things were . . .' and 'so much in love . . .' in S.C.H. 'Sammy' Davis, *My Lifetime in Motorsport:*
His Final Autobiography, ed. Peter Heilbron (Herridge & Sons, 2007), p. 13.

'never thought about . . .' Ibid., p. 14.

'Persecuted by police . . .' in S.C.H. Davis, *A Racing Motorist* (Iliffe & Sons, 1949), p. 9.

'*keel you all!*' and 'It was no good . . .' in W.O. Bentley, *My Life and My Cars* (Hutchinson, 1967), p. 38.

'Labour relations, for . . .' Ibid.
'When the men . . .' and 'The tobacco chewing . . .' and 'The subsequent white collar . . .' in S.C.H. 'Sammy' Davis, *My Lifetime in Motorsport: His Final Autobiography*, ed. Peter Heilbron (Herridge & Sons, 2007), p. 31.

Chapter 4: Smiling Through the Dust

'I hadn't the least . . .' and 'smiling through a . . .' in W.O. Bentley, *My Life and My Cars* (Hutchinson, 1967), p. 49.

Chapter 5: The Paperweight

'His cool stare . . .' in Spencer E. Ante, *Creative Capital: Georges Doriot and the Birth of Venture Capital* (Harvard Business Review Press, 2008), p. 2.
'Pretty, isn't it . . .' and 'They will break . . .' in W.O. Bentley, *My Life and My Cars* (Hutchinson, 1967), p. 54.

Chapter 6: *Le Virage du Mort*

'There was something . . .' in S.C.H. 'Sammy' Davis, *My Lifetime in Motorsport: His Final Autobiography*, ed. Peter Heilbron (Herridge & Sons, 2007), p. 43.
'curious as it may seem . . .' Ibid., p. 44.
'Life offered . . .' in John Maynard Keynes, *The Economic Consequences of the Peace* (Macmillan, 1919).
'killed stone cold . . .' in W.O. Bentley, *My Life and My Cars* (Hutchinson, 1967), p. 60.
'While the races . . .' in G.N.R. Minchin, *Under My Bonnet* (G.T. Foulis, 1967), p. 110.

Chapter 7: A Savage Elation

'begat a certain . . .' in S.C.H. 'Sammy' Davis, *My Lifetime in Motorsport: His Final Autobiography*, ed. Peter Heilbron (Herridge & Sons, 2007), p. 62.
'appallingly difficult post . . .' and 'We've got to . . .' in W.O. Bentley, *My Life and My Cars* (Hutchinson, 1967), p. 62.
'You're an officer . . .' and 'adviser, nursemaid, champion . . .' and 'What on earth . . .' Ibid., p. 63.
'would not avail . . .' in Peter Pugh, *Rolls Royce – The Magic of a Name* (Postscript Books, 2000), p. 62.
'The place was . . .' in W.O. Bentley, *My Life and My Cars* (Hutchinson, 1967), p. 64.

Chapter 8: Sent to Coventry

'What I wanted . . .' in S.C.H. 'Sammy' Davis, *My Lifetime in Motorsport: His Final Autobiography*, ed. Peter Heilbron (Herridge & Sons, 2007), p. 45.
'Then he smiled . . .' Ibid., p. 46.
'Fighting is natural . . .' Ibid., p. 47.
'a matter of . . .' and 'with everything which . . .' and 'Almost all the whole family . . .' Ibid., p. 48.

Chapter 9: Dawn Patrol

'They're to do . . .' in W.O. Bentley, *My Life and My Cars* (Hutchinson, 1967), p. 66.
'There was a . . .' in Richard Bell, *Sailor in the Air: The Memoirs of the World's First Carrier Pilot* (Seaforth Publishing, 2008), p. 156.
'A visit to . . .' in W.O. Bentley, *My Life and My Cars* (Hutchinson, 1967), p. 67.
'I wouldn't mind . . .' Ibid., p. 70.
'Their life could . . .' Ibid., p. 71.
'with grief, courage and fear . . .' Ibid., p. 69.

Chapter 10: The Morning Destroyer

'He had the most . . .' in W.O. Bentley, *My Life and My Cars* (Hutchinson, 1967), p. 73.
'We always turned . . .' and 'because no man . . .' in S.C.H. 'Sammy' Davis, *My Lifetime in Motorsport: His Final Autobiography*, ed. Peter Heilbron (Herridge & Sons, 2007), p. 49.
'cracked up entirely . . .' in S.C.H. Davis, *Motor Racing* (Iliffe & Sons, 1932), p. 54.
'feeling that older people . . .' in S.C.H. Davis, *A Racing Motorist* (Iliffe & Sons, 1949), p.10.

Chapter 11: The Invisible Foe

'with a view to . . .' in Liam McLoughlin, 'Dr J.D. Benjafield, Microbiologist, soldier and racing driver', *Journal of Medical Biography*, 2019.
'dissipate – in part . . .' in J.D. Benjafield, M.D., B.S.Lond., M.R.C.S., 'Notes on the Influenza Epidemic in the Egyptian Expeditionary Force', *British Medical Journal*, 9 August 1919, pp. 167–9.

Chapter 12: Out of the Firestorm

'leaving one numb . . .' and 'Things were somehow . . .' in S.C.H. 'Sammy' Davis, *My Lifetime in Motorsport: His Final Autobiography*, ed. Peter Heilbron (Herridge & Sons, 2007), p. 50.

Chapter 13: Best in Class

'Working out a design . . .' in W.O. Bentley, *The Cars in My Life* (Hutchinson, 1961), p. 87.
'A fast car . . .' in W.O. Bentley, *My Life and My Cars* (Hutchinson, 1967), p. 90.
'Their surface was . . .' in W.O. Bentley, *My Life and My Cars* (Hutchinson, 1967), p. 80.
'a sound designer . . .' in W.O. Bentley, *The Cars in My Life* (Hutchinson, 1961), pp. 89–90.
'thrown up a damn good job . . .' in A.F.C. Hillstead, *Those Bentley Days* (Faber & Faber, 1952), p. 28.
'take the best . . .' in W.O. Bentley, *My Life and My Cars* (Hutchinson, 1967), p. 80.

Chapter 14: Market Fever

'This usually consisted . . .' in A.F.C. Hillstead, *Those Bentley Days* (Faber & Faber, 1952), p. 27.
'Someone whilst taking . . .' in G.N.R. Minchin, *Under My Bonnet* (G.T. Foulis, 1967), p. 112.
'In build, complexion and . . .' in A.F.C. Hillstead, *Fifty Years with Motor Cars* (Faber & Faber, 1960), p. 93.
'suitably mellowed . . .' in A.F.C. Hillstead, *Those Bentley Days* (Faber & Faber, 1952), p. 28.
'We were not . . .' in W.O. Bentley, *My Life and My Cars* (Hutchinson, 1967), p. 98.
'To design and build . . .' Ibid., p. 85.
'All my ambitions . . .' Ibid., p. 100.

Chapter 15: Bentley Boys Assemble

'W.O. was still . . .' and 'A type unknown . . .' and 'Bentley Motors more or less . . .' in Clare Hay, *Bentley Factory Cars 1919–1931* (Osprey Publishing, 1998), p. 41.
'I used to look . . .' in Elizabeth Nagle, *The Other Bentley Boys* (George G. Harrap, 1964), p. 36.
'There was a large hole . . .' and 'I suppose I was . . .' Ibid., p. 30.
'Of course it was . . .' Ibid., p. 31.
'He came up . . .' Ibid., p. 29.
'At first my chief job . . .' and 'When Nobby wanted . . .' and 'I used to turn . . .' Ibid., p. 31.
'It looked like . . .' Ibid., p. 34.
'I got a pound . . .' Ibid., p. 40.
'Orders from agents . . .' in A.F.C. Hillstead, *Those Bentley Days* (Faber & Faber, 1952), p. 39.

'did not possess ...' Ibid., p. 40.
'Bentley was a hand-built car ...' Ibid., p. 33.

Chapter 16: A Lovely Sound to Die to

'W.O. pressed the starter ...' and 'Benzole ...' Ibid., p. 30.
'Almost at once ...' Ibid., p. 31.
'It was a really beautiful sound ...' in Elizabeth Nagle, *The Other Bentley Boys* (George G. Harrap, 1964), p. 32.
'giving the impression ...' in A.F.C. Hillstead, *Those Bentley Days* (Faber & Faber, 1952), p. 34.
'Well that's of some use to us ...' in S.C.H. 'Sammy' Davis, *My Lifetime in Motorsport: His Final Autobiography*, ed. Peter Heilbron (Herridge & Sons, 2007), p. 50.
'whose huge engine ...' in S.C.H. Davis, *A Racing Motorist* (Iliffe & Sons, 1949), p. 11.

Chapter 17: The Song of Rowland

'Although frowned on ...' in S.C.H. Davis, 'A Test of a 3-Litre Bentley', *The Autocar*, 24 January 1920.
'It was too good ...' in A.F.C. Hillstead, *Those Bentley Days* (Faber & Faber, 1952), p. 39.
'Where was the labour ...' Ibid., p. 36.
'We managed ...' in Elizabeth Nagle, *The Other Bentley Boys* (George G. Harrap, 1964), p. 39.
'taking tyres to be vulcanised ...' and 'It was much taller ...' Ibid., p. 40.
'We used to get ...' Ibid., p. 51.
'strain gallons of petrol ...' Ibid.
'You know, Pennal ...' Ibid., p. 46.
'It was done ...' Ibid., p. 47.

Chapter 18: Endangered Species

'tough, smart, short-set ...' in W.O. Bentley, *My Life and My Cars* (Hutchinson, 1967), p. 90.
'something of a ...' Ibid., p. 91.
'Let us know ...' Ibid.
'He had a yacht ...' in Elizabeth Nagle, *The Other Bentley Boys* (George G. Harrap, 1964), p. 91.
'The reason I bought ...' Noel van Raalte, Letters to the Editor, *The Autocar*, 1 October 1921.

Chapter 19: The Serpent of Speed

'The serpent of speed ...' in Peter Pugh, *Rolls Royce – The Magic of a Name* (Postscript Books, 2000), p. 100.

'Mine was the first . . .' Osbert Sitwell, *Great Morning*, quoted in Richard Hough, ed., *The Motor Car Lover's Companion* (George Allen & Unwin, 1965), p. 17.
'the road ahead . . .' in G.N.R. Minchin, *Under My Bonnet* (G.T. Foulis, 1967), p. 128.
'crept up the speedometer . . .' in A.F.C. Hillstead, *Fifty Years with Motor Cars* (Faber & Faber, 1960), p. 143.
'When one did . . .' Ibid., p. 142.
'an excellent salesman . . .' in W.O. Bentley, *My Life and My Cars* (Hutchinson, 1967), p. 90.

Chapter 20: The Tourist Trophy

'No one ever attempted . . .' Ibid., p. 92.
'to show the Americans . . .' Ibid., p. 94.
'We were at panic stations . . .' in Clare Hay, *Bentley Factory Cars 1919–1931* (Osprey Publishing, 1998).
'First of all . . .' in Elizabeth Nagle, *The Other Bentley Boys* (George G. Harrap, 1964), p. 72.
'You couldn't see . . .' Ibid., p. 75.
'One of the bolts . . .' Ibid., p. 78.
'proceeded in the centre . . .' in A.F.C. Hillstead, *Those Bentley Days* (Faber & Faber, 1952), p. 59.
'I kept thinking . . .' in Elizabeth Nagle, *The Other Bentley Boys* (George G. Harrap, 1964), p. 78.
'that car of yours . . .' in A.F.C. Hillstead, *Those Bentley Days* (Faber & Faber, 1952), p. 62.
'to show potential . . .' Ibid., p. 97.
'how little they understood . . .' Ibid., p. 63.
'happy and well contented . . .' and 'Had he not been . . .' Ibid., p. 66.
'resented the loss . . .' in W.O. Bentley, *My Life and My Cars* (Hutchinson, 1967), p. 88.
'having anything to do with money . . .' in A.F.C. Hillstead, *Those Bentley Days* (Faber & Faber, 1952), p. 141.
'clumsy and elaborate saloon . . .' in W.O. Bentley, *My Life and My Cars* (Hutchinson, 1967), p. 102.
'because they were undercapitalised . . .' Ibid., p. 98.
'circumvent a carefully planned . . .' in A.F.C. Hillstead, *Those Bentley Days* (Faber & Faber, 1952), p. 88.

Chapter 21: Leading from the Front

'There, now you will have . . .' in William Boddy, 'Over the Edge in a Benz', *Motor Sport*, December 2002, p. 97.

'After the first twelve ...' and 'but he was right ...' in Elizabeth Nagle, *The Other Bentley Boys* (George G. Harrap, 1964), p. 82.
'ready money was as scarce ...' and 'Will he pay ...' in A.F.C. Hillstead, *Those Bentley Days* (Faber & Faber, 1952), p. 92.
'I think the whole ...' in W.O. Bentley, *My Life and My Cars* (Hutchinson, 1967), p. 103.
'with the gravest ...' Ibid., p. 104.

Chapter 22: The Road to the Sarthe

'fleeting glimpses of towns ...' Charles Jarrott, *Ten Years of Motor Racing* (Grant Richards, 1912) excerpted in Richard Hough, ed., *First and Fastest* (George Allen & Unwin, 1963), p. 14.
'could move without ...' in Georges Fraichard, *The Le Mans Story* (Bodley Head, 1954), p. 15.
'Driving on those ...' Robert Jaraud in *L'Automobiliste*, No. 23, Mai/Juin 1971, p. 12.

Chapter 23: The Birth of Endurance

'No country enjoys ...' in Charles Freeston, *France For the Motorist* (The Automobile Association, 1927), p. 1.
'By clearing a space ...' in G.N.R. Minchin, *Under My Bonnet* (G.T. Foulis, 1967), p. 118.
'I cannot let ...' Ibid., p. 120.
'tired, without muscle ...' in Jean-Luc Boeuf and Yves Léonard, *La République de Tour de France, 1903–2003* (Seuil, 2003).

Chapter 24: Twice Round the Clock

'We went in the car ...' in Elizabeth Nagle, *The Other Bentley Boys* (George G. Harrap, 1964), p. 83.
'When it came ...' Ibid., p. 84.
'It was simply ...' Ibid.
'By Friday morning ...' in W.O. Bentley, *My Life and My Cars* (Hutchinson, 1967), p. 104.
'He refused to ...' in A.F.C. Hillstead, *Those Bentley Days* (Faber & Faber, 1952), p. 92.
'After a couple of hours ...' in R.M. Clark, ed., *Le Mans – The Bentley and Alfa Years* (Brooklands Books, 1998), p. 12.
'Before darkness fell ...' in W.O. Bentley, *My Life and My Cars* (Hutchinson, 1967), p. 104.
'All the cars ...' in Elizabeth Nagle, *The Other Bentley Boys* (George G. Harrap, 1964), p. 84.
'I was never ...' in W.O. Bentley, *My Life and My Cars* (Hutchinson, 1967), p. 105.

Chapter 25: Chasing the Phantom

'The only relaxation . . .' Ibid., p. 118.
'friendly classless people . . .' Ibid., p. 105.
'at a time when . . .' in A.F.C. Hillstead, *Fifty Years with Motor Cars* (Faber & Faber, 1960), p. 148.

Chapter 26: Neck and Neck

'found himself precipitated . . .' in A.F.C. Hillstead, *Those Bentley Days* (Faber & Faber, 1952), p. 104.
'The scrutineer who . . .' in Elizabeth Nagle, *The Other Bentley Boys* (George G. Harrap, 1964), p. 105.
'What will the fellows . . .' and 'a huge sheet' Ibid, p. 88.
'but when the actual . . .' in A.F.C. Hillstead, *Those Bentley Days* (Faber & Faber, 1952), p. 106.
'You're wrong according . . .' Ibid, p. 106.
'The evening which . . .' Ibid.
'I was very dirty . . .' in Elizabeth Nagle, *The Other Bentley Boys* (George G. Harrap, 1964), p. 90.
'a job I loathed . . .' in A.F.C. Hillstead, *Fifty Years with Motor Cars* (Faber & Faber, 1960), p. 148.
'My interest in old . . .' Ibid., p. 126.
'I suppose we . . .' and 'Because the Rolls-Royce would . . .' in *W.O.: An Autobiography* (Hutchinson, 1958), p. 120.

Chapter 27: A Presumably Respectable Doctor

'to proclaim its whereabouts . . .' J.D. Benjafield, unpublished papers.
Quotes in the remainder of this chapter are all from the same source.

Chapter 28: Sound and Fury

'The Boche have come . . .' in Elizabeth Nagle, *The Other Bentley Boys* (George G. Harrap, 1964), p. 151.
'Bertie at his most determined . . .' W.O. Bentley, *My Life and My Cars* (Hutchinson, 1967), p. 123.
'when by all rights . . .' in A.F.C. Hillstead, *Fifty Years with Motor Cars* (Faber & Faber, 1960), p. 151.
'Playing to the gallery . . .' J.D. Benjafield, unpublished papers.
'Bitterly disappointed as I was . . .' Ibid.

Chapter 29: A Diamond-Encrusted Spoon

'I was conscious . . .' in A.F.C. Hillstead, *Fifty Years with Motor Cars* (Faber & Faber, 1960), p. 151.
'something might be . . .' and 'He could take it . . .' Ibid., p. 150.

Chapter 30: That Bloody Thump

'The recent extremely dramatic ...' in Clare Hay, *Bentley Factory Cars 1919–1931* (Osprey Publishing, 1998), p. 157.
'This is the first time ...' Ibid., p. 159.
'the nearest competitive car ...' Ibid., p. 163.
'nearly always unexpected ...' in *W.O.: An Autobiography* (Hutchinson, 1958), p. 158.
'It's a very nice car ...' Ibid., p. 159.
'All our competitors ...' in Martin Adeney, *Nuffield* (Robert Hale 1993). p. 77.
'barking down a ...' in W.O. Bentley, *My Life and My Cars* (Hutchinson, 1967), p. 68.
'merely a step ...' in Clare Hay, *Bentley Factory Cars 1919–1931* (Osprey Publishing, 1998), p. 170.
'Right from the start ...' in A.F.C. Hillstead, *Those Bentley Days* (Faber & Faber, 1952), p. 170.
'hard commerce ...' in A.F.C. Hillstead, *Fifty Years with Motor Cars* (Faber & Faber, 1960), p. 159.

Chapter 31: The Brooklands Squad

'A low wage ...' in Martin Adeney, *Nuffield* (Robert Hale, 1993), p. 109.
'There's no speed ...' in A.F.C. Hillstead, *Those Bentley Days* (Faber & Faber, 1952), p. 130.
'We moved off ...' in G.N.R. Minchin, *Under My Bonnet* (G.T. Foulis, 1967), p. 136.
'It was lunchtime ...' in A.F.C. Hillstead, *Those Bentley Days* (Faber & Faber, 1952), p. 132.

Chapter 32: The Slug

'I was just ...' in Elizabeth Nagle, *The Other Bentley Boys* (George G. Harrap, 1964), p. 97.
'I would be standing ...' Ibid., p. 98.
'It was a really ...' Ibid., p. 101.
'As we were going ...' Ibid.

Chapter 33: Going All Out

'We had specially ...' in S.C.H. Davis, *A Racing Motorist* (Iliffe & Sons, 1949), p. 31.
'a colossal cumbrous machine ...' Ibid.
'the infernal hood ...' Ibid., p. 32.
'cold but thrilling ...' Ibid., p. 42.
'Every driver is ...' Ibid., p. 43.

'His corner work . . .' in A.F.C. Hillstead, *Fifty Years with Motor Cars* (Faber & Faber, 1960), p. 174.
'I have made a fool . . .' in S.C.H. Davis, *A Racing Motorist* (Iliffe & Sons, 1949), p. 44.

Chapter 34: The Desolation of W.O.

'That none of our cars . . .' in W.O. Bentley, *My Life and My Cars* (Hutchinson, 1967), p. 131.
'After a week . . .' in A.F.C. Hillstead, *Those Bentley Days* (Faber & Faber, 1952), p. 134.
'She seemed jolly glad . . .' Ibid.
'There is something . . .' Ibid.
'The elementary mistake . . .' Ibid., p. 138.
'the absolute necessity . . .' in W.O. Bentley, *My Life and My Cars* (Hutchinson, 1967), p. 170.

Chapter 35: A Bit Like an Animal

'I was very grateful . . .' in A.F.C. Hillstead, *Those Bentley Days* (Faber & Faber, 1952), p. 142.
'racing is a business . . .' in S.C.H. Davis, *A Racing Motorist* (Iliffe & Sons, 1949), p. 53.
'it was extremely . . .' in S.C.H. Davis, '24 Hour Ordeal', *Collector's Car*, September 1980, p. 17.
'We had a very firm rule . . .' in W.O. Bentley, *My Life and My Cars* (Hutchinson, 1967), p. 161.
'He couldn't do . . .' *Automobile Quarterly*, p. 370.
'and we had much ado . . .' in S.C.H. Davis, *A Racing Motorist* (Iliffe & Sons, 1949), p. 121.
'To my mind . . .' in S.C.H. Davis, '24 Hour Ordeal', *Collector's Car*, September 1980, p. 16.

Chapter 36: Carnage at Maison Blanche

'With a sharp . . .' in A.F.C. Hillstead, *Fifty Years with Motor Cars* (Faber & Faber, 1960), p. 153.
'One heard the drone . . .' in G.N.R. Minchin, *Under My Bonnet* (G.T. Foulis, 1967), p. 144.
'When we were . . .' Ibid., p. 145.
'It was a tricky . . .' in S.C.H. Davis, '24 Hour Ordeal', *Collector's Car*, September 1980, p. 17.
'A horrible sight . . .' in G.N.R. Minchin, *Under My Bonnet* (G.T. Foulis, 1967), p. 145.
'energetic and somewhat violent . . .' in S.C.H. Davis, *A Racing Motorist* (Iliffe & Sons, 1949), p. 153.

'At least I knew . . .' Ibid., p. 53.
'That second win . . .' quoted in A.F.C. Hillstead, *Fifty Years with Motor Cars* (Faber & Faber, 1960), p. 150.
'a wonderful triumph . . .' *Daily Mail*, 20 June 1927.
'Oh well, a million . . .' in S.C.H. Davis, *Great British Racing Drivers* (Hamish Hamilton, 1957), p. 33.

Chapter 37: The Schoolboy and the Playboy

'Schoolboy, send catalogue . . .' in Rivers Fletcher, *Bentleys Past and Present* (Gentry Books, 1982), p. 35.
'I felt that life . . .' Ibid., p. 36.
'What was wrong . . .' Ibid., p. 39.
'He knew his way . . .' Ibid., p. 87.
'The front compartment . . .' Ibid.
'I thought Ardenrun . . .' Ibid., p. 85.
'just for a time . . .' Ibid.
'To reach Grosvenor . . .' Ibid., p. 87.
'So off I went . . .' Ibid., p. 88.
'June got up . . .' in Diana Barnato-Walker, *Spreading My Wings* (Grub Street, 2003), p. 16.
'his numerous and mysterious . . .' in *W.O.: An Autobiography* (Hutchinson, 1958), p. 179.
'never liked lending . . .' in W.O. Bentley, *My Life and My Cars* (Hutchinson, 1967), p. 133.

Chapter 38: Full Throttle

'Maybe he was . . .' in *W.O.: An Autobiography* (Hutchinson, 1958), p. 145.
'If I blamed anything . . .' in Tim Birkin, *Full Throttle* (G.T. Foulis, 1933), p. 16.
'battalions of gendarmes . . .' Ibid., p. 37.
'they'd have all the wine . . .' in Elizabeth Nagle, *The Other Bentley Boys* (George G. Harrap, 1964), p. 134.
'The tents of eager . . .' in Tim Birkin, *Full Throttle* (G.T. Foulis, 1933), p. 36.
'I let the team . . .' in *W.O.: An Autobiography* (Hutchinson, 1958), p. 145.
'I switched off . . .' in Clare Hay, *Old Number One* (Old Number One Press, 1999), p. 11.
'looking like a prep . . .' in *W.O.: An Autobiography* (Hutchinson, 1958), p. 147.
'He loved having . . .' in Elizabeth Nagle, *The Other Bentley Boys* (George G. Harrap, 1964), p. 134.

Chapter 39: Bentley v. Bentley

'Tim ... had the constant urge ...' in W.O. Bentley, *My Life and My Cars* (Hutchinson, 1967), p. 152.
'To supercharge a Bentley ...' Ibid., p. 152.
'They would lack ...' Ibid.
'I consider this car ...' in Clare Hay, *Bentley Factory Cars 1919–1931* (Osprey Publishing 1998), p. 222.
'I climbed into the seat ...' in S.C.H. Davis, *Motor Racing* (Iliffe & Sons, 1932), p. 234.
'There was a sudden ...' Ibid., p. 234.
'That anybody could ...' Ibid., p. 235.

Chapter 40: The Other Bentley Girl

'I decided I wanted ...' in The Hon. Mrs Victor Bruce, *Nine Lives Plus* (Pelham Books, 1977), p. 34.
'Briskly I told them ...' Ibid., p. 82.
'Before they could change ...' Ibid., p. 83.
'and bought myself ...' Ibid.
'Dear Mama ...' Ibid., p. 85.
'It was so vast ...' Ibid., p. 86.
'The extra speed ...' Ibid., p. 88.
'my world shrank ...' Ibid., p. 91.
'My God what ...' in Elizabeth Nagle, *The Other Bentley Boys* (George G. Harrap, 1964), p. 134.
'Would you be ...' in The Hon. Mrs Victor Bruce, *Nine Lives Plus* (Pelham Books, 1977), p. 92.

Chapter 41: The Real Bentley Boys

'a special vaccine ...' in S.C.H. Davis, *Motor Racing* (Iliffe & Sons, 1932), p. 202.
'vin blanc, bisquet ...' in Elizabeth Nagle, *The Other Bentley Boys* (George G. Harrap, 1964), p. 152.
'We were always ...' Ibid., p. 153.
'the town was ours ...' Ibid., p. 51.
'It's a disgrace ...' in Clare Hay, *Old Number One* (Old Number One Press, 1999), p. 21.
'As to the drivers ...' in W.O. Bentley, *My Life and My Cars* (Hutchinson, 1967), p. 94.
'No sooner had ...' in S.C.H. Davis, *Motor Racing* (Iliffe & Sons, 1932), p. 206.
'which resulted in ...' Ibid.
'then the whole ...' Ibid., p. 207.

'After the race . . .' in Elizabeth Nagle, *The Other Bentley Boys* (George G. Harrap, 1964), p. 152.
'All I remember . . .' Ibid., p. 176.
'I used to sit . . .' Ibid., p. 179.

Chapter 42: The Smile of the Tiger

'We waited in the Carlton . . .' in Hugh Young, *Bentley Bedside Book* (The Bentley Drivers' Club, 1961), p. 2.
'always came to . . .' in S.C.H. Davis, *Motor Racing* (Iliffe & Sons, 1932), p. 250.
'The very fact . . .' Ibid., p. 252.
'At first things were . . .' Ibid., p. 254.
'The mere fact of seeing the cars . . .' Ibid., p. 255.
'I kept the Big Six . . .' in S.C.H. Davis, *Motor Racing* (Iliffe & Sons, 1932), p. 255.
'rousing the spectators . . .' Ibid.
'I could see the car . . .' Tim Birkin, *Full Throttle* (G.T. Foulis, 1933), p. 83.
'I knew only then . . .' Ibid., p. 84.
'limping slowly with . . .' in S.C.H. Davis, *Motor Racing* (Iliffe & Sons, 1932), p. 255.
'about as hopeless . . .' in R.M. Clark, ed., *Le Mans – The Bentley and Alfa Years* (Brooklands Books, 1998), p. 12.
'The steering was gone . . .' in S.C.H. Davis, *Motor Racing* (Iliffe & Sons, 1932), p. 257.
'In the pits . . .' in Tim Birkin, *Full Throttle* (G.T. Foulis, 1933), p. 85.
'the glare was blinding . . .' Ibid.
'Never before have . . .' W.O. Bentley, *My Life and My Cars* (Hutchinson, 1967), p. 154.

Chapter 43: *Les Camions Rapides*

'The moment has arrived . . .' Ibid., p. 182.
'I have seen . . .' in Clare Hay, *Bentley Factory Cars 1919–1931* (Osprey Publishing, 1998), p. 275.

Chapter 44: The Maharajah's Displeasure

'so we may not . . .' Ibid., p. 293.
'That is why . . .' Ibid., p. 242.
'have his fun . . .' in A.F.C. Hillstead, *Fifty Years with Motor Cars* (Faber & Faber, 1960), p. 150
'I am sorry . . .' in Clare Hay, *Bentley Factory Cars 1919–1931* (Osprey Publishing, 1998), p. 308.
'Captain Barnato is a very . . .' Ibid., p. 321.
'People can no longer . . .' Ibid., p. 321.

'The advantage to Captain Barnato ...' Ibid., p. 319.
'It was a terrible shock ...' in Elizabeth Nagle, *The Other Bentley Boys* (George G. Harrap, 1964), p. 198.
'It wasn't just the job ...' Ibid.
'We began to feel ...' Ibid.
'an odd and unpleasant ...' in W.O. Bentley, *My Life and My Cars* (Hutchinson, 1967), p. 164.
'I may have been ...' Ibid., p. 184.
'"It was Arthur ...' in W.O. Bentley, 'My Bentley Boys', *Automobile Quarterly*, Vol. VI, No. 4, Spring 1968, p. 367.

Chapter 45: Return of the Sphinx

'Regarding the Bentley ...' in Peter Pugh, *Rolls Royce – The Magic of a Name* (Postscript Books, 2000), p. 122.
'a high-speed sports ...' Ibid., p. 123.
'Of course we had ...' in J. Dudley Benjafield, *The Bentleys at Le Mans* (Motor Racing Publications, 1948), p. 39.
'He had the priceless ...' in Elizabeth Nagle, *The Other Bentley Boys* (George G. Harrap, 1964), p. 203.
'We had absolute faith ...' Ibid., p. 204.
'Eventually I went to see ...' Ibid., p. 200.
'The worst I saw ...' Ibid., p. 201.
'Of course it was all rather tame ...' in W.O. Bentley, *My Life and My Cars* (Hutchinson, 1967), p. 177

Epilogue

'Down the straight ...' in S.C.H. Davis, *Motor Racing* (Iliffe & Sons, 1932), p. 191.
'In wartime one is ...' in S.C.H. 'Sammy' Davis, *My Lifetime in Motorsport: His Final Autobiography*, ed. Peter Heilbron (Herridge & Sons, 2007), p. 140.
'not only did I lose ...' in Diana Barnato-Walker, *Spreading My Wings* (Grub Street, 2003), p. 207.
'If I blamed ...' in Tim Birkin, *Full Throttle* (G.T. Foulis, 1933), p. 116.
'If you want a good time ...' in Nick Foulkes, *The Bentley Era* (Quadrille Publishing, 2006), p. 168.
'one of the greatest automobiles ...' *Motor Sport*, September 1947, p. 427.
'Though the machines ...' in S.C.H. Davis, *Motor Racing* (Iliffe & Sons, 1932), p. 301.
'We were working ...' in Elizabeth Nagle, *The Other Bentley Boys* (George G. Harrap, 1964), p. 204.

Bibliography and Further Reading

I don't pretend to be an authority on the subject of Bentley, merely a lifelong fan, thrilled since childhood by the tale of Old No. 7. I still have my 1967 secondary school English exercise book with my first attempt to tell the Bentley story, for which I got a B, though my teacher Mr Clarke did point out that I had 'drawn too much from books'. The same could be said of this book since, just as I began it, Covid locked me out of all archives and libraries. That said, it is amazing what can be found through online second-hand bookshops and a deep trawl of eBay.

Anyone wanting to know more about Bentley cars and people has at least a year's worth of pleasurable reading ahead of them. Many of those with first-hand experience of the original company felt compelled to commit their memories to print. W.O.'s autobiographies *W.O.* and *My Life and My Cars* are, for someone so tight-lipped, remarkably revealing – though as a sometime ghostwriter myself I must pay tribute to Richard Hough's role in getting W.O. to open up.

The irrepressible S.C.H. 'Sammy' Davis wrote three autobiographies and a shelf full of other books which capture the world of motor sport in the first part of the twentieth century, not to mention all his work for *The Autocar.* A.F.C. Hillstead's accounts of his fraught time selling both Bentley cars and the company are perhaps more revealing than the author intended of just how ill-equipped he and the Bentley brothers were when it came to matters of finance. Rivers Fletcher's recollection of his arrival at Bentley Motors straight from school is wonderfully anecdotal, as is his portrait of Barnato and his magical world.

The Great War looms over this story and changed the lives of most of those discussed here. Tim Birkin's *Full Throttle*, not so much a memoir as a manifesto for patriotic endeavour, unashamedly draws a parallel between his experience of war and motor racing and sparkles with contemporary resonance. But nothing comes close to Elizabeth Nagle's exercise in oral history, *The Other Bentley Boys*. It was her inspired idea, thirty years after the demise of the original company, to sit down with a few who worked on the shop floor and in the pits and let them have their say. The result is a peerless treasure trove of reminiscence that captures so much of what made the original Bentley Motors unique.

Among those who have come along subsequently to write about Bentley men and motors, Clare Hay stands out as by far the most accomplished. Her several books on the cars and the factory leave no nut or bolt unturned. There is a wealth of technical detail and she has amassed a peerless library of photographs of the factory and construction of the cars. Nick Foulkes' *The Bentley Era* wonderfully evokes the impossible glamour that surrounded the more legendary figures of the day and this large-format book has a thrilling selection of photographs of the Bentley boys and girls at work and play.

For a wider perspective on the Great War generation and the redemptive power they perceived in feats of endurance, Wade Davis's majestic *Into the Silence: The Great War, Mallory and the Conquest of Everest* captures the mindset.

Biography and Memoir

Diana Barnato-Walker, *Spreading My Wings* (Grub Street, 2003)
Richard Bell, *Sailor in the Air: The Memoirs of the World's First Carrier Pilot* (Seaforth Publishing, 2008)
J. Dudley Benjafield, *The Bentleys at Le Mans* (Motor Racing Publications, 1948)
W.O. Bentley, *W.O.: An Autobiography* (Hutchison, 1958)
W.O. Bentley, *My Life and My Cars* (Hutchinson, 1967)
W.O. Bentley, *The Cars in My Life* (Hutchinson, 1961)
Tim Birkin, *Full Throttle* (G.T. Foulis, 1933)
The Hon. Mrs Victor Bruce, *Nine Lives Plus* (Pelham Books, 1977)
S.C.H. Davis, *Motor Racing* (Iliffe & Sons, 1932)
S.C.H. Davis, *A Racing Motorist* (Iliffe & Sons, 1949)
S.C.H. Davis, *My Lifetime in Motorsport: His Final Autobiography*, ed. Peter Heilbron (Herridge & Sons, 2007)
Rivers Fletcher, *Bentleys Past and Present* (Gentry Books, 1982)
A.F.C. Hillstead, *Those Bentley Days* (Faber & Faber, 1952)
A.F.C. Hillstead, *Fifty Years with Motor Cars* (Faber & Faber, 1960)
G.N.R. Minchin, *Under My Bonnet* (G.T. Foulis, 1967)
Elizabeth Nagle, *The Other Bentley Boys* (George G. Harrap, 1964)

Bentley Cars and People

Donald Bastow, *W.O. Bentley, Engineer* (G.T. Foulis, 1998)
Darrell Berthon, *A Racing History of the Bentley* (Bodley Head, 1956)
Malcolm Bobbitt, *W.O., The Man Behind the Marque* (Breedon Books, 2003)
R.M. Clark, ed., *Le Mans – The Bentley and Alfa Years* (Brooklands Books, 1998)

Nick Foulkes, *The Bentley Era* (Quadrille Publishing, 2006)
Michael Frostick, *Bentley – Cricklewood to Crewe* (Osprey Publishing, 1980)
Clare Hay, *Chassis 141 – The Story of the First Le Mans Bentley* (Astuto Pty Ltd, 2009)
Clare Hay, *Bentley Factory Cars 1919–1931* (Osprey Publishing 1998)
Clare Hay, *Old Number One* (Old Number One Press, 1999)
Hugh Young, *Bentley Bedside Book* (The Bentley Drivers' Club, 1961)

Beyond Bentley – Motor Industry and Motor Racing

Martin Adeney, *The Motor Makers* (Collins, 1988)
Martin Adeney, *Nuffield* (Robert Hale, 1993)
Jean-Luc Boeuf and Yves Léonard, *La République de Tour de France, 1903–2003* (Seuil, 2003)
John Bolster, *The Upper Crust* (Weidenfeld & Nicolson, 1976)
Anders Ditev Clausager, *Le Mans* (Arthur Barker, 1982)
S.C.H. Davis, *Great British Racing Drivers* (Hamish Hamilton, 1957)
S.C.H. Davis, *Memories of Men and Motor Cars* (Seeley, Service & Co., 1965)
Georges Fraichard, *The Le Mans Story* (The Sportsman Book Club, 1956)
Charles Freeston, *France For the Motorist* (The Automobile Association, 1927)
David Hodges, *The Le Mans 24 Hour Race* (Temple Press, 1963)
Richard Hough, ed., *First and Fastest* (George Allen & Unwin, 1963)
John McLellan , *Bodies Beautiful – A History of Car Styling and Craftsmanship* (David & Charles, 1975)
Andrew Nahum, *The Rotary Aero Engine* (HMSO, 1987)

Peter Pugh, *Rolls Royce – The Magic of a Name* (Postscript Books, 2000)

L.J.K. Setright, *The Designers* (Weidenfeld & Nicolson, 1976)

Rodney Walkerley, *Automobile Racing* (Temple Press, 1962)

The Wider Landscape

Wade Davis, *Into the Silence* (Vintage, 2012)

Wendy Holden, *Shell Shock: The Psychological Impact of War* (Channel 4 Books, 1998)

John Maynard Keynes, *The Economic Consequences of the Peace* (1919)

Peter Pagnamenta and Richard Overy, *All Our Working Lives* (BBC Books, 1984)

D.J. Taylor, *Bright Young Things: The Rise and Fall of a Generation* (Vintage, 2008)

Articles

J.D. Benjafield, M.D., B.S.Lond., M.R.C.S., 'Notes on the Influenza Epidemic in the Egyptian Expeditionary Force (*British Medical Journal*, 9 August 1919, pp. 167–9)

William Boddy, 'Over the edge in a Benz' (*Motor Sport*, December 2002, p. 97)S.C.H. Davis, 'A Test of a 3-Litre Bentley' (*The Autocar*, 24 January 1920)

Tony Dron, 'The Old Bentley Boy Magic Lingers On' (*Daily Telegraph*, 16 June 2001)

Robert Jarraud, 'Jean Chassagne' (*L'Automobiliste*, No. 23, Mai/Juin 1971)

Liam McLoughlin, 'Dr J.D. Benjafield, Microbiologist, soldier and racing driver' (*Journal of Medical Biography*, 2019)

Simon Read, 'The Crash at White House Corner' (*Automobile Quarterly*, Vol. VI, No. 4, Spring 1968)

Index

W.O. indicates Walter Owen Bentley.

XT 1606
MK 5206